British Film Studios

An Illustrated History

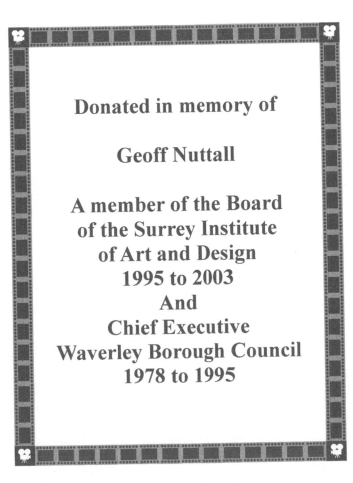

British Film Studios
An Illustrated History

Patricia Warren
Foreword by Sir Sydney W. Samuelson

B.T. Batsford Ltd, London

This book is dedicated to the people and industry who make the
movies at the British film studios, with affection and gratitude.

© Patricia Warren 1995, 2001

First published 1995
Second edition published 2001

Printed in Spain
by Bookprint, S.L.

for the Publishers
B.T. Batsford Ltd
9 Blenheim Court
Brewery Road
London N7 9NY

A member of the Chrysalis Group plc

A CIP catalogue record for this book is available from the
British Library

ISBN 0 7134 8644 9

Contents

Foreword

Sir Sydney W Samuelson

*T*he British Film Studios: An Illustrated History: an evocative title to those of us in the business and, I suspect, to many film industry *aficionados* at home and elsewhere. In a way, my own love of such places began nine years before I was born when my father opened a stately home – Worton Hall, Isleworth – as a studio in 1916. It cost all of a thousand pounds, but nevertheless, its transformation was the talk of Wardour Street and the cinema press. Vesta Tilley, a music-hall star of the time, cut a satin tape with golden scissors, and a cast and crew was put to work there and then. Such was the showmanship stuff of my father, the gathered showbiz notables saw the 'rushes' moments after they had finished their poached salmon and sherry trifle. I was nurtured on studio stories, especially those relating to the crisis-to-crisis existence of Worton Hall.

Much has happened within the British studio scene during the ensuing years, not much of it terribly satisfactory. Read on, as they say, the story will unfold as told by our indefatigable film buff/researcher/historian/author... Patricia Warren.

It is an interesting concept to write a studio survey in a geographical format, and some readers may be surprised to find that during their century of existence, British studios have established themselves and subsequently disappeared all over the UK. In fact, because of the new way of commercial thinking on the part of today's broadcasters, a clutch of modern, purpose-built studios are now available to independent film and television producers nationwide.

As Ms Warren's story unfolds, not only will readers enjoy all the fascinating star involvements, the classic film chronology and the facts and figures, but equally they will appreciate the 'funnies', many of which have been told and re-told by those lucky enough to be personally engaged in production. Some of the stories, it must be said, are apocryphal, much embellished during the telling from camera crew to camera crew. Studio stories can be happy, ordinary or dramatic: unfortunately, fire comes into the latter category, and there have been many over the years – Twickenham (1935), Elstree (1936) and the 007 stage at Pinewood (1984), which, amazingly, was rebuilt and shooting a James Bond film only 16 weeks later.

The financial story of British studios, fully recounted, would probably need 50 books like this. Some money matters are included here, others hardly need telling as the widespread demise of our studios over the period says it all. Thankfully, those studios that remain are among the best in the world; our technicians, who are the best in the world, now operate on a freelance basis – Shepperton this week, Twickenham next – and it works well.

My own relatively minor studio experiences would still take a large part of a book to report adequately. Some of them would tell of hilarious goings-on at the Manchester studio where the outrageous behaviour of Old Mother Riley (Arthur Lucan), Frank Randle and Tessie O'Shea was fully matched by the antics of the technicians they employed. As Halliwell says of Mancunian product, 'art and craftsmanship simply had nothing to do with it'. Compare this with the brilliant technique all around us at the time of writing these notes (for this book's predecessor): massive studio films like *Mary Reilly*, *Interview With The Vampire*, *Mary Shelley's Frankenstein*, *Judge Dredd* and *Restoration* prove we still know how to do it.

The frantic ups and downs of British studio and nonstudio production activity during the period covered by this book are already well known; Patricia Warren's work does much to identify where it all took place then, and where, in our relatively few remaining studios, it happens now. Although, overall, our studio stage square footage is only a fraction of what it once was, we do still have the 007 stage at Pinewood, and it is as busy as ever. The biggest in the world – seven championship tennis courts could easily fit inside – it is a national facility to be proud of. Long may it, and indeed all flourishing British studios, continue to 'be available' to those film-makers of the world who look for excellence.

I remember the little studios with considerable affection, like Carlton Hill, Maida Vale, a Victorian villa with the ground floor converted to a sound stage. The fact that there was a pillar smack in the middle of the space was accepted and thought of as a design challenge. At the long-gone Danziger Brothers studio in Elstree, I once assisted Jimmy Wilson who must have been the fastest lighting cameraman in the world, yet he was not fast enough for the punishing schedule set by the American brothers to shoot their television series for a ridiculously small amount of money. I heard the following dialogue on the set, where three actors, one a policeman, were grouped around a desk.

Director: Have you got all three in the shot, Jimmy?

Cameraman: No, not the copper.

Director: I want him.

Cameraman: No problem! (To electrician on the spotrail above) Charley, switch on that 2 K, number six.

Director: For ***** sake, Jim, no time for all that. Forget the copper. Action!

Such was the 'hurry up' atmosphere of small studio shooting, Great Britain, *Mark Saber*, circa 1958.

Introduction and Acknowledgements

The success of *The British Film Collection: British Cinema in Pictures*, an illustrated history with an emphasis on landmark British films and stars, naturally prompted an awareness of the need for a companion publication on British film studios. Not too difficult, one would suppose, given that in 1980, I had developed a potential series for Thames Television on the same subject and that I have been tucking information and stills in my files and archives ever since. How many studios were we talking about anyway: 20, 30, 50 ...?

In this book I touch on over 90. I am quite sure that I have not got them all and that someone out there is going to write and tell me about some that have escaped the net, or send me additional information that I shall be delighted to receive.

What has emerged is that every major British studio has, or has had, its own personality, clearly dominated by the man at the helm, whether it be Hepworth, Korda, Rank... I have tried to give a feel of each studio, its major personalities and protagonists, landmark films, stars, anecdotes, takeovers, development and era, with some thumb nail sketches *en route*, including, whenever possible, illustrations, stills and maps, and some hitherto unpublished material.

Importantly, I hope that I have paid sufficient tribute not only to British expertise through the decades since 1896, but have also squarely recognized the American contribution to British studios – Warner Bros at Teddington, MGM at Elstree, for instance; as well as the investment, producers, directors and stars who include Bette Davis, Henry Fonda, Marilyn Monroe, Robert Taylor, Ava Gardner, Robert Redford, Meryl Streep, Humphrey Bogart, Elizabeth Taylor, Warren Beatty, Katharine Hepburn and many more. The strong, imaginative European film and pioneer work in British studios is also gratefully acknowledged.

In the contents, I have put all of the studios in alphabetical order; all boroughs refer to current listing, not as they were in the past. I have also included notes on Northern Ireland; Mitchell and Kenyon at Blackburn and pioneer producer Walter Haggar in South Wales. The only liberty that I have taken *vis-à-vis* location is Pinewood, which is the name of the studio but is so strongly associated in people's minds as a town or borough that I have listed it as such. There may also be some instances where production dates are different to release dates.

It is important to me that this book should entertain just as the film industry has done over the decades, as well as be a source of reference for the film buff, industry and film student, and a springboard for specialized research. Given the romance, devotion, experience, joy, pathos, chutzpah, humour, brilliance, doggedness, scholarship, toughness, hardship, dedication, ambition, discipline and suicidal tendencies that emerge in this book, one should not overlook the most important characteristic of all, a sheer love of the industry and the magic of moviemaking.

My special thanks go to the following people, not only for their provision of information, stills and archive material, but also for their unstinting help and support. Every effort has been made to trace the copyright holders of the photographs and quoted material. Should there be any omissions in this respect, we apologize and shall be pleased to make the appropriate acknowledgement in future editions of the book.

Richard Attenborough Productions; Tony Bagley; Beaver Films; Blackburn Reference Library; Bray Studios; British Film Institute, Stills Department and Library and Information Department; Buena Vista International; Bushey Museum Trust Collection, Alec Just; Guido Coen, Twickenham Studios; Corbett & Keene; Cornish Studies Library, Film and Video Archives; Derby Central Museum; Devon Records Office; Ealing Studios; Elstree Studios; Eon Productions; Quentin Falk; Bryan Forbes; Hammersmith & Fulham Local History & Archive Centre; John Herron, Lumiere Pictures; Hertfordshire County Records Office; Hertfordshire Libraries, Arts & Information Service; Hounslow Library Service, Local Collection; Icon Entertainment; Intermedia; Leavesden Studios; London Film Productions; Macdonald & Rutter; Miramax; Kenneth Maidment, CBE; Manchester Metropolitan University, North West Film Archive; Mayfair Entertainment; Merchant Ivory Productions; Merton Library Service; Andrew Mitchell, CBE; National Film & Television School, Beaconsfield; National Library of Wales, Audio Visual Dept; National Museum of Photography, Bradford; Phillippa Wright, Simon Popple, New Era Entertainment; Peter Noble, Pinewood Studios; Sir David Puttnam; Richmond-upon-Thames Library, Local Studies; Rotherhithe Studios; Samuelson Productions, Sir Sydney Samuelson; Scottish Film Archive, Glasgow, Janet McBain; Patric Scott; Shadowlands Productions, 1993, Paul Olliver; Shepperton Studios, Cliff Somers; South East Film and Video Archive; *The Sunday Times* Collectors File, Peter Johnson; Fred Turner, Rank Film Distributors; 20th Century Fox; U.I.P.

(UK); Universal Pictures; Wales Film & TV; Wessex Film & Sound Archive, David Lee; Weybridge Museum; Henry Winters, Benham, Winters & Co.

My grateful thanks to my editors Tina Persaud and Helen Marsh. Last but by no means least, a very special thank you to my husband Andrew Warren, who co-ordinated the mammoth amount of material and also supplied additional research.

Alexandra Palace

Muswell Hill, Haringey, London

This studio existed for only three years. Converted from a skating rink in 1912, it had one dark and one open-air stage, and was owned by the Union Film Publishing Company, a subsidiary of the French Pathé Company whose new English trademark was Big Ben Films. A version of *David Copperfield* was made in this first year, and George Pearson was hired to produce some films for the company. The First World War curtailed production, and shortly after the outbreak of hostilities, the studio was used by Belgian refugees and later by prisoners of war. The studio burnt down in 1915.

Bayswater

Queens Road, Westminster, London

Very little is known of the one-stage Bayswater Studio which appears to have operated between 1912 and 1918. The studio was controlled by the Western-Finn Feature Film Company Limited, which had three trademarks: Regent, Pussyfoot and Piccadilly. Their productions included *The Seventh Day*, a drama about steelworkers in Northumberland, starring Arthur Finn. He was also one of the producers of the film, and engaged 3,000 extras for the crowd scenes.

Beaconsfield

Buckinghamshire

The building of Beaconsfield Studios commenced in 1921, and it was officially opened by its owner, George Clark, a Soho-based producer, in the spring of 1922. Like other producers of the day, Clark had chosen his site for three main reasons: to escape from the notorious London fog (and so have conditions for maximum daylight filming); to be within easy reach of London with a good railway service; and to have a setting with country locations for outdoor filming for his comedy two-reelers. The new studio had one dark stage of 120 sq ft x 60 ft, and a number of films were immediately initiated under the banner of George Clark Productions.

For some time, Clark had been working with Guy Newall, director and popular leading man in silent films. Newall's leading lady was the lovely Ivy Duke, and the couple married in 1922. One of their first films for Clark as a husband-and-wife team was *Fox Farm*, and shortly afterwards they made *The Starlit Garden*, both films directed by Newall. The couple had an enormous following from the press and public, and had also had their own production company; but times were hard, and although Clark continued for a short period with his comedies and leased the studios to the Britannia Film Company and Anglia Films, production had ceased by early 1925.

The studios became derelict, and by the time the British Lion Film Corporation acquired them in 1927, they were in very poor condition. British Lion had purchased Beaconsfield in anticipation of the realization of the 1927-28 Cinematograph ('Quota Quickies') Film Act. It was a new company, with Sam Smith, who had entered the industry in Canada in 1910, as Managing Director. The company's main purpose was to develop the novels of Edgar Wallace, who had agreed to give

Sydney Paxton and Sylvia Caine in *The Fair Maid Of Perth*, produced by Jack Buchanan for Anglia Films at Beaconsfield in 1923.

British Lion sole film rights and was invited to be its Chairman.

Having extensively modernized the studios, the company raced into silent film production with Wallace's *The Forger*, directed by G. B. Samuelson; *Chick*, starring Chili Bouchier; and *The Flying Squad* with Donald Calthrop and Wyndham Standing.

The arrival from America of the Warner Brothers 'talkies' *The Jazz Singer* (1927) and *The Singing Fool* (1928), both starring Al Jolson, changed the face of British film production. There was fierce competition to be the first with a British sound feature. With the added complication of different recording systems and trade show dates, there are many conflicting claims. Alfred Hitchcock's *Blackmail*, made for John Maxwell's BIP (British International Pictures) at Elstree in 1929, is usually regarded by the industry as Britain's first entry into sound film production. However, Britain's first all-talking feature was *The Clue Of The New Pin* (1929), based on a novel by Edgar Wallace, starring Donald Calthrop, Benita Hume and Fred Raines (with a small part going to a young, unknown actor, John Gielgud), made by British Lion at their Beaconsfield Studios.

Within a year of *The Clue Of The New Pin*, British Lion was in financial difficulty. Wallace left for Hollywood where he died in 1932 in considerable debt. Ironically, had he not granted British Lion the film rights to his work, but negotiated with American film companies, he would have enjoyed great wealth.

In the early 1930s, Gaumont/Gainsborough used the studios

Leading lady Chili Bouchier appeared in *Chick*, adapted from a novel by Edgar Wallace, at Beaconsfield in 1928.

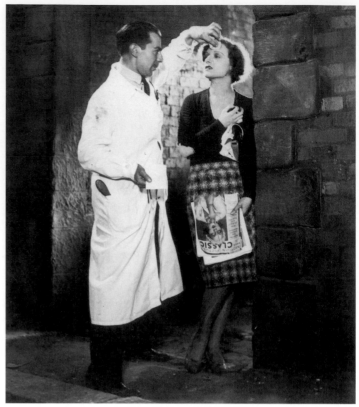

A last-minute dab of make-up for Gracie Fields on the set of *Sally In Our Alley*, directed by Maurice Elvey at Beaconsfield in 1931.

while waiting for their own new stages to be completed, and Basil Dean made *Sally In Our Alley*, starring the much-loved gawky Lancashire lass, Gracie Fields. Bill Hines's song, 'Sally', became her signature tune. As well as a number of 'Quota Quickies', films made at Beaconsfield up to the mid-1930s include *The Calendar*, which was produced by Michael Balcon and directed by T. Hayes-Hunter. The film starred Edna Best and the urbane British actor, Herbert Marshall, who cleverly managed to conceal the fact that he had lost a leg in the First World War. In 1932, Ann Todd (later to become the wife of David Lean) starred in *The Water Gipsies*, based on a novel by A. P. Herbert, which co-starred Ian Hunter; and in the same year Jessie Matthews, well on her way to stardom, appeared in *There Goes The Bride*, with Owen Nares. The film marked a change in British Lion's attitude. Up to that time, they had concentrated on the works of Edgar Wallace, but with his death it was decided to expand and experiment with other subjects, though still carrying on with the Wallace films in such productions as *The Flying Squad* and *The Frightened Lady*. This policy meant a change in the cast list away from the old 'Wallace faithfuls', and it is interesting to see the names of Sophie Tucker and Florence Desmond appearing in *Gay Love*, which was released in 1934.

It has to be said that, with few exceptions, British Lion managed to exist in the 1930s due to its production of inexpensive 'Quota Quickies' and rental of low-quality American imports. However, that it managed to survive at all in that cutthroat, highly-competitive, financially-unstable decade was proof of its tenacity.

In 1936, probably the studio's most prolific year, British Lion joined Hammer productions, headed by businessman and Liveryman of the City of London, Will Hammer, to coproduce two films starring Paul Robeson. These were *Songs Of Freedom*, also starring Elizabeth Welch; and *Big Fella*.

During the same period, Sandy Powell, the Yorkshire music-hall comic, appeared in Tom Arnold's *It's A Grand Old World*; and Margaret Lockwood was cast with Nora Swinburne in *Jury's Evidence*.

By mid-1937, British Lion, still headed by Sam Smith, was again in financial difficulties, and they ceased production until the middle of 1938. From then on, Herbert Wilcox hired the studio to make three minor productions, one of which was the Edgar Wallace vehicle *The Return Of The Frog*; Tom Arnold made another Sandy Powell film; and George King, under his Pennant banner, filmed melodramas including a remake of *The Chinese Bungalow* with Jane Baxter. The American comedy team of Bebe Daniels and Ben Lyon, who were to make a great hit on British wartime radio, came to Beaconsfield in 1938 to make *Not Wanted On Voyage*. After the outbreak of the Second World War in 1939, Beaconsfield Studios were requisitioned by the Ministry of Works for Rotax Limited who manufactured magnetos for aircraft engines.

Although Beaconsfield Studios were still leased to the Ministry of Works in 1947, the British Lion Group – which by then controlled Shepperton Studios in Surrey and Worton Hall Studios at Isleworth, as well as Beaconsfield – was sold to

Alexander Korda's London Films on the death of Sam Smith that year.

The Government then spent a massive £146,000 on refurbishing and equipping the studios for the Crown Film Unit, which produced 75 films a year for the Central Office of Information until it was disbanded during 1951-52. Shortly afterwards, Michael Balcon became chairman of Group 3, a subsidiary of the National Film Finance Corporation, with a brief to develop new talent. Their productions included *Miss Robin Hood*, a comedy with Margaret Rutherford, Richard Hearne, James Robertson Justice and Sidney James; *The Brave Don't Cry*, which was produced by the renowned documentary film-maker John Grierson; *The Oracle*, with Robert Beatty, Virginia McKenna and Michael Medwin; *Make Me An Offer*, a comedy with Peter Finch and Adrienne Corri; *The Blue Peter*, starring Kieron Moore and Greta Gynt; and *The Love Match*, a comedy with Arthur Askey, Thora Hird and Shirley Eaton, which was produced by John Baxter.

By the mid-1950s, The National Film Finance Corporation had decided that their studio base was unjustifiable. Some time later, producer Peter Rogers worked at Beaconsfield until he moved his operations to Pinewood where he founded the *Carry On* series. Independent Artists were the final production company at Beaconsfield, and left in 1964. The studios then became a warehouse for the North Thames Gas Board until 1971, when The National Film School bought the lot for £225,000. In 1983, it became The National Film and Television School, funded by a partnership of government and industry (film, television and video), offering full-time professional training leading to a NFTS Associateship (ANFTS) in the specializations of producer, director, director of photography, editor, animator, arts director, sound recordist, documentary and film composer. On 31 May 1995, the NFTS, with the tireless support of its Chairman, Sir David Puttnam and Lord Attenborough of the Foundation of Sport and the Arts, acquired Ealing Studios with a £2 million grant from the foundation which is funded by the football pools companies. The school relocated to Ealing and the Beaconsfield Studios was sold 'in order to finance the development of Ealing Studios'.

Blackburn

Pennine Film Studio, Blackburn, Lancashire

In 1936, three local men, Cuthbert John Cayley, Roland Whiteside and Eric Pollard, converted a disused cotton shuttle-making factory in Blackburn into a 'talking' picture studio. As well as making topical and scenic films, their most ambitious production was *The Samlesbury Saga*, a costume drama which involved local amateur dramatic societies and locations. The outbreak of the Second World War brought film production at the studio to a halt.

A note on Mitchell and Kenyon

There is no record that this hardy production company, formed in 1897 by James Kenyon and S. Mitchell, ever had a studio. Like Walter Haggar in South Wales, they concentrated on open air filming for maximum daylight and locations. Blackburn, an important centre in the cotton industry, became a very good 'date' for travelling film showmen and salesmen.

Mitchell and Kenyon's productions, which included animated picture shows and 'actualities' (such as a faked account of the Boer War, filmed at Blackburn) sold well in England and America. One of their most successful trick films, *Moon Man*, showing the moon rising over a hill and grimacing at the audience, was shown at the London Pavilion in 1902. The company appears to have ceased production by 1910.

Bradford

Manchester Road, Bradford, West Yorkshire

The Towers Hall Studio in Manchester Road, Bradford was occupied by the Captain Kettle Company between 1912 and 1914, and then taken over by Pyramid Films. The company appears not to have fared well at Bradford, their only film of note being *My Yorkshire Lass* (1916), a romance directed by Herbert Pemberton.

Bray

Down Place, Windsor Road, Windsor, Berkshire SL4 5UG

Akin to the studios at Pinewood and Shepperton, Bray Studios was once a splendid private residence. Down Place, a seventeenth-century country mansion, was owned by Jacob Tonson, an eminent bookseller of the day, who attracted noblemen and gentlemen to his home and formed the famous 'Kit-Kat Club' with the Earl of Dorset at its head. The club had 39 members in all, who were distinguished for their rank, learning and wit, and many held important government positions.

Down Place remained a private residence until 1949, when it was sold, and shortly afterwards it became Bray Studios. The character and mystique of the original house remain today, along (it is claimed) with the resident ghost known as 'The Blue Lady'.

Bray Film Studios will always be associated with Hammer Film Productions, which was founded in 1948 under the chairmanship of James Carreras. The original House of Hammer had been started in the 1930s by James's father, Spanish-French Enrique Carreras, and William Hinds, an ex-actor who went under the name of Will Hammer. The company worked in association with British Lion, and its fortunes came and went until after the Second World War when the new Hammer Film Productions was formed at Bray by Hammer and Carreras Senior and their sons, Anthony Hinds and James Carreras.

Hammer Film Productions was also known as Exclusive Films. In 1948, Michael Carreras (the son of James) also joined the company and became a producer and director.

In the early 1950s, Hammer Films included low-budget versions of successful radio series such as *The Man in Black, Life With The Lyons* and *PC.49*, although Paulette Goddard did make *The Stranger Came Home*; John Ireland appeared in *The Glass Cage*, and Forrest Tucker co-starred with Eva Bartok in *Break In The Circle* for Hammer/Exclusive during the same period. In the mid-1950s, Carreras secured the film rights to the television science-fiction series *The Quatermass Experiment*. The success of this film was so phenomenal that the company

Bray Studios.

Thora Birch on the set of *The Hole*, a psychological thriller directed by Nick Hamm at Bray Studios in 2000. Photo courtesy Pathé Distribution Ltd.

decided to concentrate on the remunerative horror formula, and after *Quatermass II* in 1956, they turned their attention to *The Curse of Frankenstein*. This film was to set the style for the 'Hammer House of Horror', and launched the studio – and its stars, Peter Cushing and Christopher Lee – on a long and profitable career. Set in lurid colours with close-ups of severed eyeballs, this brand of entertainment seemed to be just what the British cinema-going public was waiting for. Relishing the departure of recent bland entertainment, audiences licked their dripping lips and awaited *Dracula,* with Lee in the title role and Cushing as Van Helsing.

Throughout the 1950s, the Hammer Productions developed a cult following with such films as *The Hound of the Baskervilles,* again with Cushing and Lee; *The Mummy*, followed by *Curse Of The Mummy's Tomb* and *Blood From The Mummy's Tomb*; *Curse of the Werewolf*, starring Oliver Reed; *The Two Faces Of Dr Jekyll*; *The Damned,* directed by Joseph Losey; and *Kiss Of The Vampire*.

During their peak years, Hammer were producing eight films a year. James Carreras was the guiding force with the financial reins of the company and productions firmly in his grasp. Success of the company in the home market and in the United States enabled Hammer to claim the distinction of being Britain's most consistently profitable film company; and in 1968 the company was awarded the Queen's Award for Industry in recognition of its earnings in foreign currency. In the following year, James Carreras was knighted.

During the 1950s and early 1960s, his son, Michael Carreras, produced and directed many of the Hammer films and worked with directors Terence Fisher, Val Guest and Roy Ward. However, by the mid-1960s, film production was declining in Great Britain, and Bray, in common with a number of other studios, was in difficulties. Although they continued to make films at other locations, Hammer's last film to be made at Bray was *The Mummy's Shroud* in 1966, which Leslie Halliwell described regretfully as an: 'uninventive rehash of every other

mummy movie; too hackneyed to be saved even by a good cast and production values'.

At the end of the 1960s, Seeberg Management took over the studios from Hammer until the mid-1970s, when the then landlords, Broadway House Properties, took control. This was followed by another change of landlord in the late 1970s. In the intervening years, a number of films were made at Bray Studios. These included Ken Russell's *The Music Lovers* (1970); *Sunday Bloody Sunday* (1971), with a star cast including Glenda Jackson, Peter Finch, Peggy Ashcroft and Maurice Denham, directed by John Schlesinger; *Pope Joan* (1972), the legend of a ninth century German prostitute who discovered a vocation to preach and was made pope, starring Liv Ullmann, Trevor Howard and Olivia de Havilland, and directed by Michael Anderson; part of *The Hireling* (1973), based on the novel by L. P. Hartley, directed by Alan Bridges with Sarah Miles and Robert Shaw; and *The Rocky Horror Picture Show* (1975), directed by Jim Sharman.

In 1984, Samuelsons acquired the studios until 1990, when Bray Management Limited took over the lease in March. Production at Bray during the 1980s included special effects on Ridley Scott's *Alien*; the thriller *Loophole*, starring Albert Finney, Martin Sheen and Susannah York, and directed by John Quested; the star line-up of Gregory Peck, Roger Moore, David Niven, Trevor Howard and Patrick MacNee in Euan Lloyd's *The Sea Wolves*, under the direction of Andrew McLaglen; Euston Films' *A Month in the Country*, with Colin Firth, Kenneth Branagh and Natasha Richardson; Denzel Washington and Amanda Redman in *For Queen and Country*; and John Boorman's wonderfully evocative *Hope And Glory*, which recaptured the fears of life in London during the Blitz through the eyes of a child.

Since Bray Management Limited's acquisition of the lease, the studios have produced Derek Jarman's powerful Edward II; Double X; and numerous television series and productions which include *Inspector Morse*; *The Manageress*; *Forever Green*; *Jeeves And Wooster*; *AngloSaxon Attitudes*; and *Murder Most Horrid*.

Bray: Christopher Lee, who together with Peter Cushing and Vincent Price became one of a trio of Hammer horror film stalwarts, appears to have made more films than any other British screen actor and portrayed most of the known Hammer monsters.

Bray: Producer-director-writer John Boorman with Sebastian Rice-Edwards on the set of his wonderfully evocative *Hope And Glory* (1987), which captured the fears of life in London during the Blitz through a child's eyes.

Film productions from 1995 to 2000 included *A Midsummer Night's Dream*, directed by Adrian Noble, with Lindsay Duncan and Alex Jennings heading the cast. Originally staged by the Royal Shakespeare Company, the production did not transfer well to the screen, resulting in Matt Wolf of *Variety* commenting, 'It's so busy whipping up a stylistic storm that it lays low Shakespeare's true topic – love.' This was followed by *Mojo* (1996), *Velvet Goldmine* (1997), *The Trench* (1998) and *RKO 281* (1999).

After his Academy Award-winning performance in *The Cider House Rules*, newly knighted Sir Michael Caine arrived back in Britain for *Shiner* (2000), his fourth collaboration with producer Geoffrey Reeve, which was directed by John Irvin. Describing his role as a boxing promoter wishing to avenge the murder of his son, Caine said, 'I've been preparing for *Shiner* all my life, I grew up in the Elephant & Castle area, and I know exactly who I'm playing – but I daren't give you his name because he'd kill me!' Other productions in 2000 at Bray were part of *Captain Corelli's Mandolin*, *Unconditional Love* and *The Hole*, backed by Pathé Pictures and The Film Council. A psychological thriller adapted from a Guy Burt novel, *The Hole*'s cast included Thora Birch and Desmond Harrington and was directed by Nick Hamm.

During the same period, i.e. 1995–2000, Bray continued to play host to numerous television companies, whose productions included series such as *Murder Most Horrid*, *Pie in the Sky*, and *How do You Want Me?* and dramas as diverse as *Emma*, *Turn of the Screw*, *Poirot* and *Ruth Rendell's Harm Done*.

Situated on the bank of the River Thames, less than one hour's drive from the West End of London, Bray Film Studios offers all the facilities associated with a major studio complex for features, television, commercials, promos and rehearsal space. There are four stages of various sizes, suitable for a wide range of applications, complemented by set construction facilities, production offices, full catering, preview theatre, cutting rooms etc., all with 24-hour security and excellent parking facilities.

Although it celebrates over 50 years of film-making, Bray Studios is still dominated by the lovely old Grade II listed mansion that is set in its midst.

Brighton

The Brighton School, Brighton/Hove, East Sussex

George Albert Smith: In 1897, at the age of 33, George Albert Smith, a portrait photographer in Brighton, turned his interest to moving pictures. Like a number of his contemporaries, this brilliant film pioneer regarded his inventions as scientific developments rather than a new art form. As well as being a

Derek Jarman's powerful *Edward II* was produced at Bray Studios.

portrait photographer, Smith was also a magic-lantern lecturer, astronomer and hypnotist, and had used slides to illustrate his lectures in 1896. In the same year he devised his own cine-camera, and in 1897 he was making his own films. These first movies, called 'actualities', were just that, movement on film taken in the road, on the beach, in the back garden, of people walking, horses and carriages and so on. Smith's first 'actuality' was so profitable that by the turn of the century he had made nearly £2,000 profit, a large amount of money at that time. A leading member of the 'Brighton School', Smith led the way in the use of basic camera movement and editing techniques, as well as the close-up, which is clearly demonstrated in his *Grandma's Reading Glass*, made in 1900.

Once the public had got over the shock and novelty of moving pictures, it became necessary for these early film pioneers-producers to invent story-lines to sustain interest. Smith's offerings in the fantasy genre were *Bluebeard, Ali-Baba* and *Aladdin*; while his comedies included *The Miller And The Sweep*, and his dramas *The Little Witness*. Some of these films (and others) were made by Smith at his St Anne's Well Studios in Hove. The studios had been built for him by the Warwick Trading Company who had given him a two-year contract in 1900. Smith had also used premises at Wild Gardens in Hove. The gentleman responsible for Smith's contract with Warwick was Charles Urban who left the company in 1903 and founded the Charles Urban-Trading Company. An astute businessman and entrepreneur, he became a friend and mentor and was quick to encourage and promote Smith's invention of one of the first commercial cinematographic colour processes, Kinemacolour, which was developed and patented in 1906. This two-colour system remained popular up until 1914.

Smith's studio followed the average trend, which was to have a stage approximately 30 ft x 16 ft, set in a glass house for maximum daylight, which had sliding doors and an extended stage apron that could be pulled through them in fine weather.

Smith's neighbours and fellow pioneer film-makers of the Brighton School included James Williamson, Esme Collings and inventor-engineer-designer Alfred Darling.

The reason why these pioneers were attracted to the south coast of England was presumably the good climate and light, essential for their work. Brighton and the more refined Hove were holiday resorts after all, which would have meant a good trade in portraiture, chemistry and entertainment, from which film was a natural progression.

George Albert Smith witnessed many changes in film production during his lifetime, surviving to the era of Marilyn Monroe and dying at the age of 95 in 1959.

James Williamson: It was very common in the early days of film-making to involve the entire family in the process. In 1898, James Williamson (born 1855), decided to sell his chemist shop in Church Road, Hove, in order to concentrate on the photographic side of his business and enter the promising new industry called 'Movies'. Aided and abetted by his loved ones, he acquired premises at Western Road, Hove, and proceeded to make family-cast films in the garden, which he frequently wrote and appeared in. He would then develop, print and sell his productions to early distributing companies like Butcher, Gaumont and Urban.

Williamson's huge glasshouse studio was similar in concept to Smith's, and he also rented a large villa, Ivy Lodge, where he made his famous *Attack On A China Mission* in 1900, acclaimed as one of the earliest 'story films' with a true cinematic technique, as well as *Two Naughty Boys*, which starred his own sons. Other films from the Williamson Studios included comedies *The Rival Cyclists* (151

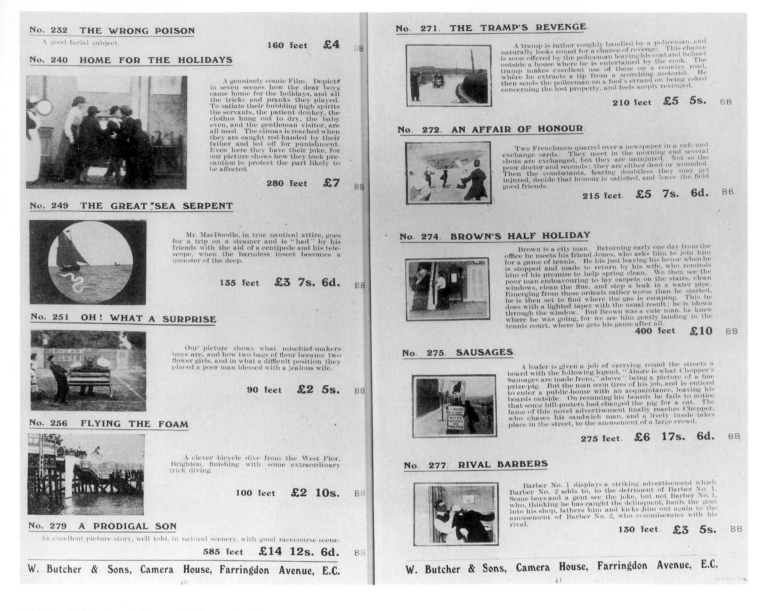

Brighton: Butcher's catalogue of Williamson's films.

ft); *Ping-Pong* (90 ft) and *Stop Thief* (112 ft). Williamson's most dramatic film was *Fire*, described as 'sensational' in his 1902 catalogue, the tale of a horse-drawn fire engine rushing to save the occupants of a burning house. The catalogue continues: 'To enhance the effect, portions of the film are stained red'.

Williamson also made a number of trick films, notable for their close-ups. In *The Big Swallow*, a photographer is ordered away but continues to approach his subject. There is then a close-up of the face, then the mouth which occupies the entire screen and then the camera-operator disappears inside. The subject retires munching, expressing satisfaction.

In *The Romance of the Movies*, Leslie Wood recounts the charming tale of ex-Sergeant Major Chart who appeared in some of the Williamson's films and set feminine hearts aflutter. Wood suggests that the ex-Sergeant Major was the first man to make audiences more interested in the actor than in the film. James Williamson abandoned film production in 1909.

Esme Collings: Little is known of Brighton/Hove portrait photographer Esme Collings, except that in 1896, before G. A. Smith, he produced over 30 short-length films. The only one of these that seems to have stood the test of time is *The Broken Melody*, one of the first films in which a professional actor – Mr Van Biene – appeared. A notice over Mr Collings's portrait photography shop announced that he was 'formerly in partnership with Mr Friese-Greene', who was also a portrait photographer and invented one of the first British practical movie cameras in 1889.

Alfred Darling: In Low and Manvell's *The History of British Film 1896–1906*, reference is made to the unpublished notebooks of James Williamson. In 1926, he states that G. A. Smith, Esme Collings and Williamson were 'Materially assisted by Mr Alfred Darling, a clever engineer who made a study of the requirements of film producers'. Williamson goes on to say that it was only after his 'floundering' with his home-made apparatus and his subsequent introduction to Darling that he was able to make successful pictures.

Brighton: George Albert Smith, an important member of 'The Brighton School', led the way in the use of basic camera movement and editing techniques, as well as the close-up, clearly demonstrated in *Grandma's Reading Glass* made in 1900.

Brighton

Brighton & County Film Company, Brighton, East Sussex

The Brighton & County Film Company ('Brightonia'), a small production company/studio, was formed by W. H. Speer, an adversary of Brighton film pioneer George Albert Smith. Its first film was *A Nurse's Devotion*, which was released in April 1912.

Brighton

Brighton Film Studios, Brighton, East Sussex

This small, post-war, two-stage studio was in operation during part of the 1950s, 1960s and 1970s, with its company and film directors B. S. Chadwick and D. C. Wynne. Some of its productions include *Alive on Saturday*, featuring Patricia Owens and Guy Middleton; *The Master Plan*, with Wayne Morris; *The Flaw*, starring John Bentley, Donald Houston and Rona Anderson; and *The Bobby Dazzler*, featuring June Thorburn and Betty Ann Davies, which was directed by Terence Fisher.

Bushey

Hertfordshire

In 1913, Sir Hubert von Herkomer, a Royal Academician anxious to participate in the creation of films as an art form, built a studio in the garden of Lululand, his Bushey house, and enthusiastically went into production with his son, Siegfried, who had gained a little experience with Pathé. It has to be said that they turned out

several 'Lulus' before Sir Hubert died a year later. The garden studio, converted from an old chapel, had a glass roof.

His first commercial film was *The Old Wood Carver* in which Herkomer starred with Archibald Forbes, Maud Milton and May Blayney. He then appeared in *The White Witch*; *His Choice*; and *A Highwayman's Honour* in which Lady von Herkomer, Miss G. Herkomer and a young actor named A. E. Matthews also acted. An extraordinarily gifted man, Herkomer seems nevertheless to have been extremely naïve in conducting his business affairs. In *Film Making in Bushey 1912–1914*, Michael Pritchard gives A. E. Matthews' account of two American entrepreneurs who rivalled the best 'con-men' in the business. It seems that having been given dinner and a private showing of *The Old Wood Carver*, they expressed their unbounded admiration for the film and proposed to take it straight back to Hollywood and sell it. They left with the negatives and the copies, and when they arrived back in London, phoned Sir Hubert to say that as they had forgotten to book their return passages, there would be a delay in getting the picture released in the States. Sir Hubert promptly ordered a suite to be put at their disposal on the *Aquitania* at his expense, and that was the last he heard of the gentlemen and the picture.

Herkomer died in 1914, and in 1915, the studio was taken over by the British Actors Film Company, which was founded by Gerald Malvern with A. E. Matthews as its Chairman. Matthews gained

Bushey: In 1920, film director Adrian Brunel formed Minerva Films with actors Leslie Howard and C. Aubrey Smith and author-poet A. A. Milne. *The Bump*, starring C. Aubrey Smith and Faith Celli, was made at Bushey in the same year.

support from the famous theatrical Green Room Club, and actors such as Donald Calthrop, Leslie Henson, Owen Nares and Nelson Keys were associated with the company. Two of their films were *The Divine Gift* and *Once Upon A Time*, both produced by Thomas Bentley, the latter starring A. E. Matthews, Nelson Keys and Dorothy Minto. It was a young and enthusiastic company with a modern-day approach, and many of the actors gave up their salaries in return for a share of the profits.

By 1920, the British Actors Film Company had merged with the Alliance Company, but the amalgamation did not go well and the company was wound up in 1922. Meanwhile, Adrian Brunel, who had worked with both Herkomer and the British Actors Film Company as scenario-editor and actor, had gone on to form Minerva Films in 1920 with actors Leslie Howard, C. Aubrey Smith and author-poet A. A. Milne. Although Minerva Films were made at different venues, one of their number, *The Bump*, starring C. Aubrey Smith and directed by Adrian Brunel, was made at Bushey. The studio was closed for long periods during the early 1920s, but Brunel came back again in 1924 to make two comedies

called *Pathetic Gazette* and *Crossing The Great Sagrada*. In 1925, he directed some Gainsborough burlesques at Bushey, which were produced by Michael Balcon, and featured *A Typical Budget*, starring Jack Buchanan; *So This Is Jolly Good*, with comedian Alf Goddard; *The Blunder Land Of Big Game*; and *Battling Bruisers*.

In 1927, the studio was bought by Randal Terraneau and was registered as a private company – that is, Bushey Studios – in 1928. In the same year, American director Lawson Butt made *Afterwards*, with Marjorie Hume and Cecil Barry.

The Terraneau purchase of the studios had obviously been made with the new 'Quota Quickies' in mind, but Bushey was a tiny one-stage studio. As productions got bigger during the 1930s, it was used less frequently; mainly for the overflow from other production companies and studios. Some of the productions during the 1930s were *The Merry Men Of Sherwood*, directed by Widgey Newman and produced by Delta Pictures, who also made *Little Waitress* with Moore Marriott at the studios; and *Heroes Of The Mine*. Bushey seems to have been something of a base for director Widgey Newman, who also directed *What The Parrot Saw* and *What The Puppy Said*, with Wally Patch and Moore Marriott in the mid-1930s. Towards the end of the decade, the studios were owned by the Bushey Film Corporation Limited, but with the outbreak of the Second World War in September 1939, the building was used to store nitrate films away from London and as an ARP (Air Raid Precautions) depot. From the mid-1940s to the early 1950s, the company was independently owned and used by Ambassador Film Productions who had Gilbert Church as Managing Director and Producer. Some of the films made during that period were *The Mysterious Mr Nicholson*; *Black Memory*, with Michael Medwin and Sidney James; and *The Greed Of William Hart*, directed by Oswald Mitchell, starring Tod Slaughter. Max Bygraves appeared in *Bless 'em All*; and Barbara Mullen made a series of short films there. The studios were also used for a period by The Children's Film Foundation.

In the 1950s, the Church family leased the old barn (part of the original Herkomer studios) and the studio to Rayant Pictures Limited, who made industrial and scientific training films as well as commercials and shorts. In the early 1970s, the lease was acquired by Cygnet Films who made training films for the Armed Services, publicity films for the British Tourist Board; and some television documentaries and commercials, and during the late 1970s–early 1980s, Michael Winner used the studios as a production base. In 1985, Cygnet moved their operations to High Wycombe and the studios were closed and later mainly demolished. The body of Sir Hubert von Herkomer, the founder of Bushey Film Studios, lies close by in the churchyard of St James Church, Bushey.

Camden

Cursitor Street, Camden, London

The three tiny stages of the Cursitor Street (Windsor) Studios in Camden were used by various independent companies between 1947 and the early 1950s to make *A Man's Affair* (Concord Productions Limited); *First Rhapsody* (International Motion Pictures Limited); *River Patrol* (Knightsbridge Films Limited);

and Paul Rotha's *History of Writing* (Films of Fact Limited); *History of Printing*; and *The World is Rich*. By the mid-1950s the premises were no longer listed as a film studio.

Catford

Bromley Road, Catford, Lewisham, London

The Windsor Studio at Catford was built in 1914 by Italian distributor the Marquis Serra, who founded the Windsor Film Company in the same year. In 1916, the company made the first movie to be based on one of Edgar Wallace's works of fiction. *The Man Who Bought London* was produced by Guido Serra and directed by F. Martin Thornton, with stars Evelyn Boucher, Roy Travers and E. J. Arundel. *Tom Brown's School Days*, again with Evelyn Boucher, was also made in 1916.

Production continued during the war years with spy stories starring Percy Moran, who had become a great favourite with the ladies in his former role of Lieutenant Daring.

In order to extend his production facilities, Walter West, who owned the Walthamstow Studio, bought the Catford Studio in 1920. An astute businessman, he had already established his own stock company with leading players of the day Stewart Rome and Violet Hopson, both of whom had formerly worked for Hepworth at his Walton-on-Thames studios. West also encouraged leading silent film comedian Walter Forde to make six two-reelers at his studio.

The small Catford Studio seems to have been used for the overflow from West's more important Broadwest Studios at Walthamstow. In 1921, after some financial upheavals, West and his financial partner, Broadbridge, agreed to part and the Catford Studio went into liquidation in the same year.

Clapham

Clapham Park, Lambeth, London

Bertram Phillips, who had made such films as *A Little Child Shall Lead Them* and *Rock Of Ages* with his leading lady Queenie Thomas at the Cranmer Court Studios at Clapham, acquired Thornton House in Clapham Park at the end of the First World War with the aim of having a manor-style studio. But Queenie Thomas married in 1919, and it seems that the house was never used for filming. However, Clapham Park was listed as a small studio up until 1955-56.

Clapham

Cranmer Court, Lambeth, London

In the early days of film-making, disused wharves, aeroplane hangers, skating rinks and greenhouses were all converted into film studios. In the case of Cranmer Court Studios in Clapham, space under railway arches was utilized for this purpose in 1913 by the Cherry Kearton Film Company. With one tiny, dark stage of just 45 ft x 30 ft, and their own film-processing equipment on the premises, they proceeded to make travel and nature documentary films, and even attempted news items at the outbreak of the First World War in 1914. However, the company quickly ran into debt and went out of business in the same year. Producers J. Payne and Sidney Morgan then leased the studio, but only made one film there, *Our Boys*, with Kathleen Harrison.

They too got into financial difficulties, and the studio was then used for a short period by the Holmfirth Company before the receivers were appointed in 1915.

In 1917, producer Bertram Phillips used the premises for a short space of time, and the studio was subsequently acquired in 1919 by Harry B. Parkinson, who made shorts starring Fred Paul until 1921.

Well abreast of the times, in 1923 De Forest Phonofilms registered to make British sound pictures, and used Cranmer Court until 1926 to experiment with short films. From time to time, they leased out the studio to Quality Plays Productions who made *Fallen Leaves* and *Constant Hot Water*, both of which were directed by George A. Cooper and featured former actor-manager John East who had co-founded The Neptune Studios, the first film studios at Elstree, in 1914. In *The Romance of the Movies*, Leslie Wood describes the experimental work on sound that was in progress at the time: 'With trains thundering past every few minutes, the Clapham Studio became the home of Lee De Forest Phonofilms, and they started producing sound-on-film talkies – that is to say, pictures with a photographic record of the actor's voice on the edge of the film. Already, in the early part of 1924, Dr Lee De Forest had produced a two-reel talking picture by the sound-on-film system in America. Called *Love's Old Sweet Song*, it featured Una Merkel and De Forest's wife, an accomplished singer. When the film was completed, its inventor expected to exploit it in a variety "turn" on the music halls. 'Production difficulties were tremendous... the room in which we worked at Clapham was just large enough to accommodate one set, and was heavily padded to keep out unnecessary noises, it also kept out fresh air. That precaution was due to the extreme sensitivity of the recorder which looked like two smoke-stacks with a connecting wire'. Use of the studio appears to have petered out by the end of the 1920s.

Craven Park

Harlesden, Brent, London

The tiny Craven Park Studio with its one dark stage, was founded by Thomas Welsh and George Pearson of The Welsh Pearson Company Limited in 1918. One of their first films was *The Better 'Ole*, with Charles Rock and Lillian Hall Davis, made in 1918. In the same year, they made *The Kiddies In The Ruins*, set in war-torn France, which was produced and directed by George Pearson. Considered quite an important company given its size, its first post-war film was *Garry Owen*, based on the novel by H. De Vere Stacpoole, a racing yarn with Fred Groves and Hugh E. Wright which did well at the box-office.

In 1920, a blonde, bubbly teenager, Betty Balfour, was introduced to Pearson by Welsh, who gave her a part in *Nothing Else Matters*, a drama with a music-hall background. Balfour became one of the most successful stars of the period.

The studio, which had been converted from a schoolhouse, was so tiny that the company was forced to hire Islington Studios for crowd scenes. It remained in Welsh-Pearson's hands until 1926 when it was forced to close due to the General Strike and high running costs.

Cricklewood

Camden, London

In 1919, Sir Oswald Stoll, theatre owner and entrepreneur, decided to enter the British film industry. Having founded Stoll Picture Productions, a public company, in 1920, he bought a former aeroplane factory in Cricklewood and converted it into the largest film studios in England. Sir Oswald regarded his new film studios as a commercial venture rather than an artistic venue, and although he installed expensive lighting and camera equipment, his productions, which followed the contemporary trend of adapting popular novels and plays, are generally thought to have been rather heavy-going.

One of Stoll's first productions was *The Yellow Claw*, directed by Rene Plaisetty, a thriller in which English and French detectives catch drug smugglers. The part of Henry Leroux was played by an actor with the rather unlikely name of Fothringham Lysons.

Cricklewood hired out its stages to other companies and producers, and one of their number who brought beauty, colour and light to the studios was American J. Stuart Blackton who directed *The Glorious Adventure* in 1922, starring society beauty, Lady Diana Manners (later Lady Diana Cooper) and Flora le Breton. This historical film, co-starring Victor McLaglen, is generally considered to be Britain's first feature in colour, and used the two-colour Prizma system. Evidently enjoying his contact with the English aristocracy, Blackton then went on to produce and direct Diana Manners as Queen Elizabeth in *The Virgin Queen*, with Carlyle Blackwell playing Lord Robert Dudley. Despite society patronage, Blackton's swashbuckling yarns did not do well at the picture houses, and in 1923 he retreated gracefully to his native America. In the same year, Stoll made *Becket*, starring Sir Frank Benson; and *Don Quixote*,

Cricklewood: *Don Quixote* (1923) was directed for Stoll by Maurice Elvey with Jerrold Robertshaw as Don Quixote and George Robey as Sancho Panza.

directed by Maurice Elvey and starring George Robey. Other Stoll productions of the decade included *Chappy – That's All*, starring Lewis Gilbert and directed by Thomas Bentley; *Confessions*, directed by W. P. Kellino; Phyllis Neilson-Terry, Lillian Hall-Davis and Clifford McLaglen in *Boadicea*; and *The Chinese Bungalow* with Matheson Lang. In 1926, Welsh-Pearson hired the studios to star the highly-popular Betty Balfour in *Blink Eyes*; and a year later they produced *Hunting Tower*, with Sir Harry Lauder – starring in his first feature – and Pat Aherne. In 1928, Pat's brother Brian Aherne (who became a major Hollywood star in the 1930s) was cast in *Shooting Stars*, co-starring Annette Benson and directed by A. V. Bramble with Anthony Asquith as assistant director. Towards the end of the 1920s, Herbert Wilcox made *The Woman In White* for his British and Dominions Company; and comedian Harry Tate filmed some of his famous sketches there.

An inevitable number of 'Quota Quickies' provided the staple diet for Cricklewood in the 1930s, with films like *Such is the Law*, with Lady Tree and C. Aubrey Smith; *Account Rendered*; and Victor McLaglen in *Dick Turpin*. In 1934, producer Joe Rock made a number of Leslie Fuller comedies, and in the same year the studios made *Irish Hearts* with Patric Knowles; and *Song At Eventide* starring Fay Compton. In 1935, Butchers rekindled the silent film hero Lieutenant Daring R.N. with Hugh Williams and Geraldine Fitzgerald; and another Butchers film at Cricklewood a year later was *Song Of The Forge*, directed by Henry Edwards (husband of Chrissie White), starring Stanley Holloway and Lawrence Grossmith. Butchers had made a number of films at Cricklewood from 1934, and were destined to make some of the last films to be shot at the studios, the Lucan-McShane *Old Mother Riley* comedies. Despite renovations to the studios in 1937 when a new sound stage was added, it was used by only a few independent producers. British film production was dwindling, and in 1938, the studios were sold.

Cricklewood: George Ridgewell directed *Becket* in 1923, which starred Sir Frank Benson as Becket, seen here preventing Queen Eleanor (Mary Clare) from stabbing Rosamund (Gladys Jennings).

Craven Park: An impish cockney humour, huge blue eyes and golden curls helped to make Betty Balfour a much-loved star of the 1920s, appearing in such films as *Blink Eyes* for Welsh-Pearson in 1926.

Cricklewood: American J. Stuart Blackton directed *The Glorious Adventure* in 1922, starring society beauty, Lady Diana Manners and Flora le Breton. This historical adventure, co-starring Victor McLaglen, is generally considered to be Britain's first feature in colour and used the two-colour Prizma system.

Croydon

The Rosie Film Company, Croydon High Street, Croydon, Surrey
Very little is known about the Croydon High Street Studio, which was set up in 1908 by Joe Rosenthal, a war film cameraman who had travelled for the Charles Urban Trading Company, and had settled in Croydon around 1906.

Croydon

Clarendon Film Company, Limes Road, Croydon, Surrey
These studios were founded in 1904 by Percy Stow and H. V. Lawley, the latter having been an associate of Cecil Hepworth. Their early comedy films, distributed by Gaumont, included *The Stolen Purse* and *Father's Hat*, and they also made adventure films like *The Stolen Bride* in 1906. The pair continued to make about one film a week, but in 1911, the studio rose to fame with the highly-popular Lt. Rose series, with P. G. Norgate as Lt. Rose. The series, commencing with *Lt. Rose And The Boxers*, was directed by Percy Stow, and wended its way through *Lt. Rose And The Chinese Pirates*; *Lt. Rose And The Foreign Spy*; *Lt. Rose And The Hidden Treasure*; *Lt. Rose And The Moorish Raiders*; and *Lt. Rose And The Patent Aeroplane*. The Marchioness of Townsend was another great publicity asset to the studio, and wrote a series of films for Clarendon including *The Convent Gate* (1913); *The Love Of An Actress* (1914); and *House Of Mystery* (1913), with Dorothy Bellew as the heroine. Clarendon seems to be one of the few film companies to have continued film output during the First World War years, mainly relying on three-to-five-reel films which were usually based on books or plays.

By the end of the war, the studio had been taken over by the Harma Company with F. Martin Thornton as head of production. Thornton's policy was to make rather more upmarket productions, such as *The Happy Warrior* with James Knight in the title role, and Leslie Howard (way down the cast list) as Rollo.

In 1928, Brian Aherne, who became a major Hollywood star in the 1930s, was cast in *Shooting Stars* at Cricklewood.

The suffragettes are made to dig roads under police surveillance in *Milling The Millitants*, a Clarendon Film Company Comedy of 1913.

By the early 1920s, the studio had two daylight stages and one dark stage, but after a dispute over his salary, F. Martin Thornton left the company and was replaced by James Reardon to direct some comedy shorts. At this time, the British film industry was suffering after the post-war boom, and Clarendon was no exception in having run into financial difficulties. Although backed by some provincial exhibitors in 1921, the studios were eventually closed in the early 1920s.

The Marchioness of Townsend was a great public relations asset for the studios at Croydon, writing a series of films for Clarendon that included *The Convent Gate*, starring Dorothy Bellew, in 1913.

Croydon

Waddon New Road, Croydon, Surrey

To the early cinema-going public, the name of Cricks and Martin and their lion's head trademark were as familiar as the name of Metro-Goldwyn-Mayer and the MGM lion would be to later generations. Mr Cricks (ex Cricks and Sharp) and Mr Martin had made a number of films at Ravensbury Lodge in Mitcham before acquiring premises at Waddon New Road, Croydon in 1910.

This studio had one stage of approximately 65 ft x 30 ft, with a glass roof, half an acre of grounds and a staff of twelve, with film-processing equipment on site. The studio appears to have made its money from crime, specializing in detective films with a series about Police Constable Sharpe from 1911 onwards, and then in 1913 a further series, *Paul Sleuth, Crime Investigator*. In *The History of British Film 1906–1914*, Rachael Low writes: 'By 1914, however, the prevailing fashion for extreme sensationalism was affecting this firm as it was many others, and their major film *Paul Sleuth And The Mystic Seven*, also included the ultra-modern thrills of flight by balloon, pursuit by an aeroplane, and the automatic operation of a cinematograph camera hidden in a car to record its route'. Quite an achievement for the time. By 1912, the Cricks and Martin partnership had dissolved, but the studio continued to derive an income principally from one-reelers. *The Wraith Of The Tomb*, made in

An early home of British films: the Cricks and Martin Studio at Waddon New Road, Croydon.

Croydon (Waddon New Road): *The Fairy Bottle* from Cricks and Martin in 1913, starring Una Tristam and Bill Hayley.

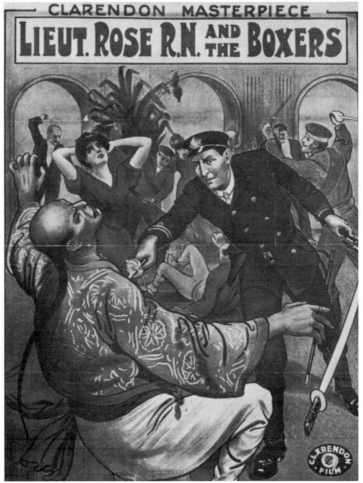

Croydon (Limes Road): Clarendon Poster, Lieutenant Rose.

1915, starring Dorothy Bellew and Sydney Vautier and directed by Carl Calvert, was, however, one of their longest and most important productions. Later that year, the Aurora Company, formed by C. H. Friese-Greene, son of film and camera pioneer William Friese-Greene, made two productions at the studio that experimented with colour, *The Earl Of Camelot* and *The Pride Of The Nation*.

Cricks, who had been left in charge of the studios, found the production of long features more and more complicated. In 1916, he let his studio to Maurice Sandground, a producer-renter who made such films as *His Uncle's Heir* and *The Walrus Gang*. Cricks retired from production in 1918, but continued to use his studio premises for his new printing business.

Crystal Palace
Bromley, Kent
Very little is known of this studio, which was part of the Crystal Palace and used by the Motograph Film Company in 1913. Two of their productions were *The Great Gold Robbery*, a crime story directed by Maurice Elvey, with Douglas Payne and Babs Neville; and *Maria Marten*, produced by Maurice Elvey and starring Elizabeth Risdon, Fred Groves and Nessie Blackford.

Denham
Buckinghamshire
The name of Denham Studios will always be synonymous with that of Alexander Korda, who created the studios in 1936. One of the most influential and flamboyant personalities to emerge on the British film industry scene in the 1930s, his contribution to the art of film is undeniable.

Born in Hungary in 1893, producer-director-film executive Korda started his career in 1912 working on a film journal, and by 1916 had directed Hungarian films including *The Duped Journalist*. Within a short space of time he became extremely successful, producing, directing and running one of Budapest's largest studios, but due to the political upheaval of 1919, he decided to leave Hungary with his protégé Maria Corda whom he had married. Korda successfully continued his career in Austria and Germany, and in 1926 went to Hollywood where he stayed until 1930. One of the films he made in Hollywood during that period was *The Private Life Of Helen Of Troy*, starring Maria Corda, a historical romance that proved to be a successful formula for many of his later pictures.

Korda was frequently accused of nepotism, and undoubtedly shaped the lives and careers of his two brothers, Zoltan, also a

Alexander Korda, who created the Denham Studios in 1936, was one of the most influential and flamboyant personalities of the British film industry in the 1930s.

film director, and Vincent, an art director who worked on his films. Probably due to their impoverished childhood and that he was the eldest of the three, Alexander always retained a dominant, paternal attitude towards his brothers, although both were extremely gifted in their own right, if without his charisma.

Wishing to return to Europe, Alexander Korda arrived in London in the autumn of 1931 with a contract from Paramount. At that time, Paramount were anxious to make a number of British films in order to comply with The Films Act, which would also allow them to import a large number of their American popular features. In 1932, Korda founded his own company, London Film Productions. He was assisted by Lajos Biro, a Hungarian playwright and novelist who became the company's scenario chief; George Grossmith, who was appointed Chairman; and Captain A. C. N. Dixie (then a Conservative MP), the joint Managing Director. Steven Pallos, the Hungarian film director, became the company's Foreign Manager. London Film's first production was *Wedding Rehearsal*, which introduced four young stars: Merle Oberon, Wendy Barrie, Joan Gardner and Diana Napier. Merle Oberon was to become Korda's second wife.

Korda's outstanding success was *The Private Life Of Henry VIII*, which cost in the region of £90,000, and opened many hitherto-locked distribution and funding doors abroad; its success and importance to the British film industry was comparable to that of *Chariots Of Fire* nearly 50 years later. Huge profits were made from the film in the United States, thus transforming Korda and Britain's standing in the eyes of US movie moguls, including those at United Artists who had invested in the production. Made at the British and Dominions studio at Elstree, the film starred Charles Laughton in the lookalike title role and his wife Elsa Lanchester as Anne of Cleves. After this triumph, Korda went on to produce a number of films including *The Rise of Catherine The Great*, starring Douglas Fairbanks Jnr, Elisabeth Bergner and Flora Robson; *The Private Life Of Don Juan*, this time with Douglas Fairbanks Snr, Merle Oberon and Owen Nares; and the extremely successful *The Scarlet Pimpernel*, starring the distinguished British actor (of Hungarian origin) Leslie Howard in the romantic title role, and Merle Oberon. It was the success of *The Private Life Of Henry VIII* and *The Scarlet Pimpernel* that attracted the attention of the financial advisers of the Prudential

Denham: Beautiful star Maria Corda was the first wife of Alexander Korda and after their divorce kept up a constant stream of bitter, reproachful letters which affected him enormously.

Assurance Company, which in the next few years invested several million pounds in the London Film Production Company, thus putting it on a secure financial footing and enabling Korda to start the construction of modern studios at Denham – a decision that was to cost the Prudential dear over the coming years.

The Fishery, near to Denham village and owned by Lord Forres, was the site that was purchased by Korda's advisers for Denham Studios. Building commenced on the 193-acre site in June 1935, and after disruption following a hard winter and a major fire during construction, the studios were completed in May 1936, an event that would not have escaped the notice of J. Arthur Rank who was planning to open his Pinewood Studios a few miles away in September of that year.

The largest film studio in Britain, Denham had seven stages, sophisticated lighting, Western Electric sound equipment, air conditioning, a private water supply and the largest electric power plant used at that time by a film studio. Additionally, the studio had plumbing, and woodworking, plasterers', painters' and electricians' departments, as well as dressing rooms and make-up salons. The most modern processing laboratories available were installed and Technicolor laboratories were also established. The Great Western Railway made special arrangements with London Film Productions to provide a fast-service train to Denham station. By Korda's own admission, there was just one thing wrong with this magnificent achievement – it was too big. Grand as the initial design was meant to be, the entire project was too large for the British film industry at that time. The workshops were too far away from the stages; the powerhouse was too close to the stages, creating noise and dirt; the cutting-rooms were a bike-ride away from the theatres; and dressing rooms and offices were linked to stages by long, draughty corridors. By the time Denham was completed, London Films had announced losses for the previous year totalling £330,000.

The Prudential, in the shape of one of their rapidly-ageing joint secretaries, a Mr E. H. Lever, begged Korda to work solely as a producer and abandon managing the company, but he refused to do so. In truth, both the Prudential and United Artists had loaned Korda too much money, and could not extricate themselves. Driven to desperation, Lever was to report in 1938: 'It is unfortunately true that on account of his temperament and opportunism in financial matters, Mr Korda is a dangerous element in any business, more particularly if he is in a position of

Thanks to the reputation earned by *The Private Life Of Henry VIII* and *The Scarlet Pimpernel*, Korda obtained the financial backing of the Prudential Assurance Company, which enabled him to build Denham Studios, officially opened in 1936.

Henry Fonda and Annabella in *Wings Of The Morning* (1937), directed by Harold Schuster at Denham with locations in Ireland.

control'. Korda was forced to relinquish command of the studios to his chief British rival, the J. Arthur Rank Organisation in 1939, who gained control. One should add that nearly 60 years on, the Rank Film Laboratory, based on the site of Alexander Korda's film processing laboratory at Denham 'invests in exploration of new techniques and processes, and has its own research and development department, plus record achieving methods that either improve quality or reduce costs'. Both achievements were recognized with an American Academy Award and by the Queen's Award for Technological Achievement.

Despite these early upheavals, Denham can point to a fine record of film production and landmark classics spanning nearly two decades.

The studios were not completed when work began on *Wings Of The Morning* (with locations in Epsom and Ireland), which was made in 1936 and starred Henry Fonda, Annabella and Leslie Banks. A 20th Century-Fox Denham production, it was the first Technicolor film to be made in the UK and was released in 1937. *Southern Roses*, with Chili Bouchier and George Robey, appears to

be the first film actually completed at Denham, while *Rembrandt*, produced and directed by Korda, followed shortly afterwards. The special quality common to the Korda films was their visual polish, which owed much to French cameraman Georges Périnal and Korda's brother Vincent, London Film's head of art direction. *Rembrandt* was a prime example of their work. Despite its artistic credentials, with Korda's star, Charles Laughton, in the lead and the presence of Laughton's wife, Elsa Lanchester, the film did not do very well at the box-office. However, it did give Gertrude Lawrence, the leading West End actress, an opportunity to measure her acting screen skills with those of the two established film stars. Three of London Film's 1937–38 productions with strong story-lines or casts were *The Elephant Boy*, based on the Rudyard Kipling story, with young Sabu; *Fire Over England*, with lovers Laurence Olivier and Vivien Leigh playing courtiers to Flora Robson's Queen Elizabeth; and *The Divorce Of Lady X*, again with Laurence Olivier, this time starring opposite Merle Oberon, supported by Ralph Richardson and Binnie Barnes. Korda made something of a coup with the

Denham: Jimmy Durante and June Clyde in *Land Without Music*, released in 1936.

appearance of Marlene Dietrich with Robert Donat in the London Film's production of *Knight Without Armour*, released in 1937. *I, Claudius*, however, was the epic that never was. Prudential and the long-suffering Mr Lever had come to the conclusion that as London Film's finances were in such an undesirable state, no further productions should be started after *I, Claudius*. One month into filming, Merle Oberon, who was to star opposite Charles Laughton in the film, appeared to have a car accident which was the ostensible reason for halting production. Korda rather cleverly was able to recover every penny that he had spent on the month's filming by claiming on his insurance which, in turn, helped him to pacify the Prudential. One should perhaps bear in mind that Miss Oberon had a very close relationship with Mr Korda at that time. Understandably Mr Laughton was not amused and the incident severed the Laughton-Korda relationship.

In the summer of 1937, Herbert Wilcox, whose British and Dominions Studios at Elstree had burnt down, secured a ten-year contract to make three 'Imperator' productions a year for RKO-Radio Productions. One of these was a remake of *The Rat*, starring Anton Walbrook. The cinematographer on *The Rat* was Oscar winner-to-be Freddie Young, who had already worked on a number of films with Wilcox. Young's career and films were to range over five decades encompassing *Bitter Sweet*; *Sixty Glorious Years*; *Goodbye Mr Chips*; *49th Parallel*; *Bhowani Junction*; *Lawrence Of Arabia*; *Dr Zhivago*; *Ryan's Daughter*; and *Nicholas And Alexandra*. Following *The Rat*, Young collaborated again with Herbert Wilcox on *Victoria The Great*, another 'Imperator' film starring Anna Neagle as Queen Victoria and Anton Walbrook as Prince Albert.

Korda and friends at a studio reception in 1936. Alexander Korda (top left) with Douglas Fairbanks Jnr, Richard Tauber, Diana Napier, Alan Hale.
(2nd row): Flora Robson, Elsa Lanchester, Marlene Dietrich, Tamara Desni, Elisabeth Bergner, William K. Conrad.
(Front): Conrad Veidt, Victor Saville (on floor), Ann Harding, Marie Tempest, René Ray, Edward G. Robinson, Googie Withers.

Despite the apparent success of Denham Studios, Korda's financial difficulties caused an exasperated Prudential Assurance Company to participate in a deal whereby the control of the studios passed to the J. Arthur Rank Organisation in 1939. A new company called D and P was set up to oversee the Denham Studios together with the neighbouring Pinewood Studios. Although Alexander Korda had lost his studio, he was now free to continue with independent film production. J. Arthur Rank, who had acquired a number of studios by the end of the 1930s, was also free to invest in other companies' productions as well as his own.

In common with other studios, Denham had been forced to close for a period in 1938 due to a slump in the industry and the imposition of new quota conditions. But in the main, the charming Mr Korda, with cigar, Homburg and spectacles, continued business-as-usual there along with other production companies. Probably anticipating the loss of control of his studio,

he had reached an agreement earlier in the year with Irving Asher (ex-Warner Bros) to launch Harefield Productions, which contracted Korda to make a number of quota films. *Q Planes*, with Valerie Hobson, Ralph Richardson and Laurence Olivier, was shortly followed by *The Spy In Black*, again with Valerie Hobson, but this time co-starring Conrad Veidt and Marius Goring. During the preparation for this film, Michael Powell, the director, encountered Emeric Pressburger who was co-scripting with Roland Pertwee; and thus the famous Powell and Pressburger partnership was launched.

In 1941, the pair worked together on *49th Parallel*, the wartime adventure drama about a ruthless German U-Boat Commander attempting to rescue his stranded crew by conveying them across Canada into neutral America. The star cast included Laurence Olivier, Glynis Johns, Leslie Howard and Eric Portman. In 1942, Powell and Pressburger founded Archer Films, which produced a number of prestigious film classics including the strikingly

Denham: *Fire Over England* (1937) starred lovers Vivien Leigh and Laurence Olivier as courtiers to Queen Elizabeth (Flora Robson).

Denham: Merle Oberon (who became the second wife of Alexander Korda) and Laurence Olivier in *The Divorce Of Lady X*, directed in 1937 by Tim Whelan.

Denham: Marlene Dietrich as Countess Alexandra in *Knight Without Armour*, directed by Jacques Feyder for London Film Productions in 1937.

visual and original *I Know Where I'm Going!* (1945), with cinematographer Erwin Hillier, starring Roger Livesey and Wendy Hiller; and *A Matter of Life and Death* (1946), with David Niven, Roger Livesey, Marius Goring, Raymond Massey and Kim Hunter.

Continuing his work with Irving Asher as associate producer, Korda produced *The Four Feathers* at Denham, which was released in April 1939. With a cast that included Ralph Richardson, C. Aubrey Smith, John Clements and June Duprez, the film was another Korda family success, directed by Zoltan Korda, with Vincent as its designer.

Denham continued to rent out its stages to incoming production companies, and one of its most valued tenants was MGM, who made three large pictures there towards the end of the 1930s. All three films had an invaluable mix of American and British stars that would appeal to the UK and US box-offices. These were *The Citadel* (1938), based on A. J. Cronin's novel of the same name, directed by King Vidor and starring Rosalind Russell, Robert Donat and Ralph Richardson; *Yank at Oxford* (1938), produced by Michael Balcon, with the incredibly handsome Robert Taylor co-starring with Maureen O'Sullivan, Vivien Leigh and Lionel Barrymore; and the much-loved *Goodbye Mr Chips* (1939), which was directed by Sam Wood, with Freddie Young as cinematographer, shooting delightful performances from Robert Donat, Greer Garson and Paul von Henreid (he later dropped the 'von').

Just prior to the passing of control at Denham from Korda to the Rank Organisation, P. C. Stapleton, a former studio manager at British International Pictures, was brought in to run a more efficient studio. Many old hands lamented the passing of the flamboyant Korda days as retrenchment replaced extravagance. One of the last films to be made at Denham in the 1930s was *The Stars Look Down*, with Michael Redgrave, Margaret Lockwood and Emlyn Williams. Graham Greene was to write: 'Dr Cronin's

mining novel has produced a very good film – I doubt whether in England we have ever produced a better'; another feather in the cap of Carol Reed, who directed the picture. A number of cinemas were temporarily closed at the outbreak of war, with half of the British studios' capacity immediately requisitioned for non-cinematograph uses. During the war years, Rank moved ahead with his production plans at the expense of Alexander Korda, who had gone to America in 1940 to supervise completion of *The Thief Of Bagdad*. Korda then stayed on to direct *That Hamilton Woman*, which made excellent propaganda for Britain, with its obvious comparison of Nelson's efforts to defeat a British foe to the then-current war with Germany. Although severely criticized by many in the UK for having 'deserted' to Hollywood, Korda made several trans-Atlantic crossings during the war, and it now seems clear that he was acting as a courier for Winston Churchill – a worthy film scenario that Mr Korda sadly missed. In 1942, he was knighted by King George VI, the first film personality to be honoured in this way.

Films with a strong national theme designed to raise morale were a strict governmental requirement in the early 1940s, and a department at the Ministry of Information was set up to boost show business propaganda. In common with other studios, Denham had been requisitioned by the government, but by the end of 1941 it was allowed to make films of its own on some of the unused stages as well as accepting overflow productions from its sister-studio at Pinewood. *In Which We Serve*, made at Denham in 1942, was the first really important film about naval aspects of the Second World War. This much-acclaimed box-office draw originated from Lord Louis Mountbatten, who had recounted some of his wartime experiences, including the exploits of his own destroyer HMS *Kelly*, to Noël Coward. Coward obtained permission to base his story on these events provided that no real names or characters were used. The film was produced by Coward, who also co-directed with David Lean, resulting in a

Rosalind Russell, the dominant American leading lady of the 1930s and 1940s who usually portrayed career women, appeared in *The Citadel*, co-starring Robert Donat and directed by King Vidor at Denham in 1938.

Robert Donat and Greer Garson in the film adaptation of *Goodbye Mr Chips* by James Hilton. The film was directed by Sam Wood for MGM-British at Denham in 1939.

In Which We Serve, made at Denham in 1942, was the first really important film about naval aspects of the Second World War. This much-acclaimed box-office draw originated from Lord Louis Mountbatten who had recounted his wartime experiences to Noël Coward. The film was produced by Coward (right), who also starred and co-directed with David Lean (left).

beautifully acted and directed picture, with a cast that included Noël Coward, John Mills, Kathleen Harrison, Richard Attenborough, Bernard Miles, Celia Johnson, Kay Walsh and many more. The film also gave John Mills (later Sir John Mills) and Richard Attenborough (later Lord Attenborough), who gave an early, fine portrayal of a terrified sailor, the opportunity to meet. Over the decades, they have worked on many films together as well as independently. *In Which We Serve* paved the way for *This Happy Breed* by Noël Coward, which was about family life between the wars and set in London. This time the film was produced by Coward, directed by David Lean and photographed by Ronald Neame. The cast included a number of players from *In Which We Serve*. With the closure of Pinewood Studios, for a period of time Denham was progressively busy, and in his book *Up in the Clouds, Gentlemen Please*, John Mills recalls that: 'Around 1943 and onwards, Denham Studios became a hive of activity and, because of transport problems, many people made their homes in the area – the Oliviers, David

Lean, Ronnie Neame, Robert Helpmann, Constance Cummings, Robert Donat and David Niven'. John Mills lived with his family in Denham village at Misbourne Cottage, just three minutes from the studios across the fields.

Meanwhile, Laurence Olivier had an invitation from the Ministry of Information indicating that a film of *Henry V* would

Denham: The incredibly handsome Robert Taylor starred with Maureen O'Sullivan and Vivien Leigh in *A Yank At Oxford*, produced by Michael Balcon in 1937/8.

Laurence Olivier as *Henry V* (1945). The Ministry of Information suggested that the film would provide both excellent propaganda and entertainment, an assumption that proved to be totally correct.

One of Denham's most famous films was *Brief Encounter* (1945), a romantic tale starring Celia Johnson and Trevor Howard, with Rachmaninov's Piano Concerto Number Two providing the heady background music.

provide excellent propaganda and entertainment. Throughout the war, J. Arthur Rank's interests in studios, production, distribution and exhibition had been escalating, as he hoped to establish a British Hollywood to rival its American counterpart when the war was over. Rank's major studio at Pinewood had been commandeered for most of the war, which meant that Denham, one of his smaller studios, took the overflow of some of the other British film productions as well as those that his organization had financed, or partly financed. He put £475,000 into *Henry V*, which brought him an international reputation as well as a quick return on his investment. Made in Ireland and at Denham Studios, the presentation of Laurence Olivier's highly-praised film was largely in the style of the Shakespearean Globe Theatre. Its admirable simplicity was matched by magnificent acting from a cast that included Olivier, Renee Asherson and Felix Aylmer. Superb costumes, and a splendid score from William Walton made this film a worthy and appropriate offering to the British cinema-goer at the end of the war. Another war film, this time in modern vein, was made around the same period

at Denham, when Carol Reed directed *The Way Ahead*, a war story set in North Africa starring Stanley Holloway, David Niven, Leo Genn and Jimmy Hanley.

One of Denham Studios' most successful films, released in 1945 and set against Rachmaninov's Piano Concerto Number Two, was *Brief Encounter*. A simple, romantic tale initiated by a chance meeting in a railway station, the film starred Celia Johnson as a suburban housewife and Trevor Howard (his third film and first starring role) as the doctor with whom she falls in love. David Lean became the first British director to be nominated for an Academy Award; the Cannes Film Festival named *Brief Encounter* Best Picture; and Celia Johnson won the Best Actress Award from the New York film critics circle. The musical director on the film was veteran Muir Matheson. *Brief Encounter* had been based on the play *Still Life*, by Noël Coward. *Blithe Spirit* was also adapted from a play by Coward, this time a brittle farce, and was again directed by David Lean. Although the production was well received, Coward was far from happy in spite of excellent performances from Rex

Rome came to Denham in 1945 with Gabriel Pascal's financially disastrous production of *Caesar And Cleopatra*. Claude Rains and Vivien Leigh are seen here in the title roles.

Harrison, Kay Hammond as his ghostly wife, Constance Cummings as his second wife and Margaret Rutherford as the superb, dotty scene-stealing spiritualist, Madame Arcati.

Rome came to Denham in 1945 with Gabriel Pascal's production of *Caesar And Cleopatra*, which proved to be a financial disaster. The sets of this fantastic production spread all over Denham Studios and quite a bit of Buckinghamshire. Palaces and banqueting halls were put up with amazing speed, along with a sphinx. There were feuds over scripts, and problems due to the weather, the illness of the star (Vivien Leigh) and the unions. After eight months, the production, plus sphinx, was taken to Egypt, where the film was completed. First-rate performances from Claude Rains as Caesar, Vivien Leigh as Cleopatra, Stewart Granger and Flora Robson, could not save the film. Alexander Korda, meanwhile, had returned from America, and working in association with MGM during 1943–45, had produced just one picture at Denham for them, *Perfect Strangers*, which he also directed, with a cast headed by Robert Donat, Deborah Kerr, Glynis Johns and Ann Todd. MGM decided not to continue their agreement with Korda, so in 1946 he re-established London Films and purchased a controlling interest in British Lion. British Lion owned Shepperton Studios in Surrey, which Korda then made his production base.

In fact, time was beginning to run out for Denham Studios in the latter half of the 1940s. John Mills returned to make *The Octoberman* and *So Well Remembered* in 1947, while another production of the same year was the famous *Odd Man Out*, a superbly-crafted film, directed by Carol Reed, about a wounded IRA gunman on the run in Belfast. The gunman was played by James Mason, with Kathleen Ryan as his long-suffering girlfriend, and the rest of the cast included Robert Newton, Cyril Cusack and Robert Beatty. This was followed by Rank's amusing *Vice Versa*, with Roger Livesey and a young Anthony Newley. However, the undoubted Denham success of 1948 was the Rank-Two Cities production of *Hamlet*. The story goes that an executive, asked by J. Arthur Rank what he thought of the first rushes, replied 'Wonderful, you wouldn't know it was Shakespeare'. Produced and directed by Laurence Olivier, it was the first British film to win an Oscar in the Best Picture category. Olivier's outstanding performance as the melancholic *Hamlet*, together with William Walton's eerie score, was fully complemented by the distinguished cast that included Eileen Herlie and Basil Sydney as the Queen and King, Felix Aylmer as Polonius, Jean Simmons as Ophelia, and Norman Wooland as Horatio. *So Evil My Love*, a curiously old-fashioned melodrama from Paramount starring Ray Milland, Ann Todd and Geraldine Fitzgerald, was released in the same year, as was

Carol Reed (left) chatting to Kathleen Ryan and James Mason on the set of *Odd Man Out*, made at Denham in 1947.

Woman Hater, a romantic comedy starring Stewart Granger and Edwige Feuillère.

By the end of the 1940s, the unthinkable had happened. The mighty Rank empire, the owner of Denham, was in ruins with an overdraft with the National Provincial Bank of over £16,000,000. Drastic measures were necessary, and were undertaken by John Davis, a former city accountant, who had become Managing Director of Rank. In order to safeguard the survival of Rank's flagship studio, Pinewood, plus that of some distribution and exhibition outlets, everything else that could go, had to go. In essence, Denham's seven stages were close to the end of their days. Production at the studios had been in the hands of Joseph Somlo and Earl St John. Somlo now departed and only a small

British leading lady Deborah Kerr appeared in *Perfect Strangers*, a comedy co-starring Robert Donat, directed by Alexander Korda for MGM/London Films at Denham in 1945.

The Boulting twins, director Roy (2nd from right) and producer John (left), with their stars of *Fame Is The Spur* (1947): Michael Redgrave (2nd from left), Rosamund John and Bernard Miles (right). A Boulting Brothers/Two Cities film made at Denham Studios.

Denham: The undoubted success of 1948 was *Hamlet*, a Rank film produced and directed by Laurence Olivier, the first British film to win an Oscar in the Best Picture category. Left to right: Felix Aylmer (Polonius), Laurence Olivier (Hamlet), Basil Sydney and Eileen Herlie (the King and Queen) and Jean Simmons (Ophelia).

J. Arthur Rank and Laurence Olivier during the filming of *Hamlet*.

part of the studios, leased to 20th Century-Fox, remained open for a short period of time. Production was to be concentrated at Pinewood Studios under the control of Earl St John who had run the Paramount circuit before the war.

One of the last big films to be made at Denham, though, more exactly, at the back of Denham, was *The History Of Mr Polly*, based on the novel by H. G. Wells, which was directed by Anthony Pelissier. The production seems to have been beset by problems. Having searched England for the right village location, it was eventually decided to build the entire set on the river behind Denham Studios. Thick fog held up the shooting, as did a strike from the production crew, and at one point, John Mills, who starred in the picture, was locked out of a union meeting as an actor but allowed in as a producer. The film also starred Sally Ann Howes (daughter of actor Bobby Howes), with Megs Jenkins, Finlay Currie and Miss Juliet Mills, aged 7, playing the part of Little Polly. A well-crafted picture, the film was not the box-office success that its producers had hoped for.

Sadly, Denham's film history came to an end in 1950–51 with Disney's *Robin Hood*. After this, it was leased to the American Air Force, then housed Rank Xerox equipment (the saving grace of Rank's fortunes). Later still, part of the complex was leased to Anvil Films; and then, despite a campaign to save the studios supported

Denham: John Mills and Margaret Lockwood, who were both under contract to the J. Arthur Rank Organisation, at the Royal Premiere of *Hamlet* in 1948. The two young actresses in the making are Miss Juliet Mills and Miss 'Toots' Lockwood (centre).

Ray Milland (Welsh-born Reginald Truscott Jones), who had become a leading Hollywood actor in the 1930s, appeared in *So Evil My Love*, a Paramount melodrama of 1948 directed by Lewis Allen at Denham.

by Francis Ford Coppola, the main buildings were demolished by the British Land Company who had acquired the site for redevelopment. In the early 1950s, the D and P Studios Limited, which had owned Denham Studios, went into liquidation.

Sir Alexander Korda died in 1956, and Lord Rank died shortly after his retirement in 1972.

Dulwich
Southwark, London
Optimistically referred to as Gaumont's 'first studio', the studio at Dulwich was operated by A. C. Bromhead who had started an English branch of the French company in 1898. The studio was a covered open-air platform at Fellow's cricket field, Champion Hill, Dulwich. The productions there included *Curfew Shall Not Ring Tonight* (1906), based on a poem by Rose H. Thorpe, a drama in which the heroine ties herself to a bell-clapper to save her lover from execution. It appears that the star of the film was a lady of ample proportions who, on leaping on to the clapper, destroyed the set. Godfrey Tearle, the star of *Romeo And Juliet* (1908), recalled that between filming the cast would put the field to its rightful use and indulge in a little cricket.

Ealing
Ealing Green, Ealing, London W5 5EP
There was never anyone quite to equal Will Barker. He was an innovative showman who moved swiftly from being a 'free show, pennies in the hat' amateur producer-director-cameraman in 1896 to a professional visionary. By 1901, he had founded the Autoscope Company, and in the same year built an open-air studio – a stage, two scaffolding rods and a backcloth – at Stamford Hill. These humble beginnings yielded a quick profit but were superseded between 1902 and 1904 by his relocation to Ealing in west London, a venue that was to earn itself a very special place in the history of the British film industry. In 1907, he bought a mansion in its own grounds, approximately on the spot of the later famous Ealing Studios, and built three glass stages for his film productions. In 1911, Barker made his first two-reeler, *Henry VIII*, in which Sir Herbert Tree starred as Cardinal Wolsey. Such was his fame, Sir Herbert was paid £1,000 for each day's work at the studio, an enormous amount of money for the period. *Henry VIII* was the first UK film for which a recognized composer (Edward German) would write the music. Barker soon became known for his lavish productions and an eye for detail which belied his seemingly casual approach to

ALLAN FIELD'S WARNING

Ealing: Will Barker groomed his actors for stardom, including Blanche Forsythe who appeared in *Allan Field's Warning* in 1913.

casting. 'Can anyone swim?', he bellowed at an attentive crowd waiting outside his casting office. 'A little', came a timid female response. 'Good', Barker replied. 'You can play Ophelia'. Barker made the first British film version of *Hamlet* in 1912, which was directed and performed by actor Charles Raymond. Ophelia was, in fact, played by actress Dorothy Foster, and shooting was completed in just two days at a cost of £180.

By 1913, Barker was grooming his actors for stardom. These included Blanche Forsythe and Fred Paul who appeared in his version of *East Lynne*, which was directed by Bert Haldane and was Britain's first six-reel feature. After the outbreak of the First World War, Barker cast his now leading lady, Blanche Forsythe, in the title role of *Jane Shore*, a historical drama based on events during the reign of Edward IV. Directed with great skill and shot with imagination by Bert Haldane and F. Martin Thornton respectively in 1915, it was a most ambitious production employing thousands of extras. Barker was quickly compared to D. W. Griffith, and, rare for the time, the American rights sold as fast as their English counterparts.

Up to 1918, Barker continued to produce films and lease his studios to other production companies. The films made during that period included *The Little Home In The West*, a drama; *Diana Of Dobson's*, with Cecilia Loftus; and *What Every Woman*

Knows, a Barker-Neptune production based on the play by J. M. Barrie, starring Hilda Trevelyan. Having been in the film industry from its inception in 1896, Barker decided to retire from production after the end of the war – having spent 22 years in the industry. In 1920, he finally sold his now famous studios to the General Film Renters Company, which soon went out of business. For a period of time subsequently, the studios were used by small independent producers and were eventually bought in 1929 by the Associated Radio Pictures Company, who built a new studio very close to the old Barker studio in 1931.

The new company was headed by chairman-actor-impresario, Sir Gerald du Maurier; Reginald Baker, a chartered accountant; Stephen Courtauld; and theatrical producer Basil Dean. Born in 1888, Dean had become an actor at the age of 18, and later produced and directed many plays and films. There is no doubt that he was the studio's guiding influence during the 1930s, and was responsible for the development of the careers of two music-hall entertainers who became Britain's highest paid film stars of the period: Gracie Fields and George Formby.

He also helped promote other comedians of that decade through the medium of film, such as Flanagan and Allen, Will Hay and Claude Hulbert. Dean's new studio claimed the title of the first British, purpose-built sound studio, and was equipped with the American RCA Photophone system. While waiting for

Ealing: After the outbreak of the First World War, Barker cast Blanche Forsyth, now his leading lady, in the title role of *Jane Shore*, based on events during the reign of Edward IV. After this ambitious production employing thousands of extras, Barker was compared to D. W. Griffith and American rights sold as quickly as their British counterparts.

Basil Dean also developed the career of toothy, northern comedian George Formby, seen here with his famous ukulele during the 1930s. Formby's films at Ealing include *I See Ice*; *Trouble Brewing*; and *Come On George*.

Basil Dean, Ealing's guiding force in the 1930s, was responsible for the development of the film career of music-hall singer-comedienne Gracie Fields, who became Britain's highest paid star of the 1930s. She is seen here in *Queen of Hearts*, produced by Basil Dean in 1936.

the studios to be completed, Dean produced *Sally In Our Alley* at the Beaconsfield Studios, which starred Gracie Fields and was directed by Maurice Elvey, another great contributor to the British film industry. Born in poverty, Elvey received virtually no education, and began working at the age of nine. He became a stage actor in his teens and, soon after, a film director. His career as a director began in 1913 and lasted 44 years during which time he turned out an amazing number of films. He became Britain's most prolific film director, and his work covered a range of genres from melodrama to comedy. He died in 1967.

Two further Elvey films with Gracie Fields during the 1930s were *This Week Of Grace* (made at Twickenham) and *Love, Life and Laughter*, while her other films for Ealing included *Sing As We Go*, with its well-known title song. The tale of an unemployed mill girl who leads workers to a successful, no-strike productivity

deal, it was based on a story by J. B. Priestley, and produced and directed by Basil Dean in 1934.

Born in 1898, Gracie Fields became a music-hall entertainer at the age of thirteen and soared to unprecedented popularity in the 1930s on stage and in films, both as a comedian and a singer. Her down-to-earth Rochdale background and sparky personality helped to create hope in the lives of British audiences during the years of the depression. She was the top box-office draw and the highest paid actress in Britain during most of the decade. Much loved, her popularity was so great that Parliament was adjourned early so that MPs could go home to listen to one of her radio broadcasts. After the outbreak of the Second World War in 1939, she joined her second husband, actor-director Monty Banks, in his exile in America, creating a furious outcry from her adoring fans who felt that she had deserted England in

Ealing: *Perfect Understanding* (1933), with Gloria Swanson and Laurence Olivier.

its hour of need. Although she made several films in America, it was more-or-less the end of her outstanding career. In the early 1950s, she went into semi-retirement on Capri with her third husband. She was created Dame Commander of the Order of the British Empire in 1979.

Her equally popular male counterpart of the 1930s and early 1940s was the toothy, northern comedian, George Formby, with his famous ukulele. Born in 1904, he started out as a boy entertainer, and then became nationally famous through radio. Although his simple, slapstick comedies were rarely exported to the United States, he was nevertheless a top UK box-office star between 1936 and 1945. Post-war audiences' tastes changed abruptly, ending his film career. He returned to the music-hall and regained some of his popularity before his death at the age of 57. His Ealing films include *I See Ice*, with Kay Walsh; *Trouble Brewing*, with Googie Withers; *Come On George*, with

Pat Kirkwood; and *Turned Out Nice Again*, which was his last film for Ealing.

A co-production agreement between Ealing Studios and RKO in the United States did not materialize in 1931, and in 1932 the studio was temporarily closed due to the breakdown of further negotiations. In 1933, the studio changed its name to Associated Talking Pictures, and in company with its fellow studios in the UK, both made its own films and rented out studio space to other production companies. One of these films, made in 1933, was *Perfect Understanding*, which Gloria Swanson produced and starred in with Laurence Olivier. Carol Reed got one of his earliest opportunities to (co-)direct with *It Happened In Paris*, starring Robert Wyler in 1935. Reed also directed *Midshipman Easy* with a young Margaret Lockwood and Hughie Green. Other films during the Basil Dean period included Ivor Novello and Fay Compton in *Autumn Crocus*; and cool, English beauty

Cool English beauty Madeleine Carroll, who appeared in *The Dictator* with Clive Brook at Ealing in 1935.

Ealing Studios in the early 1930s.

Madeleine Carroll and Clive Brook in *The Dictator*, which was directed by Victor Saville. It should also be noted that in the latter half of the 1930s, David Lean worked as an editor, and Ronald Neame became a lighting cameraman at the studio. However, life at the Ealing Studios was far from easy for Basil Dean towards the end of the 1930s. The studios were a privately backed company, and after a final disagreement with the Courtaulds, Dean left the company and the studios in 1938, returning to the theatre and ENSA (Entertainments National Service Association) for the Second World War. One of the directors of the studios, Reg Baker, recommended to the board that Michael Balcon, who had worked at Gainsborough Films, Gaumont-British and MGM, should become the new head of the studios. On his appointment, Balcon brought several former Gaumont-British colleagues to work at the studios, and these included actor-director Walter Forde and directors Sidney Gilliat and Robert Stevenson. At the same time, the studios' name was changed from Associated Talking Pictures to Ealing Studios. Balcon was a team man, encouraging ideas and initiative. During his 20 years at Ealing, Balcon developed a wide group of talented directors, many of whom had also been editors, such as Charles Crichton, Charles Frend, Robert

Hamer, Leslie Norman and Thorold Dickinson, and also writers like Alexander Mackendrick, Harry Watt and Basil Dearden, who formed a long director-producer partnership with Michael Relph. Over 90 films were made under Balcon's aegis, and very few of these were box-office disasters. In the main, his films had a distinct style of their own and were well acted, edited, written and photographed. Balcon also encouraged many new screenwriters, including T. E. B. Clarke, who scripted the famous comedies *Hue And Cry*; the Oscar-winning *The Lavender Hill Mob*; and *Passport To Pimlico*. In 1942, Alberto Cavalcanti, director, producer, screenwriter and art director, joined Michael Balcon to become the studio's feature director. Cavalcanti introduced the influence of documentary film-making into fiction films, often getting the cameras out on location to give the production a more realistic background. Among Cavalcanti's films for Ealing were *Went The Day Well*, a wartime story; *Champagne Charlie*, starring Tommy Trinder and Stanley Holloway as two Victorian music-hall rivals; and *Nicholas Nickleby*, based on the novel by Charles Dickens, which starred Derek Bond, Cedric Hardwicke and Sally Ann Howes, with the tiny role of Madeleine Bray going to Michael Balcon's daughter, Jill Balcon.

Debonair Maurice Chevalier in the 1936 Ludovico Toeplitz production *The Beloved Vagabond* at Ealing.

Headed by Michael Balcon with his brilliant team of producers, and directors, Ealing Studios made a number of comedies that are considered classics of their genre. *The Lavender Hill Mob* was directed by Charles Crichton in 1951 and T. E. B. Clarke won an Oscar for his screenplay.

EALING STUDIOS present
Alec Guinness & Stanley Holloway
with *Sidney James & Alfie Bass*
as **THE LAVENDER HILL MOB**
A MICHAEL BALCON PRODUCTION Directed by CHARLES CRICHTON Original screenplay by T.E.B. CLARKE
The men who broke the bank – and lost the cargo!

Great Gold Robbery LATEST

Jean Kent in *Champagne Charlie* directed by Alberto Cavalcanti. By the time this film was made in 1944, Michael Balcon had been firmly in charge of the Ealing Studios for a number of years.

A number of well-loved films from the mid-1940s to the mid-1950s at Ealing included *The Captive Heart* with Michael Redgrave and *Saraband For Dead Lovers*, Ealing's expensive costume drama about the sad Hanoverian Sophie Dorothea (played by Joan Greenwood) recounting her illicit affair with dashing Count Koenigsmark (Stewart Granger), which was Ealing's first Technicolor film. Both of these were directed by Basil Dearden. Other films of the period include *Scott Of The Antarctic*, directed by Charles Frend and starring John Mills as Captain Scott, which was Ealing's prestigious production of 1948 and selected for the Royal Variety Performance; *Whisky Galore*, directed by Alexander Mackendrick, a great comedy in which islanders of Todday steal the cargo of whisky carried by a shipwrecked freighter, with old faithfuls Basil Radford, Catherine Lacey, James Robertson Justice, and Duncan Macrae; *Kind Hearts And Coronets* (partly made at Pinewood), one of Ealing's classic comedies directed by Robert Hamer, with Alec Guinness playing eight members of the D'Ascoyne family; *The Blue Lamp*, directed by Basil Dearden, with the much-loved Jack Warner as P.C. Dixon in Ealing's tribute to the Metropolitan Police; *The Man In The White Suit*, directed by Alexander Mackendrick, a sharp comedy in which a young man discovers a miracle cloth and then finds that nobody wants to buy it, starring Alec Guinness with Joan Greenwood and Cecil Parker; *Mandy*, with a leading role for Jack Hawkins as a headmaster of a school for deaf children who becomes closely involved with the mother of one of his pupils; *The Titfield Thunderbolt*, directed by Charles Crichton, the first

Saraband For Dead Lovers (1948), Ealing's expensive costume drama and first Technicolor film, starring Joan Greenwood and Stewart Granger.

49

John Mills in the title role of *Scott Of The Antarctic*, which was selected for the Royal Film Performance in 1948.

Ealing: Michael Balcon on the set of *Kind Hearts and Coronets* with Alec Guinness, who played eight members of the D'Ascoyne family. The film was directed by Robert Hamer in 1949.

Ealing comedy in Technicolor, the story of a wonderful old train and a bunch of united villagers determined to keep their branchline from closure; and *The Cruel Sea*, based on the novel by Nicholas Monsarrat, one of Ealing's most successful films which consolidated Jack Hawkins' reputation as a top box-office star.

Directed by Charles Frend, *The Cruel Sea* was produced by Leslie Norman (father of film critic and author Barry Norman), who had a long and distinguished career in the British film industry as an editor, producer and director. Among his most characteristic films in the Ealing style were *The Cruel Sea*, made in 1953 and *Dunkirk*, which he directed in 1958 for Michael Balcon. But Norman was happy with a wide range of subjects, from one of his early production efforts, the breezy Ealing comedy *A Run For Your Money* (1949), to a subject in a more thoughtful vein, *Mandy*. His other films for Ealing Studios and Michael Balcon, either as editor, producer or director, include *The Overlanders*; *Eureka Stockade*; *Where No Vultures Fly*; and *The Night My Number Came Up*, which had a distinguished

script by R. C. Sherriff, and an equally distinguished cast which included Michael Redgrave, Sheila Sim, Ursula Jeans and Denholm Elliott.

With the blossoming of television in the UK in the early 1950s, together with changing public tastes, Ealing Studios started to run into financial difficulties in 1952. It lacked financial reserves and, in common with most studios at that period, existed from film to film. Disaster struck in 1955 when a massive bank overdraft led to the sale of the company's assets, of which the studio was a major part. Later that year, the studios were sold for £300,000 to BBC Television – a sad blow to the British film industry. With the demise of his studio, Balcon went into independent production, but his latter years were mainly taken up with political and financial survival in film.

In 1992, the BBRK Group purchased the studios from the BBC, the studios then being used for television series such as *Ellington*, for Yorkshire Television, and a number of commercials. *The Hour Of The Pig* and *Boiling Point* were also

Fine feathers for Lady Agatha D'Ascoyne (Alec Guinness) in *Kind Hearts And Coronets*.

Edith D'Ascoyne (Valerie Hobson) looks rather more fetching than Lady Agatha in *Kind Hearts And Coronets*.

Alec Guinness was *The Man In The White Suit* in an Ealing comedy directed by Alexander Mackendrick in 1951. The film relates the story of a chemist who discovers an indestructible fibre, to the horror of the hard-headed yarn manufacturers.

Richard Attenborough and director Basil Dearden on location for *The Ship That Died Of Shame* (1955), based on a short story by Nicholas Monsarrat.

Young Audrey Hepburn as Nora in *Secret People* (1952), directed by Thorold Dickinson.

Ealing: Jack Hawkins reports for duty on *The Cruel Sea* (1952). The film consolidated his reputation as a top box-office star.

Left to right: Jack Hawkins, Donald Sinden, Virginia McKenna and Michael Balcon on the set of *The Cruel Sea*.

A band of crooks in *The Ladykillers*, an Ealing comic masterpiece of 1955 directed by Alexander Mackendrick. Left to right: Alec Guinness, Peter Sellers, Danny Green, Herbert Lom and Cecil Parker.

Filming the comedy *Touch And Go* in the mid-1950s, starring Margaret Johnston and Jack Hawkins and directed by Michael Truman.

made in that year. In November 1993, *Screen International* announced that: 'A new attempt to resuscitate film production at London's Ealing Studios has just been unveiled', and that the BBRK Group was seeking investors via the Business Expansion Scheme, hoping to raise £750,000 in development money in addition to seeking investment of between £500–40,000 in a five-year portfolio of five or six Ealing projects. Alan Latham, managing director of Ealing Studios Productions, a sister-company to the BBRK Group, said that he hoped Ealing would ultimately be producing ten films a year.

During the summer of 1994, Peter Chelsom directed part of *Funny Bones* for Touchstone and Gary Sinyor made his low-budget *Solitaire For 2*. In the autumn of the same year, BBC Television commenced production of *Pride And Prejudice*, and Franco Zeffirelli announced that he would be making *Jane Eyre* at the studio, starring William Hurt, Charlotte Gainsburg, Joan Plowright, Anna Paquin and Geraldine Chaplin – Ealing's first international feature for many years, using its stages into 1995.

In October 1994, the industry was saddened to hear that the studios' owner, the BBRK Group had gone into receivership and that the studios were for sale. However, Vicki Harvey-Piper, the studio's operation manager, reported 'business as usual', with a continuing flow of projects for film, television and commercials either in production or pre-production. These included *Face Value*, directed by John Henderson for Freedom Pictures, and several features for Parallel Pictures. *The Secret Agent*, a Norman Heyman Production, directed by Christopher Hampton and starring Gerard Depardieu, Bob Hoskins and Patricia Arquette, was filmed in 1995. *Variety* commented that it was 'appropriately gloomy and grim, but these are not qualities that will recommend it to most audiences'.

In a complex two-stage deal, Ealing Studios was sold to the BBC on 31 May 1995. The BBC then passed them on to the National Film and Television School, who acquired them with a £2 million grant from the Foundation of Sport and the Arts, which was funded by the football pools companies. Although, from 1995 to 2000, the studios concentrated on television productions and commercials, features included *Land Girls, East is East, Mansfield Park* (also partly made at Pinewood) and *Guest House Paradiso* (director Adrian Edmondson's first feature, with Rick Mayall, Adrian Edmondson, Helen Mahieu and Vincent Cassel as its leading players).

In April 2000, Ealing Studios was purchased by Uri Fruchtmann and Barnaby Thompson of Fragile Films, John Kao of The Idea Factory and Harry Handelsman of the Manhattan Loft Corporation. They expressed their main goal as being to continue the tradition of feature film making, while also focusing

In 2000 Fragile Films produced *High Heels and Low Life*, a comedy thriller, at Ealing Studios. It was directed by Mel Smith (left) and starred Minnie Driver (right). In 2002 Ealing will celebrate the centenary of its first film studio. Photo and copyright courtesy Eugene Adebari/Buena Vista.

on television and 'new media'. One of their first films at Ealing in 2000 was *High Heels and Low Life*, directed by Mel Smith and starring Minnie Driver.

The studios have three large sound stages, one small sound stage, two non-sound low-budget stages, one model stage and on-site services that provide editing, workshops, camera/sound/lighting equipment, offices and catering facilities. Ealing is the only studio in London on the underground travel network and is well positioned between Heathrow Airport and the City of London, midway between other film studios and other production facilities in the West End of London.

East Finchley
Barnet, Hertfordshire
This studio was owned by the British and Colonial Kinematograph Company Limited, and formed in 1909 by A. H. Bloomfield and J. B. McDowell.

Before their relocation to Hoe Street, Walthamstow in 1912-13, the pair made a number of series at Newstead House in East Finchley which included *Dick Turpin*; *Don Q*; and *Three-fingered Kate*. The first of the *Lieutenant Daring* series was also produced at this studio.

Elm Park
Harrow, London
The only information on these studios appears in an advertisement in the 1947 *British Film Industry Year Book*, edited by John Sullivan. 'Elm Park Studios, 25 minutes from Baker Street Station. Our object is to meet the requirements of the small producer whose costing schedule will not stand the strain of the prevailing heavy rentals for studio space. Camera and crew, sound equipment and all the standard facilities are available on a basis affording maximum assistance to economic production'.

East Finchley: Brave Percy Moran in the title role of *Lieutenant Daring Quells A Rebellion*, the British and Colonial film of 1912 which instigated a highly successful series.

Elstree: The British Hollywood

Technically, the Elstree studios (excepting the Danziger Studios) were not in Elstree, but in Borehamwood. The first film-makers to come to this area discovered Borehamwood, adjoining the old village of Elstree, with the railway line dividing Elstree on the east from Boreham-Wood to the west (see p58). The British Hollywood was always referred to as Elstree, and is so to this day.

The second point to be made about this location is that one is not talking about one studio, but six, treated here in chronological order. Elstree was Britain's only film township where the studios operated cheek by jowl, with the producers, directors, actors and technicians working at perhaps several, or all of the studios at one time or another.

Although on a much smaller scale than Hollywood, Elstree too became a film community, with artists, directors and work-force buying property nearby, visiting each other on set, romancing each other and so on.

Elstree

Eldon Avenue, Elstree/Borehamwood, Hertfordshire

Neptune Studios; Ideal Studios; Blattner Studios; Leslie Fuller Studios; Rock Studios; British National Studios; National Studios; ATV/Central Television Studios; BBC Television, Elstree Studios. The first studio to make its appearance at Elstree was the Neptune Studio. By 1913, an actor-manager, John East, had joined the London Film Company at Twickenham and developed a friendship with a colleague, Percy Nash. The pair became convinced that, given the appropriate backing, they could produce their own films economically and quickly to meet current demands. With the help of barrister/businessman, Arthur Moss Lawrence, they succeeded in devising and attracting long-term investment and they found themselves reconnoitring London's green belt in the hope of finding a fog-free zone, which also had a good train service to London, beautiful scenery for location work and, most important of all, an excellent site for a film studio.

Neptune Films was founded in January 1914, and their new studio was the finest in England at that time, incorporating dressing rooms with running water, administrative offices, a generating plant and processing facilities. The studio stage was over 70 ft in length and devoid of glass, so claiming the title of the first dark stage in Europe.

The outbreak of the First World War in 1914 prompted many British silent films to take on a patriotic note, but, in the main, productions were adapted from popular stage plays. The studio formed its own stock company, which included Daisy Cordell, Frank Tennant and Gerald Lawrence; and Neptune's first feature was *Harbour Lights*. Ahead of their time, Neptune obtained the film rights to the works of James Barrie, the most popular piece being *The Little Minister*, filmed in 1915. Their contributions to the recruitment features requested by the government included *The Royal Naval Division At Work And Play* and *Women In Munitions*, but, as during the Second World War, there was also a need for escapism and Neptune's contributions to this genre were *The Romany Rye* and *Married For Money*.

The studio, with its permanent company and visiting stage stars like Gaby Deslys and May Whitty, prospered for its first three years. In addition, between 1915 and 1920, Neptune leased or rented their stages to other companies including Ideal Films

The original Neptune Studios at Borehamwood opened in 1914. Subsequent owners include the Ludwig Blattner Film Corporation and Joe Rock Production. In the mid 1930s, the actor Leslie Fuller would lease some studio space for several films.

and The British Lion Film Company (no connection with the later British Lion Films), while British Instructional was to start life in a hut rented on to them in turn by Ideal Films. These companies also attracted the stage and screen stars of the day, including Ellen Terry, Edith Craig, Dennis Neilson-Terry, Gladys Cooper and Matheson Lang.

The war took its terrible toll of young lives, which meant the loss of actors and technicians, while the introduction of an Amusement Tax caused further loss at the British box-office. American films flooded the home market as the British producer increasingly became the victim of circumstance. Neptune was forced to cease production in 1917, and further difficulties compelled them to mortgage two-thirds of their land in 1918. In 1920, the company went into liquidation, and by August 1921, it was all over. By 1924, nearly every British studio was closed. However, Ideal Films leased the Elstree premises until 1928, when Ludwig Blattner bought the studios for the British Phototone Sound Productions, also known as the Ludwig Blattner Film Corporation. Blattner developed the Blatnerphone, the first known commercial electro-magnetic

Updated map of all Elstree studios.

① New Elstree Studios, built 1956. Also known as the Danziger Studios.

② Whitehall Studios, built 1928, *became* Gate Studios

③ British National Studios, built 1926, *became* B.I.P. Studios (British International Pictures) A.B.P.C. Studios (Associated British Picture Corporation) EMI Studios EMI-M.G.M. Studios THORN-EMI Studios Cannon Brent Walker Entertainment Group/Goldcrest Studios

④ B. & D. Imperial Studios, built 1926. (British and Dominions Films Corporation). Adjoining the B.I.P. Studios.

⑤ Neptune Studios, built 1914, *became* Ideal Studios Blattner Studios Leslie Fuller Studios Rock Studios British National Studios National Studios A.T.V. Television Studios/Central TV BBC Elstree Television Centre

⑥ Amalgamated Studios, built 1937, *became* M.G.M. British Studios

BOREHAMWOOD

"HOLD THAT, JOHN!"

UNCLE SAM. "HELLO, BRITISHER, GOING IN FOR FILM-MAKING? DON'T FORGET OUR OLD SONG, 'WE'VE GOT THE SUN, WE'VE GOT THE STARS, AN' WE'VE GOT THE MONEY TOO.'"

JOHN BULL (registering dogged determination). "NO MATTER: I'M GOING TO HAVE A TRY."

Punch cartoon.

Ludwig Blattner, inventor of the Blattnerphone, the first known commercial electro-magnetic sound recording machine wire and tape. Blattner, who bought the former Neptune Studios in the 1920s for British Phototone Sound Productions, is seen here with actress Ellen Terry and his son Gerry.

sound recording machine wire and tape. By this time, the arrival of sound was dominating the action of every studio, and the Blattner Studio already had three neighbouring rival studios at Elstree: John Maxwell's BIP Studios; Herbert Wilcox's British and Dominions Studios; and the new Whitehall Studios, situated next to the station. Wilcox shot his first 'talkie', *Wolves*, with Dorothy Gish, at the silent Blattner Studios in July 1929, and sound was added at his own studio, which acquired recording facilities in September 1929. Blattner had already had a great success with *A Knight In London*, directed by Lupu Pick and starring Lilian Harvey, an English actress who became extremely popular in Germany. But although something of a technical genius, Blattner was commercially slow in adapting to sound, and the receivers were called in during 1932. The studio was taken on a long lease by Joe Rock, an American producer, in 1935, while later that year, Ludwig Blattner committed suicide.

Taking on Ludwig's son Gerry Blattner as his manager, Rock made a number of features, some of which starred comic Leslie Fuller, who would also set up his own production company at the studio for a short time. Other films included *The Man Behind The Mask*; *Cotton Queen*; and *Calling All Stars*. Probably one of the most distinguished films to be made at the Rock Studios was Michael Powell's *The Edge Of The World* in 1937, starring Belle Chrystal, Niall MacGinnis, and John Laurie, which established Powell as a brilliant director.

However the studios did not fare well, and by March 1938, the receivers were once again called in and Rock's backer, J. H. Iles, was declared bankrupt.

By the early 1940s, the Rock Studios had been acquired by Lady Yule, the widow of a jute millionaire, and were renamed the British National Studios. Among its productions in the 1940s was *Gaslight*, directed by Thorold Dickinson and starring Diana Wynyard and Anton Walbrook. The film was produced by John Corfield, who had long held an executive position on the British National Board. There were two *Old Mother Riley* comedies; a drama, *Love On The Dole* with up-and-coming actress Deborah Kerr, which was produced and directed by John Baxter; *The Laughing Lady*, with popular singing team Anne Ziegler and Webster Booth; and *The Ghosts Of Berkeley Square*, with Robert Morley, Yvonne Arnaud and A. E. Matthews. In 1947, the neighbouring ABPC Studios, who had not completed their post-war building renovations, borrowed the British National premises for their first post-war production, *My Brother Jonathan*, based on the novel by Francis Brett Young.

Lady Yule owned the studios until 1948, and died in 1950. The studios were to pass briefly into other hands and then darken for several years until a new proprietor surfaced in the early 1950s.

Douglas Fairbanks Jnr. had, of course, already acted in a number of films in the US and in the UK, but in October 1952, he leased the four-sound-stage British National Studios, which he now called the National Studios, and turned television producer. With British

Herbert Wilcox shot his first 'talkie', *Wolves*, with Dorothy Gish at the silent Blattner Studios in July 1929. Sound was then added at his British and Dominions Studio at Elstree.

exhibitors searching for means to counter the growing threat of television competition, 1952 marked the most important single factor in the changing face of British production – that is of film and television projects – and Fairbanks created a landmark by being head of the first British company to complete a contract with an American television corporation. This agreement was with NBC for a series of 39 films as well as additional commercials. With admirable precision and efficiency in terms of time, money and exhaustive pre-production planning, he produced six 26-minute films at the end of his first two months, with another six nearly packaged. From then on the studios were to become television oriented. In 1962, ATV Television acquired the studios, and in turn BBC Television bought them in January 1984.

Elstree

Shenley Road, Elstree/Borehamwood, Hertfordshire, WD6 1JG

British National Studios; BIP Studios (British International Pictures); ABPC Studios (Associated British Picture Corporation); EMI Studios; EMI-MGM Studios; EMI Studios; Thorn EMI Studios; Cannon Studios; Goldcrest Studios/Brent Walker Entertainment Group; Elstree Film Studios. The building of British National Studios was begun and almost completed by American film pioneer J. D. Williams. He had formed British National Films with W. Schlesinger, and invited Herbert Wilcox into the company. In 1925, the trio bought 40 acres of land at Elstree, but discord arose between Williams and Schlesinger. The conflict developed into litigation, and John Maxwell, a canny Scot, already a respected member of the industry, was called in. He provided finance and so gained control of the company and the studio. Having lost a considerable amount of his own money, J. D. Williams returned to the United States, and after a short time Herbert Wilcox left to partner top musical star of the 1920s, Nelson Keys, in the founding of a new film company, The British and Dominions Film Corporation. Mr Wilcox did not have to travel far afield for this venture. The British and Dominions Film Corporation leased studios from John Maxwell that adjoined the British National Studios which Wilcox had helped J. D. Williams to build in 1925–26. Maxwell fully acquired British National Studios in 1927, and changed its name to British International Studios (BIP). Due to Maxwell's Scottish background and the careful financial handling of the company, the BIP Studios became known as The Porridge Factory.

Maxwell's background in the industry had been in distribution, but his decision to buy the British National Studio was no doubt nudged on with the knowledge that the Federation of British Industries had inaugurated a campaign to secure statutory protection for the British film-producing industry. The Cinematograph Films Bill came to fruition in April 1927, one month after he acquired the studio. The bill stipulated that UK cinemas would be called upon to include a proportion of British films in their programmes rising to 20 per cent, while the renters were required to obtain a similar percentage of British films for distribution. The low-budget films produced to fulfil these terms became known as the 'Quota Quickies'. The bill became law in December 1927.

Although Herbert Wilcox had christened the Maxwell studio with his production of *Madame Pompadour*, with the unique Dorothy Gish in the main part, the first film under the new BIP banner was *The White Sheik* in 1927, starring former beauty queen Lillian Hall-Davis and heart-throb of the day Warwick Ward. She was to fade out of films some years later, but he went on to make a further career as a production and studio manager, and much later in 1948, to produce the company's 250th film *My Brother Jonathan*. Blonde, blue-eyed Betty Balfour, known as the English Mary Pickford, followed *The White Sheik* in *A Little Bit of Fluff*.

From BIP's inception, John Maxwell had planned that it should become an international organization; its very name reflecting the scope of its activities. A solicitor by profession, he

Alfred Hitchcock, whose *Blackmail*, made for John Maxwell's BIP, is usually regarded by the industry as Britain's entry into sound production. Hitchcock made a number of films for BIP and returned to the studio (by then named the ABPC studios) after the Second World War to make *Stagefright* (1949), starring Marlene Dietrich, Jane Wyman, Richard Todd and Michael Wilding.

Canny Scot John Maxwell was already a respected member of the film industry by the time he acquired the British National Studios at Elstree in 1927, changing the name to British International Studios (BIP).

An advertisement in *The Film Weekly*, 21 October 1929, price three old pence, inviting the audience to 'see and hear' John Maxwell's *The Informer*.

was astute enough to realize that he knew very little about film production, and that he should surround himself with people who knew the business. Accordingly, in 1927 after *Poppies Of Flanders* and *The Silver Lining*, he obtained the services of a 28-year-old director called Alfred Hitchcock for a three-year, 12-picture contract at £13,000 a year, an enormous amount of money at the time. Hitchcock's first film for Maxwell was *The Ring*, starring the Danish actor Carl Brisson. This investment was rewarded with excellent notices from *The Bioscope* and *Morning Post*.

Maxwell's next move was to appoint Walter Mycroft, a founder member of the London Film Society and the film critic of the *Evening Standard*, first as scenario editor and then as head of the studios. Mycroft, a hunchback, was always attended by a retinue of employees eager to obey his every whim. Such was his striking appearance and authority, he became known as 'Czar of all the Rushes', and Hitchcock's comment on the situation was that he managed to make films in spite of Mycroft. Shortly afterwards, Hitchcock directed another film, *The Farmer's Wife*, starring Jameson Thomas, a favourite actor of the period.

By this time, Maxwell realized that for his studio to make money, he needed to secure sound American (and, to some extent, European) distribution. To obtain American distribution

The British International Pictures studios, 1929. The sound stages on the left of the picture were the British and Dominion Studios belonging to Herbert Wilcox.

meant making films with American talent; Hollywood, after all, was already enticing British stars such as Madeleine Carroll, Ray Milland, Brian Aherne, C. Aubrey Smith and Ronald Colman to its studios.

In response, over the following years, Maxwell invited Syd Chaplin, Tallulah Bankhead, Lionel Barrymore and many others from the United States and Europe to appear in his productions. These included Maria Corda, the wife of the then little-known Hungarian, Alexander Korda. Fresh from her American appearance in *Helen Of Troy*, she starred in Maxwell's production of *Tesha*, Victor Saville's first film for BIP. Maxwell had formed Burlington Films, a private company, and invited Saville from Gainsborough Pictures to be its Managing Director and make films at the BIP studios. As was the custom in the silent days, two productions could work at the same time on the huge barn-type stages, so it was not unusual for Saville to work at one end and 'the boy wonder', as he called Hitchcock, at the other. Saville's many films for Maxwell included *Kitty* and *The 'W' Plan*.

Never a flamboyant figure, Maxwell nevertheless decided that the time had come for a display of showmanship with his 1928 trade show of *Moulin Rouge*, starring the famous Russian actress, Olga Tschechowa. It was his biggest film venture to date, and with Hitchcock and Saville already under contract, he invited E. A. Dupont, the eminent German director, to direct the production. Dupont was an extraordinarily gifted man, and would go on to direct *Piccadilly*, with Anna May Wong (Charles Laughton had his first day of film work in this production), and *Atlantic* for Maxwell. However, Dupont was extremely temperamental and preferred to work after midnight, which in turn created additional costs for his artists and workers of all grades. Maxwell, a thrifty Scot, was alarmed to hear that the budget for *Moulin Rouge* exceeded £80,000; but once again the reviews for the film were excellent and BIP's prestige increased. Thomas Bentley and Harry Lachman were others who directed films for Maxwell before the coming of sound, as did Italian comic-dancer Monty Banks, who also appeared in and directed a number of comedies for the studios. Monty's Italian temperament

Elstree (BIP): 'Gertie' Lawrence needs her glasses to sort out a problem during the filming of *Lord Camber's Ladies* (1932), watched by an attentive director, Benn W. Levy and producer Alfred Hitchcock (back only).

was exceeded only by that of his wife, Gladys Frazin, an ample American actress who always looked as if a diamond chandelier had recently descended on her. Their stormy domestic scenario far out-did anything that was taking place on the set, and technicians would await the condition of the battered husband, complete with black eye or bandaged head, with anticipation and betting slips. Tragically, Miss Frazin was eventually to commit suicide. In time, Monty Banks married Gracie Fields.

By 1928, John Maxwell had formed a subsidiary company of BIP, Associated British Cinemas, which started with 40 cinemas, a number which by 1930 had grown to 120. These included some of the most opulent cinemas of the time including the Regal at Marble Arch and the Lido at Golders Green. This was a direct challenge to C. M. Woolf at Gaumont-British, whose Gaumont cinemas numbered 280 by 1929, and who, like Maxwell, had interests in production and distribution.

In 1928, a feeling of trepidation was taking hold in the corridors of power in Wardour Street. It emanated from one word, 'sound'. In 1927, Warner Bros in the US had produced

The Jazz Singer, starring Al Jolson, though it had more singing than talking. The following year, John Maxwell's cinemas did excellent business with *The Singing Fool*, again with Al Jolson, the first American major sound feature film to be presented in London.

The artistic, technical and financial implications of this achievement were enormous. Many people thought it was just an overnight novelty that would disappear. However, once it was realized that sound was a necessary addition to all future film-making, there was a fierce competition to install varying new equipment in the studios and to produce the first British 'talkie'.

Maxwell decided to gather as much expert knowledge as possible for this venture, and coaxed two clever men from the BBC to join him. They were R. E. Jeffrey, who had had extensive experience of sound-recording and studio construction, and D. F. Scanlan, who had been one of the chief engineers at the BBC's early 2LO operation. Work began at BIP on two temporary sound stages in April 1929, and under Jeffrey and Scanlon's supervision, RCA Photophone recording equipment was

Ben Lyon (centre) filming *I Spy* in 1933 for BIP. He later became a casting director for 20th Century-Fox.

installed. With complications of different recording systems, techniques and trade show dates, there are many conflicting claims for the first British 'talkie': Herbert Wilcox with *Wolves*; British Sound Films with *Crimson Circle* and Neo-Art Productions' *White Cargo*. Industry historians tend to agree that the first 'all-talking' feature was *The Clue Of The New Pin*, produced by British Lion, but Alfred Hitchcock's *Blackmail*, made for John Maxwell's BIP at Elstree, is usually regarded by the industry as Britain's entry into sound production.

For 'talkies', and for those early recording systems in particular, the actors had to have very good voices, and the casualties are now legendary. Czech actress Anny Ondra was the star of *Blackmail*, but her thick accent and the temporary studio joined forces to give her adoring public a totally incomprehensible sound. Post-dubbing was not possible at that time, so English actress Joan Barry stood at the side of the set and read Miss Ondra's lines into a microphone as the actress mouthed them. Thus by accident, not design, *Blackmail* also

67

Elstree (BIP): Austrian tenor Richard Tauber with Jane Baxter, filming *Blossom Time*, directed by Paul L. Stein in 1934.

became the first British film to be dubbed. Sound demanded that the camera had to be silenced so that noise was not picked up by the recording equipment. Large boxes on wheels were constructed with a door at one end and a window for the camera to film through at the other. Unfortunately, the heat from the studios and the confined space made these constructions unbearably hot, and at frequent intervals, the unfortunate cameraman would be allowed out to be rubbed down, and then

Elstree (BIP): Gertrude Lawrence and Douglas Fairbanks Jnr, a romantic pair both on and off the screen, in *Mimi* (1935), produced by Walter Mycroft, the 'Czar of all the Rushes'.

put back into what were to become known as 'sweat boxes'. The Duke and Duchess of York, later King George VI and Queen Elizabeth, visited the *Blackmail* set, and the film premiered at Maxwell's Marble Arch cinema in June 1929, just one year after America's first major sound feature success at the same venue.

Maxwell pressed on with two 'Quota Quickies', *The Flying Scotsman*; and *The Lady From The Sea*, which featured a youthful Ray Milland. His next major achievement was to produce an archive classic, *Atlantic*, with Madeleine Carroll and John Stuart, which was the first British talkie produced in different language versions to be released with separate English, French and German sound-tracks. Two film extras in this production were to become major stars, Stewart Granger and Michael Wilding. There were also two new faces on the BIP stages at this time: 'clapper boy' Ronald Neame and stills photographer Michael Powell, both of whom were to have long and distinguished careers in the British film industry.

Two early 1930s productions included *Potiphar's Wife* starring Nora Swinburne and rising star Laurence Olivier (then married to actress Jill Esmond); and George Bernard Shaw's *How He Lied To Her Husband*, with Edmund Gwenn, which Maxwell obtained permission to film.

At that time, actors were generally required to perform their own stunts, and Henry Kendall, appearing in *The Flying Fool*, demonstrated just how versatile a film star had to be. Director 'Captain' Summers prepared the film – the story of a secret service pilot – with considerable enthusiasm. He built a huge tank in BIP's largest studio and prepared for a three-day shoot. Covered in lard against the cold, Kendall was called upon to dive under a grill in freezing water, wearing plus-fours which billowed out like air balloons. Later, he was required to pursue a Handley-Page aircraft along a tarmac, and jump into it on take-off, and assist with the flying and photography. Not surprisingly, he finished up in hospital with 'blood-poisoning', studio terminology for exhaustion.

Other star personalities in the 1930s were comedians Ernie Lotinga in *Josser Joins The Navy*; Leslie Fuller (who also had his own production company at another Elstree studio for a time) in *Poor Old Bill*; and Will Hay in *Those Were The Days*, an adaptation of Pinero's play *The Magistrate*. Another box-office success for BIP was *Blossom Time*, starring Viennese Richard Tauber. An important sound development was made during this film, when Tauber sang to the accompaniment of a London choir, which was relayed over the telephone, then broadcast as the background to one of the scenes.

American film stars like Charles Bickford for *Red Wagon*; Bebe Daniels for *A Southern Maid*; Ben Lyon for *I Spy*; and Douglas Fairbanks Jnr for Mimi were hired by Maxwell during the decade, as well as Buddy Rogers, whose wife, Mary Pickford, visited him on set during the making of *Let's Make A Night Of It*. From the London stage, the irrepressible Gertrude Lawrence and Gerald du Maurier arrived at BIP for *Lord Camber's Ladies*.

John Maxwell had always kept a low public profile – not for him the showmanship at which Wilcox and others excelled. The 'old man', as he was affectionately known, presented a stern but paternal image to his studio, and good Scot as he was, never had

Elstree (BIP): Mary Pickford visiting the star of *Let's Make A Night Of It* (1937), Charles Buddy Rogers, whom she married following her divorce from Douglas Fairbanks Snr.

Elstree (BIP): Patricia Neal in *The Hasty Heart*, produced and directed by Vincent Sherman in 1948. Her co-star was an American actor of whom a film magazine wrote in 1947: 'His real interest might lie in public service of another kind. Maybe politics.' The gentleman in question was Ronald Reagan.

either money or matches in his pocket. His private life always remained just that from start to finish. It came as something of a surprise, then, to the industry (and possibly to himself) to observe his fierce and public involvement in an inter-company punch-up in 1936.

Gaumont-British, his major rival, had floundered into an outsized overdraft, and Maxwell, with a keen take-over bid in hand, announced to the press that it had been successful and that henceforth he would head both Gaumont and BIP. In fact, this did not happen. 20th Century-Fox had long owned a portion of the Gaumont organization, and while Maxwell negotiated in London with the board from Gaumont, Isidore Ostrer (also from Gaumont-British), fearful of the inevitable monopoly if 5–600 cinemas fell into one pair of hands, negotiated in New York with the President of 20th-Century Fox. The outcome was a deal that did not include Maxwell. Angry and disappointed, he sued the Ostrer group and lost, then quietly bought another 130 cinemas. In the background, J. Arthur Rank, who had recently opened Pinewood Studios, watched and waited.

The film township of Elstree was to have its own disaster in 1936 when Herbert Wilcox's British and Dominions Studios, adjoining those of John Maxwell, were gutted by fire. Although anxious to help, Maxwell was not in a position to offer Wilcox the necessary backing and facilities a second time around. But someone else was,

and taking his courage and insurance money in both hands, Wilcox started afresh at J. Arthur Rank's Pinewood Studios.

The 'Porridge Factory' continued to churn out films during this era, including four musicals: *I Give My Heart*, from the operetta, *The Dubarry*, with Gitta Alpar and Owen Nares; *Invitation To The Waltz*, whose ballet scenes were devised and danced by Anton Dolin; *Heart's Desire,* with Richard Tauber and Diana Napier (who had met and married while filming at BIP); and Henry Hall with his BBC Dance Orchestra in *Music Hath Charms.*

It was Maxwell's imaginative backing of Erich Pommer's Mayflower Picture Corporation that really caught public attention in the late 1930s. With Charles Laughton featuring in each production, Pommer made three quality films with star performers. They were *Vessel Of Wrath,* based on Somerset Maugham's story, with Elsa Lanchester (Laughton's wife); *St Martin's Lane,* starring Vivien Leigh and Rex Harrison; and a film adaptation of Daphne du Maurier's novel *Jamaica Inn,* with Laughton as a villain, lovely Maureen O'Hara as the heroine, and Robert Newton, the hero.

As world attention was focusing on Europe in 1939, John Maxwell cast a speculative eye over the brand-new Amalgamated Studios at Elstree, which had been completed but was debt-laden. While Maxwell pondered, J. Arthur Rank bought, not because he wanted to use the studios but to prevent Maxwell

Elstree (BIP): Lovely star-to-be Maureen O'Hara in *Jamaica Inn*, produced by Erich Pommer and directed by Alfred Hitchcock in 1939.

from acquiring them. It was simple Rank business expertise, for if the most modern UK studios were added to Maxwell's film conglomerate, it would mean more competition and a loss of film production for his own Pinewood and Denham Studios.

Thus, in the course of three years, Maxwell was prevented from making two major deals that could well have altered the course of British film production and distribution. It could certainly not have helped Maxwell's blood pressure to pass the Amalgamated Studios each morning with the knowledge that Mr Rank had leased them to the Ministry of Works for storage purposes.

By as late as 1939, productions were still being planned for BIP Elstree, but with the outbreak of war the studios were commandeered by the Royal Ordnance Corps, and some productions were moved to Welwyn Studios which BIP/ABPC had acquired in the early 1930s. When John Maxwell died in 1940 it was the end of an era for the BIP Studios and the loss of an important influence on the British film industry.

John Maxwell had always desperately hoped that, on his death, his family would retain control of his film empire, now titled the ABPC (Associated British Picture Corporation). But it was not to be. Warner Bros acquired a number of family shares in the early years of the war, and in 1946 they bought a vast share bulk from the Maxwell estate, thus placing themselves in an unassailable position.

The transatlantic flavour of the British Hollywood was now more pronounced than ever. Of the old Anglo-Scots school, Sir Philip Warter (John Maxwell's son-in-law) became Chairman and Robert Clark, a Scottish protégé of John Maxwell, became Executive Director of Studios and Production. From the new American arm came Max Milder, Head of Warner Bros' London company and their Teddington Studios, who became Managing Director of ABPC, and was to be succeeded by C. J. Latta, an American Warner Bros executive. The new Anglo-American tie-up was to mean that, in principle, Warner Bros would distribute ABPC pictures in their 800 American cinemas and the Associated British would reciprocate by showing the Warner films in their British theatres. The new board also decided on the complete reconstruction of their Elstree Studios.

'Back to work in Britain's Hollywood', read the *Picturegoer*'s headline in 1947. Irked at not having his own stable of stars like Rank, and thus having to pay other studios for their services, Robert Clark contacted Robert Lennard who had been the studio's casting director before the war, and suggested that he should return and build up a new contracting star system for ABPC. Lennard certainly had an uncanny knack of choosing the right actor to fit the role, and top directors, including Fred Zinnemann and Stanley Donen, came to rely on his talent.

The studios' first feature after the war in 1947 was *My Brother Jonathan*, but as the studios were not ready, the film was made at the British National Studios, very close by. The film shot Michael Denison to stardom in a cast that included his wife, Dulcie Gray, and character actress Beatrice Varley; while other new stars in the studio were Ronald Howard, Stephen Murray, Beatrice Campbell, and James Robertson Justice, who had another career as a gentleman farmer and tended to arrive in a gleaming Rolls Royce with a pig in the back. By 1948, the studios were ready for production, and the first post-war film to be made

A charming study of Vera Ellen who starred in *Happy Go Lovely* at Elstree in 1950.

there was *Man On The Run* with Derek Farr and Joan Hopkins, and newcomers Laurence Harvey and Kenneth Moore in smaller roles.

Affecting all British studios in 1948 was the British government's new agreement with Hollywood, which entitled the latter to take 25 per cent only of American earnings out of the country. The British film industry received this with two schools of thought. One was that it was a wonderful opportunity to recapture the American market, since a clause in the agreement provided that for every dollar British films were to earn in the US, a corresponding dollar could be taken out of Britain. The other feared the end of the UK as an indigenous market, becoming instead part of an American production machine that would absorb their frozen assets by making American films in British studios for world sales.

Meanwhile, Robert Lennard was lining up another newcomer whom he had contracted to the studio: Richard Todd. Todd's first starring role was *The Hasty Heart*, the new studio's first international production, produced and directed by Vincent Sherman. Todd's co-stars were Patricia Neal and an American actor of whom a film magazine in 1947 wrote: 'His real interest might lie in public service of another kind. Maybe politics'. The gentleman in question was Ronald Reagan.

Elstree (ABPC): An interested visitor to the set of *The Magic Box* (1951) was Mrs Ethel Friese Barnes, eldest surviving child of British movie camera inventor William Friese-Greene, upon whose life the film was based. Robert Donat played Friese-Greene, Maria Schell the inventor's wife, and 12-year-old Janette Scott was Ethel. The film was produced by Ronald Neame and directed by John Boulting.

Although almost permanently lost to Hollywood, Alfred Hitchcock was lured back to his old (now international) studio in 1948 to make *Stagefright*, starring Marlene Dietrich, Jane Wyman (the former Mrs Ronald Reagan), Michael Wilding and Richard Todd. While Miss Dietrich swirled across the sets in costumes designed by Christian Dior, Miss Wyman became peeved at her own unattractive film personality and began to improve her appearance on a day-to-day basis, which, according to 'Hitch', was the reason for her failing to maintain her film character. Other films in the 1940s at the studio were a psychological drama, *Woman With No Name*, with Phyllis Calvert and a new film actor, Richard Burton; and *The Dancing Years*, with Patricia Dainton and Dennis Price. The new British Film Production fund had been set up to administer the Eady plan (known as the Eady Levy) by which a levy on cinema admissions would be channelled back into film production. In 1950, the fund received its first cheque of over £20,000. Helpful as this scheme was intended to be, it was a mere drop in the ocean to ABPC, who decided to sell their Welwyn studio and concentrate on Elstree.

International productions on the ABPC stages at this time were *Captain Horatio Hornblower*, with Gregory Peck, Robert Beatty and Terence Morgan; and *Happy Go Lovely*, with Vera Ellen arriving to star alongside Cesar Romero.

A classic head with enormous doe eyes had been peering from a Crookes Lacto-Calomine lotion advertisement. Its owner, Audrey Hepburn, so appealed to Robert Lennard that he signed her up for *Laughter In Paradise* and *Young Wives' Tale*. A five-year contract followed, and she was then loaned to Warner Bros for a sum far in excess of her contract figure. Again, the accountancy from a canny Scot, in the shape of Robert Clark, was showing its mettle.

For the Festival of Britain in 1951, the film doyens decided to pool their resources and produce an industry offering for the occasion. *The Magic Box*, the story of William Friese-Greene who invented and built one of the first British practical movie cameras in 1889, was their choice, and Robert Donat, though sick with asthma, was asked to play the lead. It was produced in and around the ABPC studios, distributed by the Rank Organisation, produced by Ronald Neame and directed by John Boulting.

Jack (Richard Attenborough) is anxious for May (Glynis Johns, centre) and Edith (Margaret Johnston) to see the 'pictures that move' in *The Magic Box*.

Elstree (ABPC): Barry Fitzgerald and David Niven in *Happy Ever After*, a Mario Zampi production of 1953.

Elstree (ABPC): The great John Huston during the filming of *Moby Dick*, which he directed in 1955. The film starred Gregory Peck, Richard Basehart, Orson Welles and Leo Genn.

Laurence Olivier, Michael Redgrave and Richard Attenborough were invited to play cameo performances. The star cast also included Glynis Johns, Margaret Johnston, Renee Asherson, Sheila Sim and Sybil Thorndike. Other 1951 productions included *Angels One Five*, which was partly sponsored by the National Film Finance Corporation (founded in 1949 to provide film production loans), starring Jack Hawkins; and *Twenty-Four Hours In A Woman's Life*, starring Merle Oberon and Leo Genn. Comedy actors A. E. Mathews, Margaret Rutherford and David Tomlinson also appeared in *Castle In The Air*.

Although television was to have a marked effect on the exhibition, distribution and, ultimately, production of film, the British Hollywood continued to attract American investment and stars to its studios in the 1950s. Some of the ABPC productions were *Happy Ever After*, with an impish Barry

Fitzgerald, Yvonne de Carlo and David Niven; *Duel In The Jungle*, with Jeanne Crain and Dana Andrews; the costumed *Jaws* of its day, *Moby Dick*, directed by the great John Huston with Gregory Peck as Captain Ahab; and *Indiscreet*, starring Ingrid Bergman and Cary Grant.

Two excellent, very British, war films emerged from the studios during the 1950s. They were *The Dam Busters* with Michael Redgrave as Barnes Wallis, inventor of the bouncing bomb, and Richard Todd in the role of Wing-Commander Guy Gibson; and *Ice Cold In Alex*, directed by J. Lee Thompson, starring Sylvia Syms and John Mills. Thompson also directed the critically-acclaimed *Woman In A Dressing Gown* in which Yvonne Mitchell gave an outstanding performance. Other British actors who appeared in ABPC productions during the decade were George Baker, Diana

Sylvia Syms and John Mills starred in an effective war drama, *Ice Cold In Alex* (1958), which was directed by J. Lee-Thompson for ABPC.

Elstree (ABPC): Richard Burton and Mary Ure in *Look Back In Anger*, a prime example of the 'new wave' school of film production that would emerge in the 1960s.

Dors, Bryan Forbes, Kathleen Harrison, Trevor Howard, Margaret Lockwood, Cecil Parker, Janette Scott (daughter of actress Thora Hird) and Tommy Steele.

As it became clear to the ABPC board that independent television was to become a reality in Britain, they decided to enter the stakes, and in 1955 were awarded the contracts for the Midlands and Northern programmes on Saturdays and Sundays. ABC Television Limited selected the Teddington Studios as its main base for production and administration, and the ABPC film studios at Elstree would start to make television productions with its Teddington sister company, along with its own complement of feature film projects.

With ABPC embarking on a powerful film and television line-up, the signals for the approaching 1960s indicated change. *Look Back In Anger*, directed by Tony Richardson and starring Richard Burton in 1959, was a prime example of the 'new wave school' of film production that would emerge in the next decade. In 1960, ABPC still had 319 cinemas to fill, and they decided to open up the studios further for independent productions wanting to use the studios for both feature and television films.

Among the American majors filming at the ABPC studios during the 1960s were United Artists with *The Naked Edge*, Gary Cooper's last film; MGM's *Lolita*, directed by Stanley Kubrick, the story of a teenage temptress who ensnares a middle-aged professor played by James Mason and Warner Bros's *The Roman Spring Of Mrs Stone*, starring Warren Beatty and Vivien Leigh.

Meanwhile, the ABPC corporation went on to buy back a number of the shares owned by Warner Bros and to form a joint distribution company between Associated British-Pathé and Warner Bros which became Warner-Pathé Distributors. The new company was to handle the films from Warner's Burbank Studios and ABPC's Elstree Studios as well as those of Allied Artists. Two comedians new to the ABPC studios during the 1960s were Tony Hancock, who appeared in *The Rebel*, and Charlie Drake in *Sands Of The Desert*. Other notable films of the 1960s were *The Long And The Short And The Tall*, starring Richard Harris and Laurence Harvey, which was directed by Leslie Norman; *The Trials Of Oscar Wilde*, with Peter Finch in the name part; and *Billy Budd*, with Peter Ustinov and Terence Stamp. ABC Television Production was also to have a remarkable success with *The Avengers*, starring Patrick MacNee as the immaculate, bowler-hatted hero Steed.

Over 30 years earlier at the same studios, it had been Warwick Ward or Jameson Thomas whose smile was enough to send the damsels reaching for their smelling salts. The swinging sixties were to provide heroes of another sort. These new heart-throbs were all young, groovy and loud, and their trademarks were a brilliantined quiff, a guitar and a hip-twitching action designed to dislocate the lumbar region and trousers alike. Joe Brown, Tommy Steele, Frank Ifield and Marty Wilde all made films at the ABPC Studios, as did Cliff Richard, whose successes in the 1960s included *The Young Ones*, *Summer Holiday*, and *Wonderful*

Elstree (ABPC): Cary Grant and Ingrid Bergman on the set of *Indiscreet*, a romantic comedy directed by Stanley Donen in 1957.

Life. It was not unusual for crowds of adoring teenagers to wait outside the studios in the hope of catching a glimpse of their idols, and in the main, these performers made a lot of money for themselves, their producers and their studios, and are remembered with great affection.

The film industry is rarely able to pin-point the reason for a change in atmosphere and fashion. World events and a search for new themes are always contributing factors. By the mid-1960s, the mood was beginning to veer away from the musical and the comedy, and towards the pre-historic and horrific, with lashings of sly humour. Vincent Price hypnotized his victims in a Nat Cohen-Stuart Levy production of *The Masque Of The Red Death*; and other spine-chillers of the decade included *The Fearless Vampire Killers*, directed by Roman Polanski, with the ill-starred Sharon Tate; *The Double Man*, starring Yul Brynner and Britt Ekland; and *Theatre Of Death*. By this time, Hammer Films had a production office at the ABPC Studios and they chose two of the most beautiful actresses of the period to appear in a couple of their films; Ursula Andress appeared with Peter Cushing in a tale of reincarnation and revenge, *She*; while Raquel Welch appeared

in *One Million Years BC*. In the same year, 1965, Bette Davis arrived at the studios to make *The Nanny*, and returned in 1967 to make *The Anniversary*. Another superstar, Elizabeth Taylor, came to the studios in 1968 for *Secret Ceremony* with Robert Mitchum, Mia Farrow and Peggy Ashcroft.

In 1968, there was a momentous change for the ABPC Studios. EMI (Electrical & Musical Industries), one of Britain's biggest and most influential conglomerates, purchased the remaining Warner stake in the Associated British Picture Corporation, and saw the full ownership of that company as a natural extension of their trade hardware business. After a fierce industry battle, they acquired a controlling interest in ABPC in 1969. Bernard Delfont (later Lord Delfont) was appointed Chairman and Chief Executive of ABPC. He was in turn to appoint Nat Cohen to the ABPC board, and created a new Head of Production and Managing Director of Elstree Studios, Bryan Forbes.

Forbes had started in the industry as an actor, became a screenwriter of distinction, and finally a film director of merit. Before relinquishing his position in 1971, he instigated a remarkable spate of productions at the studio which included *The Raging Moon*, starring Nanette Newman and Malcolm McDowell,

Elstree (ABPC): A tea break for director Leslie Norman, seen here with Richard Todd, who starred in *The Long And The Short And The Tall*, a Hal Mason production of 1960.

Crowds of screaming teenagers arrived at the ABPC studios to welcome rock 'n' roll star Cliff Richard who made a number of films at Elstree in the 1960s, including *The Young Ones*, *Summer Holiday* and *Wonderful Life*.

which Forbes directed; the delightful, and now classic, *The Railway Children*, based on the novel by E. Nesbitt, starring Dinah Sheridan; *The Tales Of Beatrix Potter*, with Sir Frederick Ashton and the Royal Ballet; and the Grand Prix Winner at the Cannes Film Festival in 1971, *The Go-Between*, with wonderful performances from Julie Christie, Alan Bates and Edward Fox.

There was, however, to be yet another change at the studios in 1970, when John Reed, Chief Executive of EMI, and James T. Aubrey, Junior President of MGM, announced the closure of the MGM Studios at Elstree, and the formation of the EMI-MGM Elstree Studios so that MGM could take advantage of the EMI Elstree studio facilities.

This arrangement did not continue for very long. In 1973, due to dwindling box-office receipts – and their own cut backs in production and distribution in the United States – MGM withdrew from the deal and the studio reverted to its former name of EMI-Elstree Studios.

With the withdrawal of MGM in 1973 and the declining state of the industry, massive cuts were planned at the studio and Andrew Mitchell was made Managing Director to supervise this. By November 1973, the permanent studio staff of 479 was cut to 256, and the closure of the studios seemed imminent. But Mitchell was a hardy Scot who had been a protégé of Robert Clark, who in turn had been a protégé of the studios' former owner, John Maxwell – Scots all – and he was determined to fight for their survival.

For their part, EMI decided to make their most ambitious film ever with a galaxy of international stars: Agatha Christie's *Murder On The Orient Express*, with Albert Finney, Ingrid Bergman, Sean Connery, Lauren Bacall, John Gielgud, Jean-Pierre Cassel, Richard Widmark, Wendy Hiller and many more. A John Brabourne and Richard Goodwin production, it was directed by Sidney Lumet and was very successful at the box-office as well as receiving six Oscar nominations. Another very notable film of the 1970s was Fred Zinnemann's *Julia* with two great actresses, Jane Fonda and Vanessa Redgrave.

By 1977, British cinemas were again facing a massive shut-down. Cinemas and the trade associations demanded some form of self-help legislation and better remuneration and safeguards for films shown on television. The government's Annan report brought groans of despair from the industry, which had hoped that television would be statutorily bound to plough back some of its profits into film.

The studios had been forced to close a number of stages when it was thrown a lifeline in 1976 with the 18-week shoot of the biggest blockbuster of its history. It was the 20th Century-Fox release of *Star Wars*, directed by George Lucas. With joint American and British expertise, it won Oscars for Best Sound, Best Visual Effects, Best Costume Design and Best Art Direction, and by December 1980 had grossed $510 million.

In 1978, EMI merged its distribution arm with Columbia-Warner. However, in 1979 there was yet another change when Thorn, the British electrical giant, made a bid for EMI, and with this amalgamation, the studios became Thorn-EMI Elstree Studios.

There was also welcome production news for the studio. Stanley Kubrick's *The Shining* started filming after months of pre-

Elstree (ABPC): Superstar Bette Davis as *The Nanny*, a thriller directed by Seth Holt in 1965.

production work, and EMI built an enormous silent stage on the studio's backlot for the sequel to *Star Wars*, *The Empire Strikes Back*, which commenced filming the following year. *The Return Of The Jedi*, made in 1981, completed Elstree's *Star Wars* trilogy.

In 1980, there was a further boost to the studios' fortunes. Producer George Lucas and director Steven Spielberg arrived with their stars Harrison Ford and Karen Allen to occupy five of the studios' nine sound stages for ten months' filming on another blockbuster, *Raiders Of The Lost Ark*. Its sequel, *Indiana Jones And The Temple Of Doom*, again with Harrison Ford, was made in 1983, also at the studios. In 1982, Sean Connery returned to the role of James Bond 007, but this time at Elstree, in *Never Say Never Again*; and the Monty Python team made *Monty Python's The Meaning Of Life*, which was directed by Terry Jones. Other productions in that decade included *The Great Muppet Caper*, starring Miss Piggy; Hugh Hudson's *Greystoke: Legend Of Tarzan, Lord Of The Apes*; Frederick Forsyth's spy thriller *Fourth Protocol*, with Michael Caine; *Who Framed Roger Rabbit?*, which featured a cartoon rabbit becoming involved with Bob

Hoskins in a 1930s-type thriller; and Peter Greenaway's *The Cook, The Thief, His Wife And Her Lover*. The last major film to be made at the studios in the 1980s was the third 'Indy' film, *Indiana Jones And The Last Crusade*.

There were further changes for the studios in the 1980s when it was announced at the Cannes Film Festival in 1986 that the Cannon Organization had acquired the studios. This was followed in 1988 by yet another owner in the shape of the Brent Walker Entertainment Group, who rechristened their acquisition The Goldcrest Studios.

Sadly, in the 1990s, the Brent Walker Group and Hertsmere Borough Council (whose jurisdiction covers the site of the studios) became involved in a long legal dispute. The Brent Walker Group wanted to sell the site for development but the council claimed that the conditions of sale stipulated that it should remain a film and television studio for another 25 years, with the added proviso that Brent Walker should implement a programme to upgrade the studios or forfeit a £10 million performance bond.

Elstree (ABPC): Julie Christie ponders how to coax a young boy to act as postman to her farmer lover, played by Alan Bates. *The Go-Between* was directed by Joseph Losey and won the Grand Prix at Cannes in 1971.

Elstree (ABPC): Left to right: Albert Finney, Anthony Perkins, Richard Widmark and John Gielgud in *Murder On The Orient Express*, a John Brabourne-Richard Goodwin Production directed in 1974 by Sidney Lumet.

The case provoked an outcry from the industry and the media. This once proud studio, developed in the 1920s by John Maxwell, closed its doors early in 1994. Some television series such as *Love Hurts* and *Little Napoleons* were made in 1993 and at the beginning of 1994, but by early 1995, the studio had become a ghost town, with a skeleton staff and one producer sitting out his tenancy agreement.

However, in February 1996, Brent Walker offered the studios to Hertsmere Borough Council for £1.9 million, in return for dropping all legal actions. This was accepted. Since then the studios have slowly but surely prospered under the name of Elstree Film Studios and, by July 2000, the Council had invested approximately £12 million in its facilities. As well as attracting film, television and commercial companies, a number of smaller-budgeted features have utilised the stages, including *Alien Love Triangle* with Kenneth Branagh and Courtney Cox, *Gangster No. 1* (a dark, compelling story of ambition and betrayal, played out within the hierarchy of 1960s gangland London), directed by Paul McGuigan and starring Malcolm McDowell and David Thewlis, and *Enigma*, with Kate Winslet.

Elstree's many facilities include six sound stages, one silent stage, an exterior tank, offices and on-site services.

Should this last remaining film studio at Elstree ever disappear, then (as the Hertsmere Borough Council have bravely noted), so would a large portion of Britain's film heritage, with an ensuing despair for the future of the British film industry.

Elstree

Shenley Road, Elstree /Borehamwood, Hertfordshire

Imperial Studios; British and Dominions. When Herbert Wilcox came to build the British National Studios with his colleagues American film pioneer J. D. Williams and I. W. Schlesinger at Elstree in the mid-1920s, he already had seven years' film experience in distribution and production, which included producing and directing *The Only Way* in 1925, with Sir John Martin Harvey.

Born in 1892 into a poor Irish family, he became one of the leading British film figures in the 1930s and continued to work in film production into the 1940s and 1950s.

Of his contemporaries in the 1930s – Alexander Korda, John Maxwell, C. M. Woolf, J. Arthur Rank, Basil Dean, Isidore Ostrer, Archibald Nettlefold – with the exception of Korda, Wilcox stood out as the showman of the group, having an imaginative flair for knowing what would appeal as mass entertainment as well as a good head for business.

The British National Studios ran into trouble when conflict arose between Williams and Schlesinger and John Maxwell gained control of the studio as the dispute led to litigation. Wilcox promptly formed another partnership with actor-comedian Nelson Keys and a new film company, The British and Dominions Film Corporation. He did not have to look far for a site for his new production company, leasing studios that adjoined those of BIP that he and Williams had helped to build. His new Imperial Studios (also known as the B&D Studios) had three stages and a ten-acre lot. One of the first in the British film industry to realize the importance of the coming of sound,

STAR WARS
Released by 20th Century-Fox

SW-K-55   Luke Skywalker (MARK HAMILL) and Han Solo (HARRISON FORD) protect Princess Leia (CARRIE FISHER) and Chewbacca from an impending Imperial stormtrooper attack.

SW 1B2

Vanessa Redgrave and Jane Fonda (right) in *Julia*, the story of American playwright Lillian Hellman and the fortunes of her friend Julia. Directed by Fred Zinnemann at Elstree in 1976/77.

A poster advertising *Star Wars*.

Wilcox rushed to Hollywood to obtain first-hand technical experience. On his return, he installed Western Electric Sound at a cost of £250,000, then completed his first British 'talkie', *Wolves*, with Dorothy Gish and Charles Laughton. Wilcox had already made one 'talkie' in the United States to obtain technical information and experience. By this time, he had also acquired a lovely home at Elstree, with 7 acres of garden, two cars, servants and stables, determined to be part of the Hollywood-style township that was rapidly developing. The British Hollywood was already attracting American stars to its studios, as British producers recognized that this was a necessary precaution for successful box-office receipts in the UK and the US. Wilcox's contribution was to lure Dorothy Gish, Betty Blythe and Will Rogers to his productions.

By 1931, Wilcox had already made a number of films; encouraged Michael Balcon to hire the Imperial Studios to make two Leslie Henson sound comedies; made photographic versions of two Aldwych farces, *Rookery Nook* and *The Chance Of A Night Time*, with Tom Walls and Ralph Lynn; and signed up matinée idol Jack Buchanan and a cameraman who was to win three Oscars, Freddie Young. During Wilcox's years at the studios, he also made comedy films with Sydney Howard; and *Brewster's Millions*, directed by American Thornton Freeland, with Hollywood star Lilli Damita and Jack Buchanan.

Forging ahead with his American and European contacts, Wilcox rented one of his British and Dominions sound stages in 1933 to Paramount British on a ten-year lease; and Alexander Korda found himself making *The Private Life Of Henry VIII* on a British and Dominions stage after a distribution snag whereby Wilcox had an exclusive contract with United Artists, but the astute Wilcox made an exception for Korda on the condition that his film was made at the Imperial Studios.

One of the most glamorous actresses of the day was Maria Corda, the wife of Alexander Korda. Visiting the set during filming, she had drawn his attention to a petite, striking brunette with a hint of Asian beauty. He appeared uninterested, but in fact directed the girl's screen test himself and offered her the tiny part of Anne Boleyn in the film. Her name was Merle Oberon, she became a star, and, after Alexander Korda's turbulent marriage to Maria Corda had failed, Lady Korda. *The Private Life Of Henry VIII* was an resounding success, with Charles Laughton giving an outstanding performance in the title role, and was also one of the first British films to make money at the American box-office. Korda's other films at the studios included *The Private Life Of Don Juan*, with Douglas Fairbanks; *Strange Evidence* with Leslie Banks; and *The Scarlet Pimpernel*.

The name of Herbert Wilcox will always inevitably be linked with that of Anna Neagle. Theirs was probably one of the longest

Elstree (B&D): The British actor and director, Tom Walls, decided that the successful Aldwych farces would transfer well to the screen, and they became a cult in the 1930s. One of their number was *Rookery Nook*, produced by Herbert Wilcox at his Elstree studio in 1930. Left to right: Tom Walls, Robertson Hare, Winifred Shotter and Ralph Lynn, who always played the 'silly ass'.

American producer J. D. Williams (left) and British Herbert Wilcox were the founders of British National at Elstree, which was subsequently sold to John Maxwell. Wilcox then built the British and Dominions (Imperial) Studios, which were destroyed by fire in 1936.

In 1933, Alexander Korda found himself making *The Private Life Of Henry VIII* at the British and Dominions Studios after a distribution snag with Herbert Wilcox and United Artists. With an outstanding performance from Charles Laughton in the title role, the film represented a major breakthrough for British films in terms of American box-office success and world market competition. Here Henry VIII (Charles Laughton) enjoys a wager with his 'rose without a thorn' and fifth Queen, Katherine Howard (Binnie Barnes).

romantic and professional partnerships in the British film industry. Having signed up Jack Buchanan in 1931 to appear in *Goodnight Vienna*, a musical romance, Wilcox had trouble finding a leading lady for the production. Buchanan was appearing at the London Hippodrome in the musical success *Stand Up And Sing*, and Wilcox decided to visit him one afternoon to let him know that Evelyn Laye and Lea Seidl were not available. A matinée was in progress, Buchanan was singing and Anna Neagle dancing. Wilcox was entranced and immediately signed her up for the film. They fell deeply in love, but Wilcox was a married man with a young family and there was no question at that time of a divorce. Over ten years later, they were rescued from their dilemma by Sir Alan Herbert's Matrimonial Bill, one clause of which made desertion for three years on either side an automatic reason for divorce. Wilcox and Anna Neagle were married in 1943.

Anna Neagle became Wilcox's major star, and her films during his tenure of the Imperial Studios included *Goodnight Vienna*; *The Little Damozel*; Noël Coward's *Bittersweet*; *Nell Gwyn*, in which her low décolletage got her into trouble with the Purity League in the States; and *Peg Of Old Drury*.

In the early hours of a February morning in 1936, fire swept through the British and Dominions Studios leaving a gutted ruin. Only the valiant work of the local fire brigade prevented the fire from spreading into the BIP Studios, literally yards away. Elstree was badly shaken at the demise of the studios as it had constituted a large part of its income from studio workers, shops,

Elstree (B&D): The name of Anna Neagle will inevitably be linked with that of Herbert Wilcox. Theirs was probably one of the longest romantic and professional partnerships in the British film industry. Her low décolletage in *Nell Gwyn* (1934) got her into trouble with the Purity League in the United States, who demanded that the offending scenes be taken out or re-shot.

Elstree (B&D): Another Alexander Korda film to be made at Elstree was Baroness Orczy's *The Scarlet Pimpernel* (1934). Leslie Howard was ideally suited to the role of Sir Percy Blakeney (left) while Raymond Massey gave a memorable performance as the grim Citizen Chauvelin.

hotel and attendant services. A typical show business story emerged to lighten the gloom. Wilcox had given a generous hand-out to a weary fireman, with instructions to buy a crate of whisky for the officers and ten crates of beer for the men, but both quantities and status had been reversed.

At the time of the fire, Wilcox had been filming *London Melody* with Anna Neagle and Robert Douglas. Although anxious to help, John Maxwell of BIP was not in a position to offer backing and facilities. Wilcox started afresh at J. Arthur Rank's new Pinewood Studios where the film was duly completed.

Elstree

Elstree Way, Elstree/Borehamwood, Hertfordshire

Amalgamated Studios; MGM British Studios. In 1935, film producer Paul Soskin and his uncle, Simon Soskin, decided to build their own studios at Elstree. Plans went ahead for a very modern well-designed complex, and Paul Soskin announced that

it would cost £500,000. As the building neared completion in January 1937, he returned from the United States with the news that he had made an eight-picture production programme deal for distribution with Columbia – a deal that failed to come to fruition. The building of the studio proved more costly than anticipated; additionally, the partners were unable to provide the necessary studio-operating equipment. By this time, the Soskins were in the unenviable position of being unable to redeem the mortgage to McAlpines, the builders, which had been secured to cover the cost of construction, and McAlpines foreclosed in 1939.

While John Maxwell at the Elstree BIP Studios speculated on the purchase of the Amalgamated Studios, J. Arthur Rank bought. It was simple Rank business logic – if the most modern studios in England were to be added to the Maxwell Empire at the British Hollywood, there would be little hope of success for his Pinewood and Denham Studios.

Douglas Scott as Tom Jericho and Kate Winslet as Hester starred in *Enigma*, a romantic thriller, directed by Michael Apted and produced by Michael White and Guy East, which was shot at Elstree Film Studios in 2000. Photo Jaap Buitendijk.

In the event, the outbreak of the Second World War in 1939 stopped production at both Maxwell and Rank's studios, but Rank was not in a position to know this at the time. However, he was happy to have a regular income from the Ministry of Works who leased the Amalgamated Studios from him for storage purposes for the duration of the war. By 1947, he had sold the Amalgamated Studios to the Prudential, who had lost quite heavily on their own film investments in the 1930s. Ironically, the studios were then sold to the American-backed MGM British.

The MGM British Studios always had a reputation among actors, producers and technicians of having an air of glamour and luxury, typical of a powerful American film company. While Britain was still reeling from the aftermath of war, MGM British opened its opulent doors in 1948 with a roar of publicity that gladdened the heart of the UK film industry. The old Amalgamated building was transformed into a Los Angeles-style studio, virtually self-supporting, with its own greenhouses, restaurants, generators and garages, which was to attract its contracted American stars as well as the cream of British film and theatre. These included Spencer Tracy, Deborah Kerr, Robert Taylor, Elizabeth Taylor, Greer Garson, Stewart Granger, Ava Gardner, Jean Simmons, Joan Fontaine, John Gielgud and Clark Gable. Although there was a London office and studio for MGM British, in the main, the directive came from MGM Hollywood, and over the next two decades they produced films that attracted both American and British audiences. Their first major production in 1945 was *Edward, My Son*, directed by George Cukor, and starring Spencer Tracy as a callous millionaire and Deborah Kerr as his slighted, alcoholic spouse.

The Miniver Story, made in 1950 at the studios, was a disappointing sequel to the 1942 success, *Mrs Miniver*, particularly as MGM British was still trying to make a box-office breakthrough. The cast included old favourites like Greer Garson, and Walter Pidgeon, with little James Fox, a future leading man like his brother Edward, playing their son. After appearing in a number of films as an adult, which included *The Servant*; *Thoroughly Modern Millie*; and *Those Magnificent Men In Their Flying Machines*, James Fox abandoned his acting career to become an active member of an international religious sect, but decided to re-enter films and television some years later.

Elizabeth Taylor. MGM British got its first box-office success, *Ivanhoe*, with an import of American actors, although some of their number, like Elizabeth Taylor, had been born in England. Her co-stars were Robert Taylor, Joan Fontaine and George Sanders; the film was directed by Richard Thorpe.

The MGM Elstree Studios in the 1940s.

In 1952, MGM British got its first box-office success, *Ivanhoe*, with imported American actors, though some of their number, like Elizabeth Taylor, had been born in England. Her co-stars were Robert Taylor, Joan Fontaine and George Sanders.

The following year, MGM British made their first film in Cinemascope, *Knights Of The Round Table*, with Robert Taylor as Lancelot, Mel Ferrer as King Arthur and Ava Gardner as Guinevere. This film owed a great deal to the British studios' technicians, and was another blockbuster.

In 1954, Clark Gable's 24-year star reign at MGM came to an end as the studio finally realized that he was no longer the box-office draw of former years. His last film, *Betrayed,* was partly made at their British studio in 1954. It was by no means the end of his career; he went on to work for other studios who paid him more money as an independent than MGM had done on an annual contract.

In the mid-1950s, MGM British produced two more costume dramas: *Beau Brummel* in 1954, with Elizabeth Taylor, Stewart Granger and Peter Ustinov; and *Quentin Durward*, made in 1955, which was directed by Richard Thorpe and starred Robert Taylor and Kay Kendall. In keeping with the policy of British studios at that time, MGM British leased out their studios to 20th-Century Fox in 1958 for the making of *The Inn Of The Sixth Happiness*, the story of an English servant girl who becomes a missionary and spends many self-sacrificing years in China. Its cast included Ingrid Bergman, Curt Jurgens and the renowned

veteran British actor Robert Donat. While the location shooting was done in North Wales to represent the terrain of Northern China, the studios had already built a set which was a replica of a fortified township with shops, lakes and courtyards. It covered 500,000 sq. ft. at a cost of £60,000. *The Inn Of The Sixth Happiness* was to be Donat's last film; already dangerously ill with bronchial asthma, he finished it by sheer will-power. With cast and crew near to tears, he delivered his now famous final lines to Ingrid Bergman: 'We shall not meet each other again, I think. Farewell'. He died three weeks later.

Twenty-three years after being signed up by MGM to star with Clifton Webb in *This Time It's Love*, a musical that for contractual reasons she was never able to make, Jessie Matthews appeared in *Tom Thumb* (1958). The athletic actor-dancer Russ Tamblyn played the title role, his first major assignment, while Peter Sellers and Terry-Thomas were a riotous pair of villains. The film's generous budget paid dividends as the production became a children's favourite over the years.

By the 1960s, MGM at Culver City, in common with all film studios in the US and the UK, was feeling the loss of revenue from dwindling box-office receipts due to the success of television, and also its own in-house financial and administrative problems. Nevertheless, a number of excellent films materialized from the MGM Studios in Britain during that decade. An outstanding cast appeared in *I Thank A Fool* in 1962, including Susan Hayward, Peter Finch, Kieron Moore, Cyril Cusack and Athene Seyler; and

Elstree (MGM): In 1953, another American beauty, Ava Gardner, appeared with Robert Taylor and Mel Ferrer in *Knights Of The Round Table*.

Elstree (MGM): A good-humoured historical romp, *The Dark Avenger* (1955), directed by Henry Levin, starred Errol Flynn in his last swashbuckling role (right) with Peter Finch and Joanne Dru.

in 1963, *The VIPs* with Elizabeth Taylor, Richard Burton, Louis Jourdan and Orson Welles gave British character actress Margaret Rutherford the opportunity to win an Oscar for Best Supporting Actress. A year later, an international cast headed by Omar Sharif, Jeanne Moreau, Rex Harrison, Ingrid Bergman, Shirley MacLaine, George C. Scott and Alain Delon appeared in *The Yellow Rolls Royce*. Written by Terence Rattigan, the film related three different stories about successive owners of the Rolls, and was very successful at the box-office. The most unusual and imaginative production of the decade was the award-winning *2001: A Space Odyssey*, a science-fiction film with a difference. Written and directed by Stanley Kubrick in great secrecy at Elstree, the film ranged from ape to modern scientist and included brilliant special effects and model work, with photography by Geoffrey Unsworth.

1969 was known as 'the year of the long knives' at MGM's New York headquarters. Two company presidents departed in quick succession and were replaced by James T. Aubry Jnr. Although cinema admission prices had risen both in the US and the UK, the public was still spending eight times as much on television, radio and records, and MGM had a very short production list in that year. However, one of their number which did extremely well at the box-office was *Where Eagles Dare*, starring Richard Burton and Clint Eastwood as allied fighters who parachute into a Gestapo stronghold. While the story-line became somewhat complicated towards the end of the film, the audiences obviously enjoyed the performances and action.

Sadly, however, a musical version of *Goodbye Mr Chips* with Peter O'Toole, Petula Clark and Michael Redgrave, a remake of the

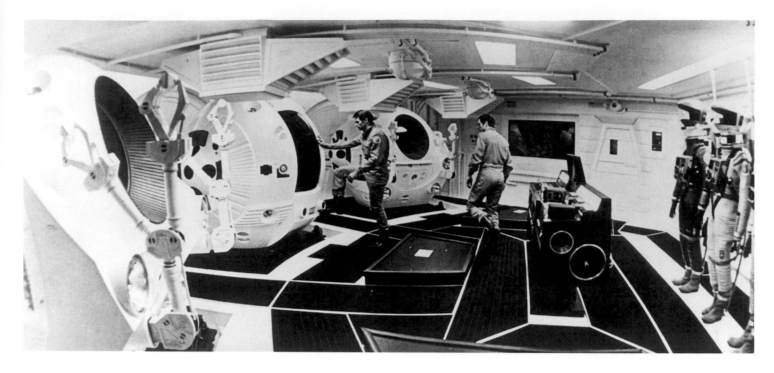

The set of Stanley Kubrick's *2001: A Space Odyssey*, a science-fiction film with a difference made at Elstree in 1968.

1939 'golden oldie' version failed to make money for the studio 30 years later. With mounting production and distribution problems, the parent company decided to reduce their losses by closing their seven sound-stage British studio in 1970. It was another sad blow for the British film industry and the British Hollywood. This was to be a little softened with the news that although MGM was to close its own studios, it would immediately take advantage of the EMI Elstree Studios' facilities forming a joint association with EMI, which would now be re-christened EMI-MGM, with MGM guaranteeing an annual subsidy of £175,000.

The once proud MGM British Studio, which had made such a splendid contribution to the industry, was allowed to deteriorate and fall into disuse. It was subsequently sold and became host to a cold storage company.

Elstree

Station Road, Elstree/Borehamwood, Hertfordshire

Whitehall Studios; Consolidated Studios; MP Studios; Gate Studios. Adelqui Millar did not conform to the usual mould of a studio Managing Director. An adventurer, he was an actor, screenwriter (which meant starring roles for Mr Millar), and subsequently, a director.

After parting from the Granger-Binger Company in the early 1920s he gained experience and contacts from independent companies both as an actor and as a writer-director of melodramas. In 1927, he formed Whitehall Films in company with two partners, and their newly-equipped studios were built by the station at Borehamwood in 1929, at an estimated cost of £35,000.

It was not the best location for a film studio. With the coming of 'talkies', even the best soundproofing was no defence against a busy railway line close by. In time to come, it would be necessary for the studio to employ a man for the sole purpose of standing on the roof in order to signal an approaching train, so that the filming could stop until it had passed. Given that the studios never had a strong parent company or guiding personality for any length of time, it is remarkable that the building remained a film studio until 1952. Mr Millar did not have comparable stamina. In 1929, the company ran into serious financial difficulties and he was removed from the board by his two partners, Charles Lapworth and N. A. Pogson.

As at the neighbouring BIP Studios, the decision to build a studio had been taken with the knowledge that the new Cinematograph Films Bill of 1927 stipulated that a quota of British films must be shown in British cinemas. Hence a number of UK productions (known as 'Quota Quickies') needed to be made quickly and cheaply. Some sound equipment was installed at the Whitehall Studios, and sound-tracks were given to two silent films that had been made at Julius Hagen's Twickenham Studios: *The Rising Generation*, with Jameson Thomas; and a melodrama, *White Cargo*. However, the pressing financial problems of the studios could not be alleviated, and the company went into receivership later in 1929.

For a period of time in the early 1930s, the studios were leased by Audible Filmcraft Limited, a contradiction in terms as they were listed as 'not acoustically equipped'. Again, the studios went dark for a period before being renovated in 1933 and renamed Consolidated Film Studios Limited in 1934, when Alexander Korda's *Things To Come* with Raymond Massey commenced shooting. The production was then moved to Worton Hall Studios and then to Denham for location work.

In 1935, Twickenham Studios were partially destroyed by fire. Julius Hagen formed JH Productions and bought the studios. Films made during his short occupancy include *Skylarks*, with comedians Jimmy Nervo and Teddy Knox, and Eddie Gray; and *Tomorrow We Live*, a drama with Renee Gadd and Godfrey Tearle; while work was due to start on *Impromptu Voyage*. But by the following year, Hagen's studios at both Elstree and Twickenham had gone into receivership. In 1937, J. Banberger formed a company, MP Studios Limited, and took over the old Consolidated/ Whitehall site.

From the end of 1936 to 1939, in the main the studios were used for 'Quota Quickies' by independent companies, and overflow filming and productions from the British National Film Company who had acquired the Rock Studios at Elstree in the early 1940s. Some of the productions in the late 1930s included *Dr Sin Fang*, with Harry Agar Lyons and Anne Grey; *Sister To Assist 'er*, from sketches based on stories by John le Breton; *Secret Journey*, with Basil Radford; *Old Mother Riley Joins Up*, starring Arthur Lucan as Old Mother Riley, a conniving washer-woman with a shrill Irish accent and a long-suffering daughter, Kitty, played by his wife Kitty McShane; *What Would You Do, Chums?*, from a radio series *Walker Wants To Know*; and *Trunk Crime*, produced by John Boulting and directed by Roy Boulting.

The MP Studios were requisitioned during the war and were later known as the Gate Studios. By 1947, the J. Arthur Rank Organisation had acquired the studios with their two sound stages for their GHW Productions.

While the studio was primarily concerned with the production of religious films (the reason for Rank entering the film industry in the 1930s), it was occasionally leased both to other units of the Rank Organisation – Sydney Box produced *Cockpit* there in 1948 – and to other companies – the costume drama *Decameron Nights*, with Joan Fontaine and Louis Jourdan was partly made there in 1951.

By 1952, the studios were sold, and in turn bought by Andrew Smith Harkness, who, coincidentally, manufactured cinema screens.

Elstree
Elstree Road, Elstree, Hertfordshire

Danziger Studios (The New Elstree Studios). After watching television in 1933, Sam Goldwyn was to prophesy that within three years every home would turn into a private kinema. A war and old traditions slowed the British conversion, but in 1956 there was a new addition to the British Hollywood Studio scene – the new Elstree Studios built by brothers Edward and Harry Danziger. An optimistic venture, this five sound-stage studio mainly turned out American television productions and series, although a few feature films were also made there. Their features included *Satellite In The Sky*, a science-fiction film with Bryan Forbes, Keiron Moore and Donald Wolfit; and *The Spanish Sword*, a costume drama with June Thorburn and Nigel Green. Television productions included *The Moving Finger*; *Bamboo*; and *Triangle*; while series made at the studio included the popular *The Vise*, *Richard The Lionhearted* and *Ali Baba And The Forty Thieves*. The studios closed in 1965.

Esher
Portsmouth Road, Esher, Surrey

This specially-designed one-stage studio was built in 1913 by the directors of MLB Productions: Reginald Michaelson (business adviser), J. Welfear Lloyd (technical manager) and Warwick Buckland (producer). Although the company hired stock players from the Hepworth Company, their films did not do well and they were taken over in 1915 by the Broadwest Company, who moved shortly afterwards to larger studios at Walthamstow. As production became increasingly difficult during the First World War, in 1917 the studio was turned into a training studio, and it was announced in *The Picture-Play* magazine that the studio would 'train thoroughly and efficiently.. there is a big boom in the British film industry.. producers cannot secure the talent they need... we are in touch with the leading British producers.. our students are trained by eminent producers in our large, well-appointed, and properly equipped studios'. This description varies somewhat from the one given by Leslie Wood in his book, *The Romance of the Movies*, in which he calls the studio 'a gigantic green-house, originally intended for the cultivation of tomatoes, situated behind a row of little shops in the Portsmouth Road and called 'Coleby's Conservatory'. This name came from the producer A. E. Coleby, who used the studio from time to time.

In 1918, actor-director A. V Bramble made *Bonnie Mary* for Master Films, and in the early 1920s, Henry Ainley appeared in a series of short films produced at the studio.

Glasgow
Black Cat Cinema Studio, Glasgow, Strathclyde

In 1984, producer Paddy Higson bought the former Black Cat Cinema in the east end of Glasgow, and converted it into a film studio. Although it was mainly used for television productions, Paddy Higson produced two feature films at the studio: *The Girl In The Picture*, directed by Cary Parker, with John Gordon-Sinclair and Irina Brook, released in 1986; and *Silent Scream*, based on the life and writings of Larry Winters, which was directed by David Hayman and starred Iain Glen. The film won a Silver Bear Award in 1990, and the first Michael Powell Award in Edinburgh in the same year. The studios were sold in 1991.

Glasgow
Elder Productions Studio, Glasgow, Strathclyde

In the early 1950s, Elder Productions, who as Elder-Dalrymple Films had previously owned a small studio in Ayr, converted a Gothic-style building behind the Saracen's Head pub in Glasgow into a film studio. They produced a 60-minute story starring Campbell Hastie, *The Little Singer*, but it failed to secure national release, apparently due to the unintelligibility of the Glasgow accent, although it did well on local screenings.

Glasgow
India Street, Glasgow, Strathclyde

Two film companies were to dominate non-fiction production in Scotland from the 1930s onward: Campbell Harper Films, based in Edinburgh, and Scottish Film Productions Limited, who had established studios in India Street at Charing Cross, Glasgow,

In 1984, producer Paddy Higson bought the former Black Cat Cinema in the east end of Glasgow and converted it into a film studio. In 1990, one of her films, *Silent Scream*, won a silver Bear Award and the inaugural Michael Powell Award in Edinburgh.

where they did all their own processing, editing and printing. Under the guidance of Malcolm Irvine, Scottish Film Productions developed the Albion Truphonic Sound System in 1934, which they sold to a number of cinemas. Irvine instigated the production of a number of short films starring Scottish entertainers, but despite the talents of Dave Willis, Meg Buchanan, and Alec Finlay, the films were not commercially sound. Following the appointment of Stanley Russell as Irvine's partner, the company embarked upon a long and successful period in the production of sponsored and commercial film, which included *Glasgow: City Of Achievement*, and *The Romance Of Engineering*. Much later, in the 1960s, Stanley Russell (who by then had a film company, Thames and Clyde, in the west end of Glasgow) advertised for a trainee. Bill Forsyth answered the advertisement and learned his filmcraft on the documentary and sponsored film. His first major success was the delightful *Gregory's Girl* (1980), which he wrote and directed.

Glasgow
Rouken Glen, Glasgow, Strathclyde

In 1911, a disused tram depot situated at Rouken Glen on the southern side of Glasgow was used as a film studio by producer James Bowie for his film *Rob Roy*, directed by Arthur Vivian and starring local actors John Clyde and Theo Henries. This was the first three-reel feature to be made in Scotland.

Janet McBain, archivist of the Scottish Film Archives, writes of the studio: 'The building's lighting was still linked to the electrical current from the tramway power station. Every time a tram passed it caused an automatic 'fade out' and then 'fade in'. If two trams passed at the same time, the power faded out altogether!'

After the end of the First World War, the Ace Film Producing Company took over the studio, and in 1919, having invested in a new lighting system, they produced the five-reeler *The Harp King*, a slender drama based in Scotland with Nan Wilkie, W. R. Bell and Jack Baker. The film enjoyed an excellent Scottish trade showing in spite of the fact that 'a slight fog filled the hall'. Shortly afterwards, Ace Films went bankrupt, and in 1921, the studio was taken over by Broadway Cinema Productions who made *Fitba Daft*, adapted from a comedy sketch by James Milligan. Film-making had ceased in Rouken Glen by 1924. In the Autumn of 2000, *Screen International* and *The Times* reported that Scotland was still to learn whether its first big studio complex was to be positioned in Glasgow, at the Pacific Quay site opposite the new Clyde Auditorium, or in Edinburgh, through a private consortium led by Sean Connery. Both sites were seeking public funding.

Greenford
Grip House Studios, Greenford, Ealing, London

Purpose-built in 1981 as a film facilities house, in 1985 the Grip House Studios at Greenford diversified into television production, commercials and shorts. In 1994, these five-stage studios produced their first feature film, *Tom & Viv*, which won a BAFTA award and received two Academy Award nominations. Based on the true love story of poet T. S. Eliot and his first wife Vivienne, the film starred Willem Dafoe and Miranda Richardson. Directed by Brian Gilbert, the film's producers were Harvey Kass and Marc and Peter Samuelson, the grandsons of producer G. B. Samuelson, founder of the Worton Hall Studio at Isleworth in 1914, and the sons of Sir Sydney Samuelson, Britain's first Film Commissioner.

Hackney
Tuileries Street, Hackney, London

Converted from a disused gasworks, this one-stage studio was used by Lawrence Cowen's Union Jack Film Company between 1913 and 1920. Productions at the studio included Britain's first colour feature, *The World, The Flesh And The Devil* (1914), directed by F. Martin Thornton and produced by The Union Jack Photoplays and Natural Colour Kinematograph Company (Kinemacolor 1914), with Frank Esmond; and *It Is For England*, which starred Baroness Helene Gingold and was produced by Lawrence Cowen.

Greenford: Willem Dafoe and Miranda Richardson in the title roles of *Tom & Viv*, directed in 1993/4 by Brian Gilbert and produced by Harvey Kass, Marc Samuelson and Peter Samuelson.
© New Era Entertainment

Hammersmith

Riverside Studios, Hammersmith & Fulham, London

At the end of 1935, Twickenham Film Distributors, headed by Julius Hagen, the owner of Twickenham Studios, purchased the newly-built, two-stage Riverside Studios at Hammersmith from the PDC-New Ideal Film Company. Hagen's objective was to use Riverside for the overflow from his 'Quota Quickie' productions. The low-budget offerings made there include *Can You Hear Me, Mother*, with Sandy Powell; another comedy, *Don't Rush Me*, which was produced by Fred Karno and directed by Norman Lee, starring Robb Wilton; *Her Last Affaire*, which was directed by Michael Powell and featured Hugh Williams; *Path Of Glory*, with Valerie Hobson; and *Vicar Of Bray*, directed by Henry Edwards, starring Stanley Holloway, Margaret Vines and Esmond Knight.

However, by January 1937, Julius Hagen Productions and his film studios had gone into liquidation. Riverside Studios floundered until a new owner appeared in the late 1930s in the shape of the elegant, debonair, song-and-dance man of stage and screen, Jack Buchanan. Although Buchanan starred in *The Gang's All Here*, and *The Middle Watch* in 1939, they were not made at his studio. However, Anson Dyer who had formed a company in 1935 to make coloured cartoons featuring Stanley Holloway, appears also to have used the studio until the outbreak of war in 1939.

Hammersmith: Stanley Holloway in *Vicar Of Bray* (1937), directed by Henry Edwards for Julius Hagen Productions.

Matinée idol Jack Buchanan became the owner of the Riverside Studios at Hammersmith in the late 1930s.

Muriel and Sydney Box's reputations were firmly established with their Oscar-winning story, *The Seventh Veil*, in 1945. Ann Todd played the schoolgirl who develops into a brilliant pianist under the tutorship of her handsome but 'Svengali'-type guardian (James Mason, already a huge box-office star).

The studio seems to have been used little during the war years, apart from odd overflow work if another working studio was full as in the case of the model work for *One Of Our Aircraft Is Missing*. However, towards the end of the war and during the immediate post-war period Sydney Box made some excellent films at the Riverside. These included the highly-acclaimed *The Seventh Veil*, a splendid melodrama concerning a concert pianist romantically torn between her guardian and her admirers, starring Ann Todd and James Mason, which won an Academy Award for its script by Muriel and Sydney Box. Herbert Lom gave a notable performance as the psychiatrist, and the music was recorded at the studio. *The Years Between*, starring Michael Redgrave, Valerie Hobson and Flora Robson, was directed by Compton Bennett; *The Brothers*, a sombre tale set in a Skye fishing village, starred Patricia Roc, Maxwell Reed and Duncan Macrae; while the psychological thriller, *The Upturned Glass*, featured James Mason, his wife Pamela Kellino and Rosamund John.

In 1948, Jack Buchanan sold the Riverside Studios which were then acquired by the Alliance Film Studios Limited, who also controlled the Twickenham and Southall Studios. Their

Hammersmith: Patricia Roc, Maxwell Reed and Finlay Currie in *The Brothers* (1946-47).

productions towards the end of the 1940s included *The Brass Monkey*, a thriller with Carole Landis; and *No Orchids For Miss Blandish*, starring Jack La Rue and Linden Travers, which Milton Shulman of the *Evening Standard* described as: 'A most vicious display of sadism, brutality and suggestiveness'.

Among the films produced at the studios during the first half of the 1950s were *Delayed Action*; *The Embezzler*, with Zena Marshall; *The Golden Link*; *Contraband-Spain*, with Richard Greene and Anouk Aimée; and two rather more well-known films, *The Sea Shall Not Have Them*, directed by Lewis Gilbert, starring Dirk Bogarde, Michael Redgrave, Bonar Colleano, Nigel Patrick, Jack Watling, Anthony Steel and Sidney Tafler; and *Father Brown*, based on a story by G. K. Chesterton, with Alec Guinness playing the detecting Catholic priest who retrieves a priceless relic from a master thief. By the end of 1954, the BBC Television Film Unit was using the Riverside Studios, which were no longer employed for feature film productions for outside companies.

Hastings
East Cliff House, Hastings, East Sussex
There is very little information available about this studio at East Cliff House, Hastings, which is known to have been used by Harry Furniss in 1913 to make cartoon films.

Highbury
Islington, London
Producer-director Maurice J. Wilson entered the film industry in 1926, built the Highbury Studios in 1937 and founded the Grand National Company in 1938. From 1937 to the outbreak of the Second World War in 1939, the studio was leased to independent producers and production companies for such films as *Everything In Life* (Tudor Films), produced by the Marquis of Ely, with music by Hans May, starring Gitta Alpar; *Midnight At Madame Tussaud's* (Premiere Sound Film Productions), directed by George Pearson with James Carew; *Sam Small Leaves Town* (British Screen Service), starring Stanley Holloway and June Clyde; and *Law And Disorder* (British Consolidated), featuring Alastair Sim and Diana Churchill; the earlier films being mainly intended to fulfil the 'Quota Quickie' requirement.

In 1947, Frank Sherwin Green was appointed production manager by the Rank Organisation, who had acquired the studios after the war. One of the Rank films made at the studio in 1948 was *To The Public Danger*, starring Dermot Walsh, Susan Shaw and Patricia Hayes, directed by Terence Fisher. Other films of the late 1940s to early 1950s include *Colonel Bogey*, with Jack Train; *Song For Tomorrow*; *Penny And The Pownall Case*, with Christopher Lee and Diana Dors, directed by H. E. H. 'Slim' Hand; *Fly Away Peter*, with Patrick Holt; and *Trouble In The Air*, co-produced by George and Alfred Black and directed by Charles Saunders.

By the start of the 1950s, the Rank Organisation was in difficulties. Production at their Pinewood Studios was drastically diminished, while their smaller studios were gradually wound down, and then leased or sold off. By 1956, Highbury had become a full-time television studio.

Holmfirth
West Yorkshire
The family firm of Joseph Bamforth Limited was founded in the 1860s to produce lantern slides and hand-coloured picture postcards.

By the turn of the century, Joseph's son, Edwin, had a small studio at Holmfirth and had branched out to produce greeting cards which combined 'real-life' photographs with a quotation from a hymn or worthy tract. He then went into partnership with the Riley Brothers of Bradford who manufactured lantern equipment, and together they made a number of comic films with local talent which they then sold mainly in the north of England. By 1914, they had become famous for their *Winky* series, which starred comedian Reggie Switz as Winky in such titles as *Winky's Insurance Policy*; *Winky Takes To Farming*; and *Winky's Lifeboat*. The studio's new stars during the First World War years were child star 'Baby Langley' and comedian Bertie Wright. However, it was Hettie Payne who was to give the studio its most daring success in 1915 in the title role of *Paula*, a drama about a widow who follows her sick lover to Italy and dies after donating blood. Later in that year, the Bamforth Company was absorbed into the Holmfirth Producing Company, who then decided to move their production base to a London venue, Cranmer Court in Clapham.

Holmfirth: *Winky* film advertisement for Bamforth Films, 1914.

The official opening of the Worton Hall Studios at Isleworth in 1914. Left to right: Director George Pearson; producer and owner, G. B. Samuelson; his brother Julian Wylie; and cameraman Walter Buckstone (seated).

Although Bamforth's film production at Holmfirth ceased in 1915, their postcard business continued into the 1990s. By 1939, the original religious themes such as 'Rocked in the Cradle of the Deep' and 'Rock of Ages', had given way to the famous 'fat bums and bad puns' cards which were selling at the rate of 20,000,000 a year. Their success then declined as 1990s holidaymakers demanded rather more subtle themes on their postcards.

Hounslow

Hatton Road, Hounslow, London

Very little information is available about this studio, but it is known that Frank Newman, a well-known natural history cinematographer, occupied the premises for a period in 1914, when it was announced in the trade press that he would be making a number of dramas for the Dreadnought Company.

Isleworth

Worton Hall, Hounslow, London

Opening of a Magnificent Studio

Mr Samuelson's Fine Speech

It would require a poet to adequately describe the beauties of Worton Hall, Isleworth, which has been acquired by the Samuelson Film Manufacturing Company Limited. Suffice it to say, therefore, that it is an old English mansion, with terraces, lawns, wooded glades, orchards, and fields, affording opportunities for some of the finest exterior pictures which it is possible to conceive.

To this abode of bliss a large party was carried in motor cars on Wednesday, July 1st, in order to take part in inaugural proceedings. These were graced by the presence of that most charming and gracious lady, Miss Vesta Tilley who, after cutting with a pair of golden scissors the ribbon guarding the magnificent studio, declared it open amidst scenes of intense enthusiasm.

After the luncheon was served in a large marquee erected on the lawn in front of the house, Mr Walter de Freece presided, being supported on his right hand by Mr Samuelson, the Managing Director, and on his left by Mrs de Freece (Miss Vesta Tilley), while Mr Samuelson had his mother on his right hand. The Chairman, having proposed the loyal toasts, turned his attention to the subject of "The Firm".

It might appear, said Mr de Freece, that, in proposing the toast, he was going back on himself, being concerned as he was in such large music-hall concerns. But in his opinion, the cinema theatres were educating the public for other forms of amusement, and that there was ample room for all. Mr Will Barker, in proposing a vote of thanks to Miss Tilley, struck a remarkable note, reminding his audience that he stood there that day as the first man in the world to manufacture films, wishing the best of luck to the latest recruit.

Mr Samuelson, on rising to respond, was received with the greatest enthusiasm, the audience rising as one man and singing 'For he's a jolly good fellow'. When quiet had been restored Mr Samuelson said: In directing this studio, I shall produce films which will compare favourably with those on the American market. I want the English to be on top. There is a big fight ahead in the film business. We mean to win. But one thing I promise you, Ladies and Gentleman, it is this if we fail we'll give in like sportsmen!

And who are the people who will be responsible for the working of this ambitious undertaking? There are many, because it will be readily understood that a very large staff is necessary to carry on a concern on the lines of which the Samuelson Manufacturing Company are doing. We must therefore content ourselves with picking out a few of them, and with very much pleasure introducing them to our readers.

Mr George Berthold Samuelson Mr Samuelson is the Managing Director and Chairman of the company. As is well known, he was previously in business both in Southport and Birmingham. It is to his inventive faculty that we owe the great production 'Sixty Years A Queen'. The success which attended this venture gave him the idea which has now materialised in the formation of the new business. Mr Samuelson is keen as mustard on his work. The fighting blood in him is up and he means to win. But we know that he is a sportsman, and if the gods are not pleased to give him success, he'll accept failure with a smile on his face. For our part, we decline for one moment to believe the gods will be so unkind.

Mr Harry Engholm In Mr Engholm, (Director and Secretary), Mr Samuelson has found a strong lieutenant. A journalist by profession, he, in a brief rest from the work of Fleet Street, joined Barker's as a scenario writer. In all he wrote about forty scenarios, among them being 'East Lynne' and 'Sixty Years A Queen'. Mr Engholm pays a high tribute to Mr Barker, and frankly acknowledges that to that wonderful cinema school, Barker, he owes all that he has learned about cinematography. After leaving Barker's, Mr Engholm returned to Fleet Street, but finally met Mr Samuelson and joined him. May the happy partnership last long.

Mr George Pearson Mr Pearson's hobby is painting. From this it follows that he has an artistic temperament. And surely this must be a considerable asset to a producer. The company undoubtedly therefore made a wise choice when it fell on Mr Pearson as their chief producer. He started in the trade by writing scenarios for Pathé, and then joined the Union Film Publishing Company, for which he has worked for the past three years. Mr Pearson has now been engaged in producing for two years. He is bound down by no hard-and-fast conventions, but will strive to turn out the most artistic productions possible. After talking to Mr Pearson, and actually seeing him at work, we have no doubt that he will do quite his fair share in placing the firm under which he now serves, in the first rank of English manufacturers.

Mr Fred Paul In securing this gentleman to play 'leads' the firm have acquired the services of one who has all-round experience in both theatrical and picture worlds. Mr Paul has not only had much acting experience but he also was for a time stage manager for Mr Cyril Maude, and produced 'Her Son' for Miss Winifred Emery at the New Theatre. He started his career as a cinema actor with Cricks and Martin, playing small parts. He has also been with Pathé, the B.C.M and Barker's, before joining the latest manufacturing firm. He is an actor who brings a very high intelligence to bear on his art. Handsome and debonair, he is indeed an ideal 'leading man', and bids fair to become known as an English Kerrigan and Costello rolled into one.

Mr Jack Clare There is a well-known saying 'experientia docet', and if that is so (we have no reason to doubt it) then the company have found the right man in Mr Jack Clare, their stage manager. Formerly on the music hall, Mr Clare has, since 1904, devoted himself to 'Picture Land' both as an actor and staff officer. Amongst other firms for whom he has acted we select Pathé Hepworth, and Cricks and Martin. He was engaged by Union as their stage manager. Knowing the business backwards, as naturally he does, we shall look forward to hearing, in good time, of Mr Clare's promotion in the firm.

In conclusion, we would add that the trademark of Samuelson's films is singularly appropriate, namely, a picture of Samson pulling down the house, under which are the words, 'Samson Films Bring Down the House'.

'May this be a true prophesy' is the sincere wish of 'The Cinema'.

The Cinema, July 9, 1914

Born in 1889, G. B. Samuelson entered the film industry as a film renter in Southport in 1909, and in that year also made a brief excursion into exhibiting. In 1910, he moved his renting agency to Birmingham and developed it with great success. He had, however, a strong desire to use his creative gifts more fully, and in 1913 conceived the idea of producing an epic film about the reign of Queen Victoria, whom he greatly admired. Using his acquired capital, he financed and played a major part in the production of *Sixty Years A Queen* at Will Barker's Ealing Studios.

The film was an outstanding success and, with additional finance behind him, Samuelson felt that the time had come to acquire his own studios and produce his own movies. He learned that the house and estate of Worton Hall, Isleworth, which had been occupied by Colonel Cecil Paget, was for sale, and early in 1914, 'Bertie' Samuelson rented the Hall with an option of buying it for the incredible sum of £200.

Set in nine acres, the Hall had 40 rooms. The ground floor of the centre of the mansion was converted into offices, and also contained property and wardrobe rooms, a projection theatre, a cutting- and joining-room and a canteen. The first and top floors, which had eleven bedrooms between them, were converted into flats to accommodate those who might need to stay overnight, while the ballroom and dining-hall were left intact and used for filming though they were later converted into property rooms. The left wing was converted into dressing rooms for the actresses, and the right wing for the actors. The grounds comprised terraces, lawns, paddocks, orchards, vineries and several acres of farm land, while ancient cedar trees and wooded areas gave the appearance in parts of dense forest – all of which offered excellent facilities for shooting outdoor scenes.

Although the studios were officially opened on 1 July 1914, filming had already commenced on 8 June. Samuelson had engaged Walter Buckstone as his cameraman, and through him had met former headmaster, film director George Pearson, who described Bertie as 'a young man with amazing enthusiasm and boundless energy; his excitement regarding his adventures was infectious'. Samuelson, Buckstone and Pearson explored the grounds of

Isleworth: Distinguished stage actress Ruby Miller, who appeared in British and American films including *Little Women*, produced and directed by G. B. Samuelson in 1917.

Worton Hall to find the ideal site on which to build a glass studio of 50 ft x 40 ft for maximum daylight filming. Within a month, the studio was completed and equipped for a little over £1,000.

The film that had commenced on 8 June 1914 – the first from the new studio – was Conan Doyle's *A Study In Scarlet*, for which Samuelson had bought the film rights, first presenting Sherlock Holmes and Dr Watson to a delighted cinema-going public. The story had been written by Conan Doyle when, as a young doctor in Southsea, his small earnings had driven him to despair and a determination to earn a fortune by his pen. The character of Sherlock Holmes was based on one of Conan Doyle's tutors, Dr Joseph Bell, whose lectures on deduction in diagnosis were famous. *A Study In Scarlet* was an exciting tale of Mormon mystery, murder and implacable revenge that roamed from Salt Lake City to the London suburbs. Some ambitious locations were called for, and Pearson decided to shoot some scenes at Cheddar Gorge. In *Flashback: An Autobiography of a Film-maker*, Pearson describes how he needed a shot of the leading man, Fred Paul, sitting quietly on horseback, then suddenly hearing a cry for help and spurring his horse into a furious gallop. The horse in question had been acquired from a local man who had enthusiastically described her as 'a real bloodmare'. The only problem was that the beast did not seem to want to move. Pistols were fired, trays were banged, but the animal appeared unmoved and just 'stiffed'. Enlightenment came when a villager eventually called out, 'She won't budge, Guv'nor, 'til you rings a bell... she's our old 'bus-'orse'.

A Study In Scarlet was a great success in the UK, and Samuelson sold it to the US for a four-figure sum. In high spirits, he involved Pearson in a new film story, *A Cinema Girl's Romance*, but the storm clouds that had been gathering over Europe burst in August 1914 with the outbreak of the First World War. According to George Pearson, as crowds moved towards Buckingham Palace, shouting that the German navy would be at the bottom of the North Sea in a week, Samuelson, tremendously excited, rushed up to him in the street with: 'Come on, George, we'll take a room for the night at Frascati's... write a script... *The Great World War*... and start filming tomorrow'. *A Cinema Girl's Romance* went straight into cold storage, and the following day, Samuelson's loyal band of workers listened with growing excitement to his startling new venture: a fictitious newsreel brought bang up-to-date with material provided by the headlines of the daily press, which was to commence in two days' time. There was a frantic rush to engage every available out-of-work actor, hire costumes from Nathans the costumiers and buy up old medals, swords, flags, rifles, wigs and all usable bits of stage property from 'dummy bodies to lycopodium pots!' In *Flashback*, George Pearson also recalls that 'Fred Paul, the studio's leading man, by skilful make-up, rang the changes on the Kaiser, Kitchener, and a Serbian fanatic. By sheer good luck, our own scenic artist, Bernasconi, was very like the Austrian Emperor and, with ample face-crepe and other fungus, he went about all that week dressed in the gorgeous trappings of Francis Joseph, much to his discomfort when coping with the constant calls made on him for painting jobs'. Samuelson had decided to have a dramatic opening screen title, 'The Spark That Set The World In Flames';

Isleworth: G. B. Samuelson undoubtedly made a star of Lillian Hall-Davis, who appeared in a number of his films including *The Hotel Mouse*; *The Faithful Heart*; and *Brown Sugar*.

stiff wire was bent into the words of the title, which were then swathed with thick bands of cotton wool well soaked in petrol, the idea being to set the wool alight against a black background. Unfortunately, when the cotton wool was lit, a draught blew the flames on to a nearby drape which in turn set some of the set on fire. All studio hands were required to douse the blaze, prompting one of their band to suggest a change of title to 'The Spark That Set The Studio In Flames'. *The Great European War Day-By-Day* played to record audiences, and was followed by *Incidents Of The Great European War*. The films were so successful that the market soon became saturated with imitations, seriously threatening the originator's box-office receipts.

During the following year, 'Bertie' Samuelson and George Pearson worked non-stop, producing films that played to packed houses; very often working on two or three at the same time – far easier in the silent days. These included *Christmas Day In The Workhouse*, based on the poem by George R. Sims, with Fred Paul as the pauper who tells the workhouse visitors of his wife's death from starvation; *The Life Of Lord Roberts*, VC, with Hugh Nicholson in the title role, supported by Agnes Glynne and Fred Paul; *A Cinema Girl's Romance*, with a scenario from Harry Engholm, a melodrama again starring Fred Paul and Agnes Glynne; *Buttons*, the tale of a page who trails some burglars and is saved by a dog; an adaptation of Elizabeth Craik's novel *John Halifax, Gentleman*, with Fred Paul in the title role, and co-

Isleworth: *A Bioscope* article of 1925 depicting G. B. Samuelson as Napoleon against a film world globe.

MAN OF THE WEEK.—XXI.

G. B. Samuelson.

Urbane, smiling and genial—with cloth cap and mackintosh. A real test for tip-ups! He has made many outstanding films—"If Four Walls Told" and "A Royal Divorce," to mention but two, as diverse as the Poles. He has now made "She"—that is to say, he has now made it immortal, a lasting tribute to a great British author whose loss we mourn. "G. B. S." has artistic sense, precision, a brain that conceives and works quickly. He is one of our greatest producers (in two senses of the word), and "She" is one of his greatest films. He is the Napoleon of public sentiment—and gets there every time. Somebody once told him that his initials stood for Get Busy Sam—and he has taken it to heart ever since.

starring Peggy Hyland and Harry Paulo; and *The Lyons Mail*, an intriguing version of a famous French criminal trial, with Fred Paul this time changing course from actor to director, although George Pearson certainly also worked on the film.

By late 1915, Pearson was an exhausted man, and his one-year contract was coming to an end. Much as he admired Bertie, he felt that he was no longer able to sustain his 'frantic pace' and still keep abreast of his family commitments. While always acknowledging the debt he owed Samuelson, he left Worton Hall to become the Chief Film Director at Gaumont's Lime Grove Studio at Shepherd's Bush.

With the directional bit firmly between his teeth, Fred Paul now took over Pearson's duties at Worton Hall, and *The Adventures Of Deadwood Dick* went into production. There were six adventures of Deadwood Dick, based on the exploits of an Englishman in the Wild West, all, as one might have guessed,

starring Fred Paul as Dick Harris, with Joan Ferry listed simply as 'Girl' in the credits.

In 1916, Worton Hall was enlarged, and from that year until 1919 earned an enviable reputation for producing high-quality two-reel adaptations of classic books and plays. As well as working on his own productions, which included *A Pair Of Spectacles*; a version of Arthur Conan Doyle's *The Valley Of Fear*, directed by Alexander Butler; *Little Women*, which Samuelson also directed, starring Ruby Miller, Milton Rosmer, Vivian Tremayne and Roy Travers; J. M. Barrie's play *The Admirable Crichton*, with Basil Gill and Lillian Hall-Davis; and *Damaged Goods*; Samuelson also leased out part of his studios to other companies.

The Ideal Film Company's first film at Worton Hall was *Whoso Is Without Sin*, which was followed by versions of Arthur Wing Pinero's *The Second Mrs Tanqueray*; Oscar Wilde's *Lady*

Windermere's Fan; and Oliver Goldsmith's *The Vicar Of Wakefield*, starring Sir John Hare, Laura Cowie and Ben Webster. Thomas Bentley directed Arnold Bennett's *Milestones* for G. B. Samuelson, which starred Owen Nares; and Maurice Elvey directed *Hindle Wakes* for producer William Baker.

There is no doubt that by 1919 Samuelson had overcome wartime difficulties, had also achieved a meteoric rise to fame, and was regarded by many as the great hope of British film production. It therefore came as something of a shock for Wardour Street to read in the trade press of November 1920 that Samuelson's had been bought outright, 'taken over', by General Film Renters. What exactly the 'take over' of Samuelson's studios meant is hard to assess. General Film Renters announced a programme for 1921 of 80 feature films comprising the outputs of Swedish Biograph, the Norwegian firm Nordisk, Samuelson's and Barker's. But it is known that the General Film Renters Company had, almost from its inception, suffered what was later described as gigantic losses. In *BERTIE – The Lift and Times of G. B. Samuelson* commissioned by the Samuelson family, Harold Dunham writes: 'It is unlikely that the reported sale of Worton Hall and the Samuelson Company to G.F.R. ever took place – a conclusion which was supported by the fact that when Bertie formed a new company in association with Sir William Jury, early in 1922, under the title of British Super Films, Bertie was clearly named as the vendor in the sale of Worton Hall to the new company'. According to Dunham: 'The implication behind the formation of the new company must surely be that Bertie was unable, after the losses in another venture, a motor coach business, to maintain the Worton Hall Estate and studios and to undertake production, without financial backing. He now found himself a partner in the new enterprise, no longer the sole owner and fountain-head of a production company. Nevertheless, he had the controlling interest in British Super Films, with 13,500 shares as against Jury's 10,000. The great gain to Bertie was the guarantee of distribution'.

It should also be said that the early to mid-1920s was a slump period in the British film industry when studios and producers fought for survival; after the post-war industry boom had declined, production costs accelerated and foreign competition was flooding the home market. Samuelson had also courageously attempted to make Hollywood his production base in 1920 and so break into the American market by converting it into his 'home' market.

The first film under the new banner was *Stable Companions*, produced by Samuelson and starring Lillian Hall-Davis and Clive Brook, a distinguished British leading man, who usually played the role of the perfect English gentleman and became extremely popular, particularly in Hollywood, during the 1920s and 1930s. Samuelson quickly followed this with *Game Of Life*, Britain's first ten-reeler, and then went on to make *The Right To Strike* with a scenario by 'Captain' Walter Summers (later a film director), which was directed by Fred Paul. This team of Samuelson, Paul and Summers went on to make three more films together, all starring Lillian Hall-Davis: *The Hotel Mouse*, a crime story; Monckton Hoffe's *The Faithful Heart*, with Owen Nares and Cathleen Nesbitt; and *Brown Sugar*.

Samuelson undoubtedly made a star out of the immensely popular, elegant blonde, Lillian Hall-Davis, who also appeared in his *A Royal Divorce*, a historical drama co-starring Gerald Ames, which was directed by Alexander Butler. Samuelson's and Miss Davis's most controversial film was to follow. *Maisie's Marriage*, with Sam Livesey and his son Roger, caused an outburst of outraged indignation from the British Board of Film Censors in 1923, who objected to a book which was construed to have the glorification of free love as its main theme being turned into a film. The daring book in question was *Married Love* by British birth control campaigner Dr Marie C. Stopes, who also wrote the screenplay for the film adaptation.

By 1925, Samuelson, along with every other major producer and studio, was fighting for survival. Nevertheless, he enterprisingly made a screen version of Sir Henry Rider Haggard's *She* with an international cast at a studio in Berlin. Difficulties with his American star, Betty Blythe, resulted in a law suit, and, although his name was completely cleared, the colossal legal expenses, plus the extra production expenditure due to this disputed claim, resulted in yet another financial setback. At the same time, the *Bioscope*, depicting him as Napoleon against a film world globe, hailed him as 'one of our greatest producers... and *She* is one of his greatest films. He is the Napoleon of public sentiment [a reference to Napoleon Films which he had founded in partnership with S.W. (Sam) Smith] – and gets there every time. Somebody once told him that his initials stood for Get Busy Sam – and he has taken it to heart ever since'. However, a courageous short spurt of film-making could not prevent the sale of Worton Hall to British Screen Productions in 1928.

Although Bertie Samuelson continued to work in films for a number of years, mainly as a director, he mourned the loss of his studio and possibly never appreciated the contribution he had made to the industry. The coming of talkies to the UK in 1929 revitalized Worton Hall, which survived Samuelson's death in 1947 by five years. An additional legacy of which he would have been justly proud was the continued involvement of his family in the film industry. His son, Sydney Samuelson was appointed Britain's first Film Commissioner in 1991 and knighted in 1995, and his grandsons Peter and Marc have followed their grandfather into feature film production with *Tom & Viv* (1994).

British Screen Productions, the new owner of Worton Hall, was headed by George Pearson, who had worked with G. B. Samuelson during the First World War. In *Film Making in 1930s Britain*, Rachael Low comments that the company made 'a handful of inferior silent films', and went into liquidation in the early 1930s. In 1931, the Hon. Richard Norton, who was to later have a considerable involvement with Pinewood Studios at Iver Heath in Buckinghamshire, organized a production schedule of six low-budget 'Quota Quickies' on behalf of United Artists. The studios were also leased out to other companies, and some of the early films of the decade at Worton Hall included *Madame Guillotine*, which starred a young Madeleine Carroll and Brian Aherne; *Birds Of A Feather*; Guilt, directed by Reginald Fogwell, starring James Carew and Anne Grey; and *Jealousy*, which was directed by G. B. Samuelson.

In 1936, Douglas Fairbanks Jnr and his fellow directors acquired the Worton Hall Studios at Isleworth.

In 1933, Worton Hall had yet another change of ownership in the shape of J. W. Almond and Edward Gourdeau, and by 1934, the studios had been fully modernized and the Western Electric Sound System installed. Although indifferent 'Quota Quickies' had been the lot of the studio in the early part of the 1930s, its fortunes were about to change.

Alexander Korda, having had enormous success with *The Private Life Of Henry VIII* decided at the end of 1934 to lease Worton Hall at £35,000 per annum, a huge sum at that time. This was achieved with the helpful backing of the Prudential Assurance Company, who had been most impressed with the receipts from *The Private Life Of Henry VIII*. Later, the 'Pru' was to back the building of Korda's studio at Denham, which would cost them and their shareholders a vast sum of money. Two onlookers who had been notably impressed with the success of *The Private Life Of Henry VIII* were the great silent film star Douglas Fairbanks Snr and his son, Douglas Fairbanks Jnr. They struck a deal with Korda in which Fairbanks Snr was to offer Korda an interest in United Artists, while his handsome son would appear in Korda's film *Catherine The Great*. Fairbanks Jnr was the darling of the UK's aristocratic social set and through his connections, he was able to secure backing as well as to reach a distribution agreement with United Artists. In 1935, he founded Criterion Film Productions with Marcel Hellman, Paul Czinner and Lady Mountbatten's brother-in-law, Captain A. Cunningham-Reid. Early in 1936, after lengthy negotiations with the Almond family, Douglas Fairbanks Jnr and his fellow directors acquired Worton Hall Studios at Islington.

What of the films made by Korda, Fairbanks Jnr and independent producers in 1935–36? The delightful comedy *The Ghost Goes West* starred Jean Parker (she of the delicious throaty chuckle) and Robert Donat, and was directed by René Clair. In his biography of Alexander Korda, Paul Tabori recounts the story that Korda was not sure whether the audiences would appreciate this comedy, and insisted on going with some friends to the Leicester Square Theatre where the film was showing, though he would not let them go inside the auditorium. "'You know the scene where Robert Donat looks up at the sky and asks 'Where am I, Father?' If the audience gets it – we have a success, if it doesn't...", he shrugged elegantly'. Fortunately loud laughter greeted the sequence to which Korda had referred, and he turned on his heels with 'We can all go home now, it's a success'. Another production by Korda was *Moscow Nights*, based on an unpublished novel by Pierre Benoit. It was directed by Anthony Asquith and starred Penelope Dudley Ward and Laurence Olivier. While Korda was waiting for Denham Studios to be finished, the interior shots of *The Man Who Could Work Miracles* were completed at Isleworth. Based on the novel by H. G. Wells and directed by Lothar Mendes, the film drew delightful performances from Roland Young, Ralph Richardson and Joan Gardner. Korda used another of Wells's novels, *Things To Come*, to produce one of his most impressive artistic films which was also filmed at Elstree and Denham. With a score by Sir Arthur Bliss and a fine cast headed by Raymond Massey, it was directed by William Cameron and used a newly-erected stage at Worton Hall, one of the largest in Europe, as well as splendid special effects. Korda also completed some scenes of *Sanders Of The River* at Worton Hall, which was directed by his brother Zoltan Korda and starred Paul Robeson, Leslie Banks and Nina Mae McKinney. Three of the Criterion films produced in 1936–37 by Marcel Hellman were *Accused*, with Douglas Fairbanks Jnr and Dolores Del Rio; *Crime Over London* with Margot Grahame and Paul Cavanagh; and *Jump For Glory*, again with Douglas Fairbanks Jnr and Valerie Hobson. Sadly, the films were a box-office disaster and Douglas Fairbanks Jnr returned to the US.

Production continued at Worton Hall until the outbreak of war in 1939. Sam Spiegel produced *The Invader* in 1936 as a 'Quota Quickie' for MGM under the direction of Adrian Brunel. The Austrian actor and director, Erich Von Stroheim – whose dictatorial extravagance had harmed his career in Hollywood in the 1920s – starred in *Madmoiselle Docteur* with John Loder and Clare Luce. Other Worton Hall productions of the late 1930s included H. F. Maltby's play *Bees And Honey*, which was adapted as *His Lordship Regrets* with Claude Hulbert, Jean Malo and Winifred Shotter; *Captain's Orders*; *Too Many Husbands*; *Special Edition*; *Mistaken Identity*, directed by Walter Tennyson; and *You're The Doctor*, with Googie Withers and Gus McNaughton.

The film producer Maurice Wilson leased Worton Hall in 1939 for a short period, but later in the year, the studios were commandeered by the Ministry of Works and were closed for the duration of the war. During that period, a number of the studios' scenic artists were engaged in camouflage preparation for the Ministry. Late in 1944, the British Lion Film Corporation negotiated the purchase of Worton Hall from Captain A. Cunningham-Reid of Criterion Film Productions.

The first full-length film to be released under the new British Lion banner was *The Shop At Sly Corner*, which was directed by George King and had a cast headed by Oscar Homolka with Muriel Pavlow, Derek Farr, Kathleen Harrison and Irene Handl. Although some scenes of *Piccadilly Incident* starring Anna Neagle and Michael Wilding were shot at Worton Hall, the next major production from British Lion was *White Cradle Inn*, starring Madeleine Carroll, Michael Rennie and Ian Hunter. However, the studios were to experience yet another change of ownership when Alexander Korda bought controlling shares in British Lion, which also operated Shepperton Studios, in 1946–47.

By the end of 1947, Korda's London Films had produced *Mine Own Executioner* at Isleworth. The film was based on Nigel Balchin's novel and directed by Anthony Kimmins with a cast that included Burgess Meredith, Kieron Moore and Dulcie Gray. Richard Winnington was to describe it as: 'The first psychoanalytical film that a grown-up can sit through without squirming'. *Night Beat* followed shortly afterwards, directed by Harold Huth and with Anne Crawford, Maxwell Reed and Christine Norden in the cast.

From the end of 1946, the lives of Shepperton Studios and Worton Hall at Isleworth had become inexorably linked; for example, some scenes from Carol Reed's *The Fallen Idol*, mainly shot at Shepperton, were filmed at Worton Hall; and overflow productions from the much larger Shepperton would often find

Isleworth: *The Ghost Goes West*, an Alexander Korda production directed by René Clair in 1935, starring Jean Parker and Robert Donat.

themselves at Worton. Richard Burton made his screen debut in *The Last Days Of Dolwyn*, which was written and directed by Emlyn Williams at Worton Hall, and Michael Powell and Emeric Pressburger's *The Small Back Room*, adapted from Nigel Balchin's suspense thriller, was also made there.

1949–50 saw a spurt of activity at the studios. Robert Donat made *The Cure For Love*, a London Films production which also starred Renee Asherson, Dora Bryan and Thora Hird; and this was briskly followed by Frank Launder's *The Happiest Days Of Your Life*, with a wonderful comedy team comprising Alastair Sim, Margaret Rutherford, Joyce Grenfell and Richard Wattis, partly made at Shepperton Studios. Veteran directors Herbert Wilcox and Maurice Elvey also came to Worton Hall during this period, the former to make *Into The Blue*, and the latter, *The Late Edwina Black*, starring Geraldine FitzGerald and David Farrar. In 1950, Douglas Fairbanks Jnr came back to the studio that he had once owned to star in British Lion's *State Secret*, which was directed by Sidney Gilliat, and of which Leonard Mosley was to write: 'One of

the best thrillers a British Studio (any studio, for that matter) has made for years'. This was followed by a visit to the studio from the incomparable Katharine Hepburn and Humphrey Bogart to shoot some scenes for the great John Huston's *The African Queen*, which was also partly made at Shepperton.

However, the life of the Worton Hall Studios at Isleworth was about to come to an abrupt end. Alexander Korda's British Lion Film Corporation, the owners of both Shepperton Studios and Worton Hall, had received a massive loan from the National Film Finance Corporation in the 1940s. When the time came for the loan to be repaid in October 1951, it was announced that 'no repayment could be made without curtailment of production'. Part of that 'curtailment' meant the selling of Worton Hall Studios. During 1951, the National Coal Board had come to realize that the existing resources at the Central Research Establishment near Cheltenham were insufficient for future requirements. One of several properties inspected for a second establishment was the Isleworth Studios. Negotiations for the

The incomparable Katharine Hepburn and Humphrey Bogart filmed some scenes of John Huston's *The African Queen* (1951) at Worton Hall, Isleworth. The film was also partly made at Shepperton.

From the end of 1946, the lives of Worton Hall and Shepperton Studios had become inexorably linked. Carol Reed's *The Fallen Idol* (1948) was mainly shot at Shepperton but he also filmed some scenes at Worton Hall. This story of an ambassador's son (Bobby Henrey) who almost incriminates his butler friend (Ralph Richardson) in the accidental death of his shrewish wife won Academy Award nominations for Carol Reed and writer Graham Greene.

Isleworth: Richard Burton made his screen debut in *The Last Days Of Dolwyn*, written and directed by Emlyn Williams in 1949.

acquisition of the property commenced in March 1952, and the contract between the National Coal Board and the British Lion Film Corporation was signed in May of that year. British Lion vacated the premises on 30 June, and, on the following day, the acting-director of the Central Research Establishment moved into his office in the old Manor House, Worton Hall.

Islington

Poole Street, Islington, London

In order to comprehend the history of the Islington Studios, it is necessary to appreciate their close association with the Shepherd's Bush, Lime Grove Studios, and to understand that Gainsborough films were made at both locations. There is a sad lack of Gainsborough business records, and, according to the *BFI Dossier 18*, 'The formal documents normally deposited at Companies House have been destroyed, and those more interesting confidential documents, if they still exist, lie deep within the bowels of the Rank Organisation and appear to be completely inaccessible'.

At the end of the First World War, American producers and studios cast a speculative eye over the poor UK production and exhibition scene with a view to development. One of their number was the Famous Players-Lasky Company of America, who founded the Famous Players-Lasky British Producers Limited in 1919 when they acquired a former railway power station at Islington, and converted it into a two-stage film studio with workshops and offices. The company also invested in good lighting, a rare commodity in British studios in the post-war years.

Two early productions released in 1920 and directed by the American director Hugh Ford were *The Great Day*, a drama with Arthur Bourchier and Mary Palfrey; and a romance, *The Call Of Youth*, starring Mary Glynne, Ben Webster and Jack Hobbs. These were followed by *Three Live Ghosts*, a so-called comedy about three dead prisoners of war who return to find themselves caught up in a tale of murder and intrigue (there was a lot of amnesia in the story-lines at that time); a drama, *The Man From Home*, directed by George Fitzmaurice, with Anna Q. Nillson, a reigning star of the 1920s, and James Kirkwood; and a melodrama, *Spanish Jade*, with Evelyn Brent and David Powell.

However, with another industry slump in the early 1920s, J. C. Graham, the company's Managing Director, was forced to announce that the parent company in the US headed by Jesse L. Lasky had decided to withdraw from their British investments. In 1924, the studios were sold to Michael Balcon and his associates.

Michael Balcon had entered the film industry in 1920, forming a small renting company with Victor Saville in Birmingham. Some time later, they met director Jack Graham Cutts who had already made films with Herbert Wilcox at Islington Studios: *Flames Of Passion* and *Paddy-The-Next-Best-Thing*, released in 1923 and starring Mae Marsh, Darby Foster and Marie Ault. Later in that year, Balcon, Saville and backer John Freedman decided to make their own productions with Cutts as director. They managed to obtain investment and distribution from C. M. Woolf, who had his own renting company, and their first film, shown in 1923 and made at Islington, was *Woman To Woman*. In common with other producers of the time, Balcon hoped for US as well as UK

Islington: American screen star Betty Compson and romantic lead Clive Brook in *Woman To Woman*, produced in 1923 by Victor Saville and Michael Balcon.

distribution for his films, and invited American screen star Betty Compson, a stunning blonde, to play the lead, paying her £1,000 a week, a huge remuneration at that time for a British studio. The distinguished suave leading man of the period, Englishman Clive Brook, played opposite Miss Compson, but there appears to be no record of how much he was paid. A romance, the film was set in 1914 with the storyline, 'an amnesiac officer weds a barren socialite and adopts his son by a French ballerina', and was a great success. Hoping for an additional hit, the same team went quickly into production, again at Islington, with *The White Shadow*, but it proved a disappointing follow-up to its predecessor and did not do well at the box-office. At this point, Woolf was unwilling to invest further, and withdrew from the company.

In 1924, Balcon founded a new company, Gainsborough Pictures, a name and logo that was to become famous in the British film industry. With the creation of this company, Balcon's reputation as a producer was established as, indeed, was that of Reginald Baker, his accountant, with whom Balcon had a long professional relationship. Their first film was *The Passionate Adventure*, which was produced by Michael Balcon and directed by Graham Cutts, with a scenario by Alfred Hitchcock.

Hitchcock had started his film career as a sign-writer at Islington Studios when they were owned by the Famous Players-Lasky Company of America. The American draw for this film was actress Alice Joyce, playing opposite Clive Brook, together with popular British star Lillian Hall-Davis and Victor McLaglen, who had five brothers who were also film actors – Arthur, Clifford, Cyril, Kenneth and Leopold.

Victor's own background equates to a film scenario. Born in 1886, a boy soldier in the Boer War, then a prize fighter in Canada, and subsequently a vaudeville and circus performer, he served as a captain with the Irish Fusiliers during the First World War and for a while was Provost Marshall of Baghdad. After starring in a number of silent British films of the 1920s, he went on to Hollywood, where he became a favourite of director John Ford who used him in a number of films, including *The Informer* (1935), for which he won an Academy Award playing the title role of Gypo Nolan. He was also the father of film director Andrew V. McLaglen.

Another Islington success, released in 1925, was *The Rat*, starring American actress Mae Marsh and Ivor Novello. The hint of Rudolph Valentino in Mr Novello's appearance and

The young Alfred Hitchcock worked as an assistant to director Graham Cutts at Islington Studios. An Islington success of 1925 for Graham Cutts was *The Rat*, starring American actress Mae Marsh and Ivor Novello. The hint of Rudolph Valentino in Mr Novello's appearance and performance was enough to have the ladies queuing at the box-office, and producer Michael Balcon decided to place Novello under contract.

performance was enough to have the ladies queuing at the box-office, and Michael Balcon decided to place him under contract.

By this time, Alfred Hitchcock had already worked as assistant on Graham Cutts' early films at Islington. He was given the opportunity to direct Gainsborough's *The Lodger*, which was released in 1926 and established his reputation. *Downhill*, produced by Michael Balcon and directed by Hitchcock and *Easy Virtue*, with the same producer and director, followed shortly afterwards in 1927, the latter starring Isabel Jeans, Ian Hunter, Eric Bransby Williams and Enid Stamp-Taylor.

1928 saw the release of *The Constant Nymph*, produced by Michael Balcon but this time directed by Adrian Brunel, with the new Gainsborough star, Ivor Novello, and Mabel Poulton. In the same year, Gainsborough was absorbed into the Gaumont-British Picture Corporation, a conglomerate which owned the Shepherd's Bush, Lime Grove Studios as well as

interests in distribution and exhibition. Between 1928 and 1932, while the Gaumont Studio at Shepherd's Bush was undergoing renovation in readiness for the talkies, Gainsborough, with its two-stage studio in Islington, served as the production arm of Gaumont-British. The RCA Photophone sound-on-film system was installed at Islington in 1928, and by 1931, Balcon was dividing his responsibilities between the two studios.

Early Islington films of the 1930s included *Sunshine Susie*, directed by Victor Saville and starring light comedian Jack Hulbert; a remake of *The Ghost Train*, directed by former silent film comedian Walter Forde, which was another vehicle for Jack Hulbert and his comedienne wife Cicely Courtneidge; *Friday The Thirteenth*, with star Jessie Matthews and her now-husband Sonnie Hale, a drama released in 1933; and two more comedies for the Courtneidge and Hulbert team, *Jack's The Boy*, and *Soldiers Of The King*.

Islington: January 1933 saw the release of *The Man From Toronto* with Jessie Matthews and Ian Hunter.

Islington: Flanagan and Allen, part of the British comedy institution The Crazy Gang, appeared in *O-Kay For Sound* in 1937.

Balcon produced two further films at Islington: a historical drama based on fact, and a vehicle for Boris Karloff. *Tudor Rose*, directed by Robert Stevenson and released in 1936, starred Cedric Hardwicke (father of the actor Edward Hardwicke) as the Earl of Warwick and Nova Pilbeam as the ill-fated Lady Jane Grey, with a young John Mills playing her husband, the Earl of Dudley, who was beheaded in the third reel, in Mills's opinion 'not a moment too soon'. The Karloff vehicle, *The Man Who Changed His Mind*, inevitably a horror film, depicted a mad doctor who exchanges his mind with that of someone else, and starred Cecil Parker and a popular actress of the period, Anna Lee, who was married to the director Robert Stevenson. However, for some time Balcon had been experiencing difficulties with the Gaumont-British board, which included the Ostrer brothers who Balcon felt relied too much on outdated styles of humour and over-theatrical performances. Added to this, his bosses usually gave him star contracts to deal with, and Balcon little relished their many foibles. George Arliss, an actor

of the old school who demanded and got a huge salary, always stopped for a nice cup of tea at 3.45 pm precisely; Tom Wall's shooting schedules were frequently interrupted by visits to the racecourse; while Jack Hulbert, according to Mr Balcon, had 'the persistence of a road-drill and the staying power of the Pyramids'. Balcon left Gaumont-British in December 1936 with a two-year contract to work for MGM at a much higher salary. His decision to leave the company was probably influenced by foreknowledge of the impending financial disaster for Gaumont-British in the following year. After Balcon's departure, the studios were reorganized under Balcon's former assistant, Edward Black, who proved to be a very successful producer.

By the beginning of 1937, disaster had struck the British film industry, due in the main to its inability to capture the American market. Isidore Ostrer was forced to announce that: 'Unless we can get a bigger return from the American market for British pictures, Gaumont-British will be compelled to abandon production'. Further trouble hit the studio later in the year when

Gaumont-British star Nova Pilbeam, whose films at Islington included *Tudor Rose* (1936), in which she played the ill-fated Lady Jane Grey with John Mills as her husband, the Earl of Dudley.

Will Hay was one of Britain's best-loved character comedians of the 1930s. One of his most famous films made at Islington in 1937 was *Oh, Mr Porter*, which also featured his two wonderful stooges, Moore Marriott and Graham Moffatt.

the Gaumont-British trading figures were released showing giant losses, with their subsidiary studio, Gainsborough at Islington having a loss of nearly £100,000. C. M. Woolf and J. Arthur Rank came up with a rescue package which stipulated that the Gaumont-British Studios at Shepherd's Bush would be closed and all its productions moved to Pinewood Studios, while Maurice Ostrer would be allowed to make a few films at the Gaumont-British's subsidiary Gainsborough Studios at Islington. This meant that within a period of time, the J. Arthur Rank Organisation would own both Shepherd's Bush, Lime Grove Studios and the Islington Studios – a tough but fair bargain, given the state of the industry at that time.

Ironically, it was Pinewood Studios that were to close a year later in 1938, while Islington Studios received a new lease of life in that year from 20th Century-Fox who decided to make films there up to the outbreak of war in 1939, very often utilizing the studios' excellent resident technicians and staff. Two of these productions were *A Girl Must Live*, a comedy produced by Edward Black and directed by Carol Reed, who was fast establishing his reputation, starring Margaret Lockwood, Lilli Palmer, veteran music-hall star Sir George Robey and Renée Houston; and *Shipyard Sally*. This was the last film that Gracie

Fields was to make in Britain, and it was directed by Monty Banks whom she later married.

One of Britain's best-loved character comedians of the 1930s was Will Hay, who had been a music-hall artist with incomparable timing and then a film actor. Two of his most famous films made at Islington in 1937 were *Oh, Mr Porter*, an Edward Black production directed by Marcel Varnel; and *Good Morning, Boys*, based on one of Hay's music-hall sketches. However, much of the success of the Will Hay films was due to his two stooges, Moore Marriott and Graham Moffatt.

The Crazy Gang were another British comedy institution, consisting of three pairs of music-hall comics, Flanagan and Allen, Nervo and Knox, and Naughton and Gold. Audiences adored the saucy innuendo and risqué ad-libbing at their appearances at the London Palladium, which the comics managed to convey in their Gainsborough film *O-Kay For Sound* in 1937. In 1938, Alfred Hitchcock directed what was to be one of his last films in the UK for many years. It was *The Lady Vanishes*, a thriller made for MGM at Islington, with an impressive cast including Michael Redgrave, Margaret Lockwood and Dame May Whitty. In the same year, Carol Reed directed a successful low-budget film, *Bank Holiday*, an enjoyable family feature which captured a pre-war Brighton on holiday, again starring Margaret Lockwood, but this time with Hugh Williams and John Lodge. At the outbreak of war in 1939, producer and studio boss, Ted Black, called everyone on to the set and explained that there would be no more production at Islington as, in the event of an air raid, a huge power chimney would probably collapse and crush everything and everyone. *Band Wagon*, an Arthur Askey film, was half-way through production, and was transferred to Gaumont-British's other studio at Shepherd's Bush, Lime Grove. The original two-stage Islington Studios had always been much smaller than Lime Grove, and their production backgrounds were heavily entwined. Although Black was to be made a director of the company, he would leave Gaumont-British in the mid-1940s to join Alexander Korda's London Films. It appears that Islington Studios were closed for most of the war, superintended by a skeleton staff; although the studios' tank was used for *The Young Mr Pitt* and services training films were made there for the Ministry of Defence. It seems likely that George Black's much-loved family saga of 1943 *Dear Octopus*, directed by Harold French, with a cast that included Michael Wilding, Celia Johnson, Roland Culver, Nora Swinburne and Athene Seyler was partly made at Islington, as was the Gainsborough classic *Fanny By Gaslight*, which was directed by Anthony Asquith and released in 1944.

Born in 1902 and from an aristocratic background, Asquith had worked on silent films and developed his directorial reputation in the late 1930s. At the beginning of the war, he worked on documentaries and propaganda features as his contribution to the war effort. Although some of his best work was done in the post-war years – *The Winslow Boy*; *The Browning Version*; and *The Importance Of Being Earnest* – he will perhaps be best remembered for his tribute to the Royal Air Force, *The Way To The Stars* (1945).

In 1938, Alfred Hitchcock directed *The Lady Vanishes* for MGM at Islington, one of the last thrillers that he made in the UK for many years, starring (left to right) Basil Radford, Michael Redgrave, Dame May Whitty and (kneeling) Margaret Lockwood.

Islington: Anthony Hulme assists Phyllis Calvert with her make up for her screen debut with Will Fyffe in the Twentieth Century production, *They Come By Night*, made in 1939 just before the outbreak of the Second World War.

Islington: Glynis Johns, the daughter of actor Mervyn Johns, played the title role in *Miranda*, a tale of a sexy mermaid produced by Betty Box in 1947–8.

Fanny By Gaslight, a Gainsborough classic partly made at Islington, was directed by Anthony Asquith in 1944. These three stills show: insult from star James Mason; retribution from heart-throb Stewart Granger; and gratitude from heroine Phyllis Calvert, watched over by Jean Kent.

Islington was reopened after the cessation of hostilities by the J. Arthur Rank Organisation which had acquired full control of the studios during the war years. A number of other UK studios opened around the same time, presenting opportunities for both lesser-known actors and established stars. Among these were Richard Attenborough, Dirk Bogarde, Derek Bond, Michael Denison, Diana Dors, Bryan Forbes, Dulcie Gray, Joan Greenwood, Sally Ann Howes, John Mills, Kenneth More, Anthony Newley, Laurence Olivier, Sheila Sim, Jean Simmons, David Tomlinson and Glynis Johns.

The daughter of actor Mervyn Johns, the delicious husky-voiced Glynis Johns, played the title role in *Miranda*, a sexy mermaid, which was a Gainsborough film produced by Betty Box in 1947–48. Other films produced at Islington around this period were *When The Bough Breaks*, a Sydney/Betty Box production starring Patricia Roc, Rosamund John, Bill Owen and

Islington: Betty Box and brother Sydney co-produced *When The Bough Breaks*, starring Patricia Roc, in 1947.

Islington: The star line-up and director (Ken Annakin) of *Here Come The Huggetts*, which was produced in 1948.

Patrick Holt; *Dear Murderer*, another Sydney/Betty Box production starring Eric Portman, Greta Gynt, Dennis Price and Jack Warner; and *The Blind Goddess*, starring Anne Crawford, Eric Portman and Hugh Williams.

In 1946, Sydney Box had become production head of the Gaumont-British/Gainsborough Studios at Shepherd's Bush and Islington. His sister and one-time assistant, Betty Box, had also become a producer. For many years, she made comedies and dramas with great box-office appeal and worked in close association with director Ralph Thomas. One of her most popular films for Gainsborough was *Here Come The Huggetts*, directed by Ken Annakin in 1948 and starring the much-loved character actors Jack Warner and Kathleen Harrison. Sadly, however, with the collapse of the Rank Film Empire at the end of the 1940s, the only course open to the Rank Organisation was to sell off studios and commodities in order to ensure the survival of their flagship Pinewood Studios. Islington and Shepherd's Bush were sold in 1949, and with their demise so too, for a time, went the famous Gainsborough trademark, based on a Thomas Gainsborough portrait of Mrs Siddons who, in a delightful picture hat, bowed graciously from her frame to an anticipating audience.

Kensington

St Mary Abbotts Place, Viking Street, Kensington & Chelsea, London

The St Mary Abbotts Place Studios at Kensington were primarily used between 1947 and 1950, and also known as the Viking Studios. The small three-stage studios' productions included *Fortune Lane*, produced and directed by John Baxter; *Nothing Venture*; *Bank Holiday Luck*; and *The Last Load*. John Baxter Productions Limited also used the studio to make such films as *Mr Jolly's Journey*; and *The Great Escapade*; while Five Star Films productions included *Death In The Hand*; and *The Hangman Waits*. By the early 1950s, the studios were making advertising films, commercials and television programmes, and by 1955, they were listed as a television studio.

Kew

Kew Bridge, North Side, Hounslow, London

Converted from a one-floor theatre in 1919 by Lucky-Cat Films, this studio was leased out to independent companies. Productions included *A Little Bit Of Fluff*, with Ernest Thesiger; and *Castles In Spain*, with Lilian Braithwaite and C. Aubrey Smith.

In 1921, Walter West, formerly of Broadwest Productions, leased the studio to make his own films which included Victor McLaglen in the 1923 production of *In The Blood*.

Many years later, the studios were converted back to the well-known Kew 'Q' theatre.

Kew

Kew Bridge, South Side, Richmond-upon-Thames, Surrey

Formerly a ballroom above the Boat House Hotel, this one-stage studio was used from 1915 until 1919 by Billy Merson in partnership with W. P. Kellino for their Homeland Films Syndicate Limited. The pair produced a series of two- and three-reel comedies, all featuring Billy Merson, who, it was hoped, would become a second Chaplin, such as *Bill's Stormy Courtship*; *Billy Strikes Oil*; *Billy The Truthful*; and *Billy's Spanish Love Spasm*. West End artist Lupino Lane also appeared in some of their productions including *The Missing Link* (1917).

Kingsbury

Hertfordshire

In 1919, film production commenced in a converted hangar at Kingsbury for Zodiak Film Limited, who made a number of Walter Forde comedies.

Leavesden

P.O. Box 3000, Leavesden, Herts. WD2 7LT

A former aerodrome responsible for the assembling and flight testing of Wellington bombers, Mosquito fighter bombers and Handley Page Halifaxes during the Second World War, in 1966 it was sold to Rolls Royce, who, after years of generating world class aero-engines, stopped production in 1993.

In 1994 Eon Productions, searching for the ideal location to film their latest James Bond adventure, (the blockbuster *Goldeneye*) discovered the airfield, with its forgotten factory buildings, and realized that it would be ideal in terms of interior and exterior space, with a location that would afford them the necessary proximity to all industry-related services and facilities. Produced by Michael G. Wilson and Barbara Broccoli, (the daughter of producer Albert R. – 'Cubby' – Broccoli, one of the instigators of the Bond films), *Goldeneye* starred Pierce Brosnan, Sean Bean, Izabella Scorupco, Judi Dench and veteran Bond actor Desmond Llewelyn (who always played Q). Taking over $219 million at the box office, the producers would not have been too disheartened when an *Entertainment Weekly* critic wrote 'Fast cars! Exotic games of baccarat! Double entendres that might have been cribbed from a 20-year-old copy of Playboy! Are we having fun now or what?'

During the filming of *Goldeneye* in 1995, George Town Holdings (G.H.T.), a subsidiary of a Malaysia-based conglomerate, set in motion a plan to acquire the premises in order to develop film studios, a studio tour, business park and residential complex. Their application was granted in November of that year.

Leavesden Studios' entry into British film production was impressive. In 1996 pre-production work for *Titanic* was followed by an eight-month shoot on another blockbuster, *Star*

Mabel Chiltern (Minnie Driver) eventually gets her man, Lord Arthur Goring (Rupert Everett) in the screen adaptation of Oscar Wilde's *An Ideal Husband*, directed by Oliver Parker at Leavesden in 1998. Copyright The Ideal Company 1999. Photo by Alex Bailey.

Wars: Episode One – The Phantom Menace, which was directed by American George Lucas, one of the most commercially successful contemporary film-makers and producers. Starring Liam Neeson and Ewan McGregor, with stirring music from John Williams, when the film was released in the month of July 1999 it took £26.9 million at the UK box office.

1998 productions included exterior filming for *Eugene Onegin*, which Ralph Fiennes starred in as well as produced, and which was directed by Martha Fiennes; Oscar Wilde's *The Ideal Husband*, which received two Golden Globe nominations and of which Rex Reed of the New York Observer wrote, 'Writer-director Oliver Parker's adaptation is superbly stylish, literate and immensely entertaining. Impeccably acted by Rupert Everett, Julianne Moore, Cate Blanchett and Minnie Driver, and Jeremy Northam is excellent. The film is rich in decor and sumptuously photographed (David Johnson).'

In the following year Leavesden played host to the production of *Longitude*, directed by Charles Sturridge for Granada Film Productions; *The Beach*, directed by Danny Boyle and starring Leonardo DiCaprio; *The Final Curtain*, requiring a six-month shoot for director Patrick Harkins; and Washington Irving's classic tale of *Sleepy Hollow*, directed by Tim Burton for Paramount British Pictures. This legend of the hero (Johnny Depp) confronting a headless horseman, in 1799, in order to win the heart of the heroine (Christina Ricci) was well received for its imagery and originality.

Warner Bros started the new millennium by taking over the entire Leavesden Studios for part of 2000 and then into 2001 for the pre-production and filming of J.K. Rowling's best-selling

Warner Brothers took over the entire Leavesden Studios in 2000 and part of 2001 for their pre-production and filming of J.K. Rowling's best-selling children's story *Harry Potter and the Sorceror's Stone*, starring (top to bottom) Rupert Grint, Daniel Radcliffe as Harry Potter and Emma Watson. Photo Terry O'Neill. Copyright: Warner Brothers Pictures.

children's story, *Harry Potter and the Sorcerer's Stone*, starring Daniel Radcliffe as Harry Potter, Rupert Grint as Ron Weasley and Emma Watson as Hermione Granger.

From 1997 Leavesden has developed a strong Television/Music Videos/Commercials slate, with projects as diverse as *The Alchemist* for Red Rooster Entertainment and a Nestlé Nescafé Gold Blend commercial.

Based in the heart of the English countryside, Leavesden Studios rapidly earnt itself a reputation as one of Europe's leading film studios. Set within a 286-acre site, it offers seclusion with accessibility, space with security and boasts extensive facilities to meet the needs of both film and television productions. Its substantial stages and clear horizons have attracted major, international film productions, leaving Rick McCallum, producer of the *Star Wars* (TM) prequels to comment, 'Leavesden Studios is one of the only facilities in the world which could accommodate a film on a scale such as ours. It is a unique environment which offers tremendous space, complete privacy and flexibility to utilise the emerging digital technologies developed by Industrial Light & Magic and Skywalker Sound.'

The Studios are within easy reach of central London via the M1, M25, and A41 highways. Excellent international air links are accessed easily through London Heathrow, London Stansted and Luton airports. Although the entire complex is surrounded by countryside, the industry-related services and facilities are all within 45 minutes of the site, affording the necessary proximity to ensure production efficiency.

Eight acres of this unique studio complex are completely covered under one huge roof, allowing cast and crew to move from workshop to stage, office to canteen, without having to face either the elements or prying eyes – an advantage for productions that demand tight security and a closed set. The studios' four sound stages and two silent stages (at time of going to press) are operated within a flexible environment by a friendly and efficient team, and secure easy adjustment to the various needs of directors and producers. In addition, the workshops accommodate complete in-house production. Encompassing 100 acres of vast backlot, Leavesden Studios possesses the unparalleled advantage of 180 degrees of clear and uninterrupted horizon.

Leyton
Lea Bridge Road, Waltham Forest, London
This studio was converted from an old horse-tram shed, and was used from 1914 until the mid-1920s. Owned by the I. B. Davidson Film Company, productions included *The Mystery Of The Diamond Belt*, a Sexton Blake thriller starring Percy Moran.

Producer A. E. Coleby, an ex-bookie and actor who commenced his film career in 1905, also used the studio during the First World War years, and then spasmodically until about 1924–25. A colourful character, Coleby would often cast himself in his own films such as in *The Call Of The Road* (1920), in which he co-starred with Victor McLaglen whom he had discovered at the National Sporting Club.

Victor McLaglen also appeared in *The Gay Corinthian* with Betty Faire, directed by Arthur Rooke and produced by I. B. Davidson at the Leyton Studio in 1924.

Producer A. E. Coleby discovered Victor McLaglen at the National Sporting Club and cast him in his own productions. One of McLaglen's films at Leyton was *The Gay Corinthian* with Betty Faire, which was produced by I. B. Davidson.

Manchester
Lancashire Film Studios, Rusholme, Greater Manchester, Lancashire
In 1919, Gerald Somers, who had worked in his family cinema business and advertising films, decided to make feature films at his two-stage Lancashire Film Studios at Rusholme, Manchester. In 1920 he produced *Annie Laurie*, in which his wife Lily appeared.

It seems unlikely that the studios survived for more than a few years, but Gerald Somers' career continued as a film producer, scenartist, cartoonist, cameraman and director. In the 1930s, he took a staff job with British Pictorial Productions, and during the Second World War he worked for Pathé.

Manchester
Dickenson Road, Rusholme, Greater Manchester, Lancashire
This two-stage studio was converted from a Wesleyan Church in 1947 by John E. Blakely. The studio pursued a policy of having its own contract artists who, in the main, were popular music-hall stars. These included Frank Randle, Tessie O'Shea, Sandy Powell and Jimmy Clitheroe. The Frank Randle comedies were

extremely successful at the box-office. Productions in the late 1940s and early 1950s included *Cup-Tie Honeymoon*; *Holidays With Pay*; *It's A Grand Life*; and *Somewhere In Camp*.

By 1954, television was having a marked effect on cinema attendances and Blakely was forced to sell his studios. Ironically, they were purchased by the BBC, their first television studios outside London.

Marylebone
Westminster, London

This two-stage studio was operational in the late 1930s with productions that included *Paris In The Spring*; and *Governor Bradford*, produced by Widgey Newman with Hetty Sawyer. Most features seem to have been made after the war, in 1947, when the studio was owned by Henry G. Halsted, who was also in charge of production. Films up to 1950 include *Death In High Heels*; *Crime Reporter*; *Walking On Air*, with Susan Shaw, produced by Michael H. Goodman; *Who Killed Van Loon?* produced by Gordon Kyle and James Carreras; and *My Hands Are Clay*.

Exclusive Films Limited, which had William Hammer, Enrique Carreras, James Carreras and Anthony Hinds on its board, also produced a number of films at Marylebone which included *Dick Barton – Special Agent*; *Ray Of Death*; and *There Is No Escape*.

By 1950, Henry Halsted had relinquished direction of the studios, though they continued to be used by independent producers and by 1955–56 had come under the direction of Eric Veendam. From then on, the studios produced commercials, documentaries and training and television films, but were no longer listed as a feature film studio.

Merton
Kingston Road, Merton Park, London

In 1931, Sound Services Limited took over commercial and industrial premises in Merton and transformed them into a film and sound-recording studio. In the early 1930s, Julius Hagen used the studio for some overflow production work from his Twickenham Studios, and in 1937, a new company, Merton Park Studios Limited, was formed with a capital of £100 in £1 shares. Publicity Films leased part of the premises, and the remaining part of the building was used as a private school by the Misses Brocklesby and their family until the outbreak of the Second World War in 1939.

After the war, the studio made advertising and promotional films, but by 1947–48, the Merton Park Studios production company had moved into making feature films that included *Circus Boy*, with James Kenny and George Stephenson and *The Secret Tunnel*.

By the late 1940s, a number of independent companies, who jointly formed the Film Producers Guild Limited, were working out of Merton Park, including Green Park Productions Limited who made a number of documentaries such as *Tale In A Tea Cup* for the International Tea Marketing Board; and *Down To Sea*. Some of the scripts for these documentaries were by Laurie Lee.

In the early to mid-1950s, Edgar Lustgarten made his popular crime series at Merton, reconstructed from actual cases recorded at Scotland Yard. These included *The Missing Man*, and *Persons Unknown*. For the remainder of the 1950s and during the early 1960s, this three-stage studio produced the *Brain Machine*, with Elizabeth Allan and Maxwell Reed, directed by Ken Hughes; *Little Red Monkey*, with Richard Conte and Rona Anderson; and *Confession*, with Sydney Chaplin; as well as a number of sponsored documentaries and shorts. By the mid-1960s, the studios seem to have gone over almost entirely to the production of commercials and television programmes. Work finally ceased at the studio in March 1967 with the film *Payment In Kind*, an Edgar Lustgarten thriller, produced by Jack Greenwood. The film library and projection services continued until the mid-1970s, when the site was sold for redevelopment.

Merton
Quintin Avenue, Merton Park, London

J. H. Martin (ex-Cricks and Martin) built the Merton Park Studios in Quintin Avenue in 1912. The studios were purpose-built with two glass stages, and were set in half-an-acre of land. By 1914, the studios were producing specialist and trick films typical of that period. However, by 1917, Martin had run into financial difficulties and film production came to a halt, although for many years he used the premises for the film processing side of his business.

Mitcham
London Road, Merton, London

C. H. Cricks, who had formerly been employed by R. W. Paul, founded the Cricks and Sharp studio at Mitcham in partnership with H. M. Sharp in 1901. The 'studio' was in fact an outdoor stage in the grounds of a country cottage that was used as a laboratory and office. An innovative cameraman, Cricks would employ the close-up and the chase, and was even known to place a series of oil-burning search lamps over a kitchen scene to supplement an obstinate sun. The cottage grounds were also used for his comic films. By 1908, the partnership of Cricks and Sharp was dissolved as J. H. Martin replaced Sharp. The company was renamed Cricks and Martin, and filmed at Mitcham before moving to the Croydon Studios in 1910.

Muswell Hill
Barnet, Hertfordshire, London

A pioneer of the British film industry, Robert W. Paul was one of the first to show films commercially, charging an admission fee to an early 'motion pictures' performance at Olympia in March 1886. A clever inventor, he regarded film-making as secondary to his scientific instrument business. His most successful period of film production was from the turn of the century until 1905. His one-stage studio, expressly designed for trick photography, produced *Dancing Girls*, specially hand-painted by a Mr Doubell; *The Egg-Laying Man*, with trick photography showing a conjurer producing eggs from a head and arms; *The Tea Party*, a comedy in which guests upset a tea table; and *Trilby Burlesque*, a dance scene from a production at the Alhambra Theatre. R. W. Paul paid a daily wage of five shillings to Britain's first professional film actor Johnny Butt. The premises were also known as the New Southgate Studio. Paul formally retired from film production in 1910.

Muswell Hill: R. W. Paul, a pioneer of the British film industry, was one of the first to show films commercially, charging admission to 'Motion Pictures'. His one-stage studio at Muswell Hill was expressly designed for trick photography. These pictures are from his 1898 catalogue and are entitled *Kitchen* (left) and *Exhibition*.

Northern Ireland

There is no available information on feature film studios in Northern Ireland, and the author would be most grateful to receive any information on this subject via the publishers.

Paignton

Drill Hall, Paignton, Devon

These premises at the Drill Hall at Paignton were used in 1919 by the Torquay and Paignton Photo Plays Limited.

Penhow Castle

Gwent

A small studio was built in the 1990s opposite Penhow Castle, but there are no listings of any feature films made there. The author would be most grateful to receive any additional information about Welsh film studios via the publishers.

Pinewood

Iver Heath, Buckinghamshire, SLO 0NH

Born in 1888 of a wealthy flour and milling family, J. Arthur Rank was to become a major force in the history of British film-making. An astute businessman (and devout Methodist), he entered the British film industry in the 1930s with Lady Yule and British National Films, intending to make films with a religious or strong moral theme. Unable to find a satisfactory release circuit for these productions, he formed General Film Distributors with C. M. Woolf, and then joined forces with Charles Boot, head of a building company, who had acquired Heatherden Hall, a magnificent 156-acre estate near Iver Heath in Buckinghamshire, 25 miles west of London. Rank and Boot formed a new company, Pinewood Studios Limited, and commenced building a new studio on the site in 1935, retaining the old mansion for administrative purposes. The new studio was opened on 30 September 1936.

The board of the new studio was strengthened in 1936 with the addition of Herbert Wilcox, whose British and Dominions Studios at Elstree had been destroyed by fire. Having collected the insurance money, the board of British and Dominions became part owners of Pinewood with a 50 per cent investment.

The first film to be completed at Pinewood, although started at the destroyed British and Dominions Studios, was *London Melody* with Anna Neagle and Tullio Carminati, while the first film to be entirely made at Pinewood was Carol Reed's thriller, *Talk Of The Devil*, with its American stars, Ricardo Cortez and Sally Eilers.

However, even this most optimistic opening could not halt the film industry's slump of 1937–38, which affected all of Britain's studios. Herbert Wilcox, who had moved to Pinewood, experienced financial difficulties, and it was often left to the Honourable Richard Norton, Pinewood's first Managing Director, to cajole the bank into meeting the new studio's massive weekly bill. Even with Norton's strategy of having a production co-operative, the studio was closed in 1938 for a period of time.

But J. Arthur Rank had not been idle. At the end of 1938, he acquired Korda's financially troubled Denham Studios and in 1939 took the Amalgamated Studios at Elstree from under John Maxwell's nose. Thus, by 1939, Rank owned three of Britain's largest studios, though two were closed and one was fighting for survival, an incredible speculative venture given the state of the industry and the European political climate at that time.

Before production moved to Denham at the outbreak of the Second World War, Pinewood Studios had completed 47 films. These included Britain's musical leading lady, Jessie Matthews, in *Gangway* and *Sailing Along;* Alfred Hitchcock's *Young And Innocent*, with 1930s star Nova Pilbeam; a successful film adaptation of George Bernard Shaw's *Pygmalion*, with Leslie Howard as the definitive Professor Higgins and Wendy Hiller as his star pupil; and *The Mikado*, Pinewood's first Technicolor film, with Kenny Baker, Sidney Granville and Martyn Green.

Once war was declared, the British government requisitioned a number of British studios, either as military bases or with the vast stages becoming camouflaged warehouses for storing emergency food supplies and equipment. For six years, Pinewood served variously as offices for Lloyds of London; as a base for the Royal Air Force and Crown Film Units; and as an out-station of the Royal Mint, which prompted rival studios to comment that it was the first time that Pinewood was making money.

By 1942, J. Arthur Rank had gained control of both the Odeon and Gaumont-British cinema circuits, making a total of 619 Rank cinemas with the rival ABPC organization owning 442.

Although the studio was not officially re-opened until April 1946, eleven months after the Armistice, 32 films were made at Pinewood during the remainder of the 1940s, including David Lean's classics *Great Expectations*, with John Mills and Valerie Hobson; and *Oliver Twist*, with such a powerful performance from Alec Guinness as Fagin that the film was banned in the US on the grounds of anti-Semitism. Powell and Pressburger's successful *The Red Shoes*, starring ballerina Moira Shearer and Leonide Massine, was notable for its use of the 'Gunn-shot' technique (named after its inventor, George Gunn) which allowed Shearer to dance a sequence with a figure made of newspaper. Although classified as an Ealing Comedy, due to the overcrowding at Ealing Studios at that time, Pinewood sets were used for the making of *Kind Hearts And Coronets* starring Dennis Price and Alec Guinness, who played eight members of the D'Ascoyne family.

Rank passionately believed in British films, and hoped to establish a post-war industry that could compete with that of the US. He invested in films such as Laurence Olivier's *Henry V*; and *In Which We Serve*, one of the most successful British war films in America. By the mid-1940s, Rank also controlled the Gainsborough and Lime Grove Studios, and had acquired a 50 per cent stake in Ealing Films. It is interesting to conjecture as to whether Rank's dominance of the British film industry in the 1940s was a matter of luck or brilliant business acumen; probably it was a mix of both. Certainly, three of his major rivals had disappeared from the scene by 1942: John Maxwell had died in 1940; Oscar Deutsch of the Odeon Circuit in 1941; and Isidore Ostrer, Chairman of Gaumont-British, retired from the film industry in 1941. However, the new Rank film empire, with its complex diversifications and intertwining studios, distribution and cinemas, could only have been achieved by someone with an inborn brilliant business acumen.

Pinewood Studios.

In 1947, Britain underwent a severe balance of payments crisis. About £18m was leaving the country to American producers exhibiting their films at British cinemas, and the UK industry was horrified to learn of the government's imposition of a 75 per cent tax on the box-office earnings of American films screened in UK theatres. Naturally, America retaliated by placing an embargo on the release of British films in the US.

By 1949, Rank had a debt of £16m, and the following year, Rank's Managing Director, John Davis, was forced to slash budgets, lay off staff and reduce the salaries of the remaining executives. The Rank empire appeared to be collapsing, as the Islington and Shepherd's Bush Studios were closed and part of Denham leased off. All production was now to be concentrated at Pinewood Studios, and independent producers and companies were encouraged to make films there.

With the televised coronation of Elizabeth II in 1953, and the establishment of independent television in 1955, the number of British domestic television sets had increased dramatically providing a marked effect on cinema audience admissions and, in turn, British film production. However, Davis's streamlined efficiency paid dividends, and a number of competent and excellent films emerged from Pinewood in the 1950s including

Pinewood: J. Arthur Rank, who built a screen empire and became a major force in the history of British movie-making, opened his Pinewood Studios in September 1936.

Pinewood: Professor Henry Higgins (Leslie Howard) encounters his future pupil, cockney flower girl, Eliza Doolittle (Wendy Hiller), in *Pygmalion*, produced by Gabriel Pascal and directed by Anthony Asquith in 1939.

Valerie Hobson as Estella and John Mills as Pip in *Great Expectations*, directed by David Lean at Pinewood in 1946.

The Browning Version, with Michael Redgrave, Jean Kent and Nigel Patrick; and Anthony Asquith's *The Importance Of Being Earnest*, with Joan Greenwood, Dorothy Tutin, Michael Denison, Michael Redgrave and Edith Evans as the definitive Lady Bracknell. A further boost to production was *Genevieve*, one of Pinewood's most popular films, a simple tale of a veteran car and two bickering, competitive couples who make a wager to race each other from Brighton to London. The impeccable performances of Dinah Sheridan, John Gregson, Kenneth More and the zany Kay Kendall made the film a smash hit for Rank.

More comedy came to Pinewood in the 1950s when Ralph Thomas and Betty Box had a great success with *Doctor In The House*, the first of the *Doctor* series, starring Dirk Bogarde, Kenneth More and James Robertson Justice as the irascible surgeon, Sir Lancelot Spratt.

The *Carry On* series, initiated in 1958, was another of Pinewood's comedy successes. The first film, directed by Gerald Thomas and produced by Peter Rogers, was *Carry On Sergeant*. From then on, the *Carry On* films usually featured members of a brilliant repertory company which included Kenneth Williams, Sidney James, Hattie Jacques, Barbara Windsor, Kenneth Connor, Jim Dale and Charles Hawtrey. Budgets were low, situations predictable and the burnout bawdy, while the locations were often on the Pinewood backlot. However, these pictures became a British film institution, and their audiences adored them. After a break of 14 years, *Carry On Columbus* was made at Pinewood in 1992.

Gregory Peck made two films at Pinewood during the 1950s: *The Million Pound Note* and *The Purple Plain*. Other notable films of that decade were *The Kidnappers*; *A Town Like Alice*, with Peter Finch; Kenneth More as Douglas Bader, the legless RAF ace, in *Reach For The Sky*; *The Prince And The Showgirl*, starring Laurence Olivier and Marilyn Monroe (such was her sexual magnetism, the entire workforce was drawn to the set); *Carve Her Name With Pride*; and *The League Of Gentlemen*, with a star cast including Jack Hawkins, Bryan Forbes, Richard Attenborough, Nigel Patrick, Kieron Moore and Roger Livesey.

In 1960, great excitement and publicity surrounded what was to be the most expensive non-event of Pinewood's history with the announcement that a multi-million dollar epic, *Cleopatra*, starring Elizabeth Taylor, Richard Burton and Rex Harrison, would be made at Pinewood. Massive sets depicting ancient Rome and Egypt were built on the backlot, but the production was doomed when a dangerously ill Elizabeth Taylor was rushed to hospital for a tracheotomy and followed up her stay by a long period of convalescence. The English bad weather added to the mounting costs, and the production was transferred to Italy.

Alec Guinness gave a masterly performance as Fagin in *Oliver Twist* (1948), the second film adaptation of a Dickens novel to be directed at Pinewood by David Lean.

British leading lady, lovely Jean Simmons, married Stewart Granger and later settled in Hollywood. She appeared in a number of Pinewood films including *So Long At The Fair* (1949) and *The Clouded Yellow* (1950).

The 1960s did give birth to the hugely successful *James Bond 007* series based on Ian Fleming's sexy British secret agent. Canadian and American producers, Harry Saltzman and Albert R. – 'Cubby' – Broccoli formed EON Productions, and cast Sean Connery in the first Bond film, *Dr No*, which was made in 1962, co-starring Ursula Andress. The films became famous for their technical expertise and incredible sets. For *You Only Live Twice*, directed by Lewis Gilbert, a gigantic volcano was built at Pinewood at a cost of £400,000. The role of Bond has been played by Sean Connery, George Lazenby, Roger Moore and Timothy Dalton (although one should not forget the Bond spoof *Casino Royale* starring David Niven), and in June 1994, *Screen International* announced that Pierce Brosnan would be the fifth James Bond, in *Goldeneye*, the seventeenth Bond movie.

The 160 films made at Pinewood during the 1960s include *Whistle Down The Wind*, produced by Richard Attenborough and directed by Bryan Forbes, starring a young Hayley Mills; *Those Magnificent Men In Their Flying Machines*, made by 20th Century-Fox in Todd-AO; *The Ipcress File* with Michael Caine, based on Len Deighton's story; Jack Cardiff's *Sons And Lovers*, with Wendy Hiller and Trevor Howard; and *Chitty Chitty Bang Bang*. The world-renowned Charles Chaplin returned to England in 1966 to direct *The Countess From Hong Kong*, starring Sophia Loren and Marlon Brando; and Maggie

Smith played the charismatic Scottish schoolmistress in Ronald Neame's *The Prime Of Miss Jean Brodie*. Sidney Poitier also visited Pinewood to star in *To Sir With Love*, directed by James Clavell. The 1960s also saw the beginning of television production at Pinewood, unthinkable in the early 1950s, and this trend increased in the 1970s with titles such as *The New Avengers*, *The Persuaders* and *Space 1999*. Nevertheless, 125 films were made at Pinewood during the 1970s, and two of the visiting directors from Hollywood were Billy Wilder to make *The Private Life Of Sherlock Holmes*, and Alfred Hitchcock for *Frenzy*. The script of the latter was by Anthony Shaffer who also adapted the long-running play *Sleuth* for the screen, giving Laurence Olivier and Michael Caine the opportunity to compete for acting honours. In 1976, Pinewood built the world's largest sound stage, the 007 stage on the backlot. In keeping with the demands of the times, equipment and facilities for television and video production were added along with the new H, J, K, L and M stages. A new pattern of film-making was being instigated at Pinewood with the Alexander and Ilya Salkind production, *Superman: The Movie*. Previously, the studios had needed to make 20 films annually to keep in profit, but the scale of *Superman* broke the mould, for now it took only two massive blockbusters to occupy all of the stages as well as the

One of Pinewood's most successful films was *Genevieve*, the story of the traditional veteran car race from London to Brighton and two bickering couples, (top) Dinah Sheridan and John Gregson, (bottom) Kenneth More and Kay Kendall. The film was produced and directed by Henry Cornelius in 1953.

Pinewood: Michael Redgrave seems a little stunned at hearing of *The Importance Of Being Earnest* from the lips of his intended bride, Joan Greenwood.

supporting services. It is also interesting to note that even with the drastic reduction of American investment in British films and studios in the 1970s, it was still the most economical option for Paramount to move their production of *The Great Gatsby*, directed by Jack Clayton and starring Robert Redford and Mia Farrow, to Pinewood after location shooting in the US. Apart from the *Bond* and *Carry On* films of the 1970s, other productions of that decade include *Superman 2*; *Fiddler On The Roof*; Alan Parker's feature film debut, *Bugsy Malone*, produced by David Puttnam and Allan Marshall, a spoof on the 1930s gangster period played by a cast of very adult children; *The Slipper And The Rose*, a Cinderella story starring Richard Chamberlain with the 1940s star Margaret Lockwood playing a not-so-wicked stepmother; and the star-studded John Brabourne and Richard Goodwin production of *Death On The Nile*, an Agatha Christie thriller with Bette Davis, David Niven, Angela Lansbury and Peter Ustinov.

Cyril Howard was appointed Managing Director of Pinewood in 1977 after the death of his predecessor, Kip Herren. Howard started his career at the age of 15 at Denham Studios in 1941, and went to Pinewood seven years later. He retired in 1992 after a remarkable 51 years in the British film industry.

Lord Rank, founder of the studios and of the organization that bore his name, died in 1972, the year of his retirement. John

Davis, who was knighted in 1971, became Managing Director of the Rank Organisation in 1948 and continued to diversify and extend Rank interests into television sets, scientific equipment and hotels, as well as to 10-pin bowling and ballrooms. In the 1970s, Davis brought City Wall properties, Butlins and Oddenino's Property, an investment company, into the organization. He became one of Britain's most formidable businessmen, and by 1969, total profits had reached £60m, and by 1972, £80m.

Davis's financial management was certainly competent, but what really tipped the scales as far as profits were concerned was his decision to enter the Xerography (photocopying) market. The Rank Xerox arm of the organization eventually came to account for over 40 per cent of the group's sales turnover. Sir John Davis, whose third wife was Dinah Sheridan, the actress, retired as President of the Rank Organisation in 1983, and died in 1993 aged 86 years.

Mainly due to the government's introduction of the capital tax allowance scheme, there was a resurgence of investment in British films in the late 1970s, and it was a major set-back to the industry when the scheme was phased out in April 1985.

Up to the late 1970s, there had always been a sharp division between British film and television in terms of both industry politics and interests, but as the decade drew to a close, it became

Director Anthony Asquith on the set of *The Importance Of Being Earnest* (1952) with Dorothy Tutin and Michael Denison.

Simon (Dirk Bogarde) gives the unsuspecting Sir Lancelot (James Robertson Justice) a check up, but how do you tell the Big Chief that he is only love-sick? *The Doctor* series, based on the novels by Richard Gordon, were top money-makers for Rank/Pinewood. *Doctor In Distress* was directed by Ralph Thomas and produced by Betty Box in 1963.

clear that the future of the film industry would inevitably be linked with the new communications explosion and would have to embrace many forms of technological entertainment. In the future, the producer of any major film would automatically have to consider its distribution pattern in terms not only of cinema exhibition, but also of video, television and cable sales.

Although fewer than 50 films were made at Pinewood during the 1980s, these included blockbusters such as *Superman 3*; *Octopussy*; *A View To a Kill*; *The Living Daylights*; *Batman*; *Aliens*; David Puttnam's production of *Memphis Belle*; and Ridley Scott's visual extravaganza, *Legend*, whose stage burnt down during its last week of filming. As with other studios, it was vital for Pinewood to adjust to the demise of the British film industry; the studio was already making a number of television productions, and in the mid-1980s it began to promote its services to companies specializing in the making of commercials. It came as no surprise to the industry when in

1987 Pinewood decided to become a four-waller, following the path already taken by other UK studios. This meant that producers were able to hire freelance labour to make their films at the studio. Pinewood's conversion from Britain's sole fully-serviced studio to one of three large UK four-wallers took effect in May of that year; inevitably there were job losses, though about 170 personnel were retained. Given the financial climate of that time, and the tendency for more and more producers to film on location, it was the only option left to the Rank Organisation.

As Pinewood moved into the 1990s, the Managing Director Steve Jaggs, Cyril Howard's successor, faced the major challenge of ensuring that Britain's largest studio continued as a thriving production centre. The early 1990s saw the making of *Alien III*; *The Secret Garden*, starring Maggie Smith; David Puttnam's production of *Being Human*, starring Robin Williams and directed by Bill Forsyth; part of *Little Buddha*; and *Black Beauty*

The *Carry On* series initiated in 1958 was another of Pinewood's comedy successes. 'Britain's answer to all past dramas of passion in the bush' said the publicity blurb for *Carry On Up The Jungle*, produced and directed by Peter Rogers and Gerald Thomas in 1970. Left to right: Frankie Howerd, Kenneth Connor, Joan Sims, Sidney James and Jacki Piper.

for Warner Bros. The 1994–95 Pinewood productions included *Interview With A Vampire*, starring Tom Cruise; *First Knight*, with Sean Connery and Richard Gere in the leading roles; Julia Roberts in *Mary Reilly*; *Hackers*; and *Mission Impossible*, again with Tom Cruise. Television productions included *The Borrowers*; *Minder*; *Parallel 9*; and a version of *The Phoenix And The Carpet* for US television, while 182 television commercials were shot at Pinewood during 1993.

In 1992, press speculation suggested that Rank might be 'giving up the gong', a reference to their famous film trademark, a bare-torsoed man striking a massive gong, but by January 1994, Michael Gifford, Rank's Chief Executive, was proud to announce that the Rank Organisation, Britain's biggest leisure group, had more than doubled its profits in the previous year when pre-tax profits rose from £125.8m to £276.6m. Film productions at Pinewood from 1995 included, in 1996, *The Fifth Element* and *The Jackal*, a thriller directed by Michael Caton-Jones starring Bruce Willis, for Universal Studios. In 1997, Warner Brothers' *Eyes Wide Shut* was the last film made by Stanley Kubrick (American writer-producer-director) – he died in 1999. He began shooting in 1996 and continued for over one year with Harvey Keitel and Jennifer Jason Leigh, who both had to withdraw due to other commitments and were replaced by Nicole Kidman and Tom Cruise. His films included such classics as *Dr Strangelove*, *2001: A Space Odyssey*, and *A Clockwork Orange*. In 1968 Andrew Sarris wrote of him, 'His tragedy may have been that he was hailed as a great artist before he had become a competent craftsman. However, it is more likely that he has chosen to exploit the giddiness of middlebrow audiences on the satiric level of *Mad* magazine.' *Sliding Doors* (also partly made at Shepperton) was also filmed for Paramount/Miramax in 1997 and resulted in a clever comedy-drama, with parallel story-lines starring Gwyneth Paltrow and John Hannah.

Just back from filming in Hollywood, Pinewood star Dirk Bogarde chats on the set of *Conspiracy Of Hearts* (1959) with producer Betty Box and its star, Sylvia Syms.

Pinewood: The one and only Marilyn Monroe starred with Laurence Olivier in *The Prince And The Showgirl* (1957), based on a play by Terence Rattigan. Laurence Oliver also directed the film.

In 1962, Harry Saltzman and Albert R. – 'Cubby' – Broccoli formed EON Productions, and cast Sean Connery in the first of the James Bond, 007, films to be made at Pinewood. The phenomenonally-successful *Dr No* co-starred Ursula Andress and was directed by Terence Young.

Michael Caine, the internationally-renowned British leading man, appeared in a number of Pinewood films including *The Ipcress File*, based on Len Deighton's story of counter-espionage (1965) and *Sleuth* (1972), in which he co-starred with Laurence Olivier.

Pinewood: The celebrated Charles Chaplin returned to England in 1966 to direct *The Countess From Hong Kong,* starring Sophia Loren (seen here) and Marlon Brando.

In 1998 Pinewood played host to Catherine Zeta-Jones and Sean Connery for the production of *Entrapment* for 20th Century Fox and were home to the filming of *Mansfield Park,* an adaptation of a Jane Austen novel, for writer/director Patricia Rozema. During the following year Merchant Ivory Productions completed a beautiful adaptation of Henry James's *The Golden Bowl*, which was a British entry for the Cannes Film Festival in 2000. James Ivory's direction elicited classic under-stated performances from Nick Nolte, Uma Thurman, Kate Beckinsale, Jeremy Northam and Angelica Huston. Also in 1999, Eon Productions again cast Pierce Brosnan as the lead in their James Bond thriller *The World is Not Enough*. The combination of Brosnan and the spectacular special effects wizardry, plus great stuntsmanship, made the film follow in the footsteps of the other Bond films and become a huge commercial success.

In February 2000, *Screen International* announced that the Rank group had sold its chain of Odeon Cinemas to Cinven, a private equity firm, for $448 million and had followed this action with the sale of Pinewood Studios for a 'cool' $99.2 million, thus breaking a 64-year British movie-making tradition with Rank. This was followed by a press release from Pinewood Studios that stated, 'Michael Grade has joined Ivan Dunleavy to form a management buy-in team to acquire Pinewood Studios from the Rank Group Plc. 3i led the transaction, supported by the Royal Bank of Scotland and Intermediate Capital Group, which will fund the total consideration of £62 million; the management team were advised by HSBC.'

Steve Jaggs, the Managing Director of Pinewood, had developed key relationships with the world's leading film-makers and continued to play an integral role alongside the new team, which comprised Ivan Dunleavy as Chief Executive and Michael Grade as Chairman. Ivan Dunleavy had been the Chief Executive of VC1 plc and Michael Grade the former Chief Executive of Channel 4. The focus of the new management team was to build on the existing film relationships, while developing new ties with the television and commercial sectors. They also envisaged that with the varying sizes of their stages, they would be able to offer a flexible service for all production needs, from a

Christopher Reeve as *Superman*. The first three *Superman* films were made at Pinewood in 1978, 1980 and 1982. In 1984, *Supergirl*, starring Helen Slater, Faye Dunaway and Peter O'Toole, was also made at Pinewood.

two-day commercial shoot, to a Bond epic such as *The World is Not Enough* (at the peak of which, Pinewood accommodated over 800 Bond crew). As well as being home to the 007 stage (with its vast interior water tank), Pinewood offers production houses a range of services, including Europe's largest exterior water tank, an historic mansion and 50 acres of landscaped gardens and backlot, which enable producers to recreate venues as diverse as Camelot for First Knight and downtown New York for *Eyes Wide Shut*. By February 2000 it had completed two new state-of-the-art, large sound stages, which increased its ability to simultaneously accommodate several large film projects.

At the time of going to press, the Pinewood film production and release listings for 2000/2001 included *Birthday Girl*, backed by

Miramax Films and Film Four, directed by Jez Butterworth and starring Nicole Kidman, Ben Chaplin and Vincent Cassel in a tale of a British man who orders a Russian bride through the Internet; *Tomb Raider* for Paramount Pictures, with a cast that included Angelina Jolie, Iain Glen and Leslie Phillips (veteran star of character/comedy roles who started his career as a child actor in 1935); *Revelation* (working title), a Cyclops Vision Production, directed by Stuart Urban; *Jack and the Beanstalk*; *Dinotopia* for Hallmark productions and *Below* for Miramax Films.

On Sunday 11 February 2001, Europe's two leading film and television studios, Pinewood and Shepperton, announced their merger, valuing the combined business at more than £100 million. The combination of the two studios created a facility that

Pinewood: Left to right: David Niven, George Kennedy, Peter Ustinov, Lois Chiles, Simon MacCorkindale, Bette Davis, Jack Warden, Maggie Smith and Angela Lansbury, giving their undivided attention to I. S. Johar in *Death On The Nile* (1978), based on the novel by Agatha Christie. A John Brabourne and Richard Goodwin production, directed by John Guillermin.

Pinewood: The Queen talks to Lois Chiles (left) and Angela Lansbury at the Royal Premiere of *Death On The Nile*.

Pinewood: *Octopussy* poster, 1982.

The World is Not Enough (directed by Michael Apted 1999): Inside the test chamber Bond (Pierce Brosnan) holds his gun to the back of Renard's (Robert Carlyle) head. Photographer Keith Hamshere.

Nicole Kidman, star of *Birthday Girl*, talks to director Jez Butterworth on the set of Pinewood Studios, 2000. Photo Liam Daniel. Copyright Miramax Films.

In 1999 Merchant Ivory Productions completed a beautiful adaptation of Henry James's *The Golden Bowl*, starring Nick Nolte and Kate Beckinsale (with Baby), and Uma Thurman and Jeremy Northam as the star-crossed lovers. Photos Seth Rubin (Courtesy Buena Vista).

In February 2000 Michael Grade, former Chief Executive of Channel 4, joined a management buy-in team to acquire Pinewood Studios from the Rank Group Plc. Photo Phil Rudge.

American leading lady Gwyneth Paltrow starred in *Sliding Doors*, which was partly made at Pinewood in 1997.

can compete on a global scale for Hollywood productions and offers producers an unrivalled level of service, flexibility and comfort. 3i, Europe's leading venture capital company is the majority shareholder in the combined business.

Michael Grade, executive chairman of the enlarged group, said: 'The two studios have been competing for years against each other. In an increasingly global market, this makes no sense. Together, we can enhance Britain's share of the international movie making business.'

Shepperton was acquired in January 1995 by an investor group headed by Ridley Scott and Scott and Candover Partners. Since the acquisition, more than £17.9 million has been invested in Shepperton studios. Candover is selling its interest in Shepperton to Pinewood's shareholders. Ridley and Tony Scott will remain active shareholders in the enlarged group and continue as co-chairmen.

Ridley Scott said: 'Britain remains a great place to make movies – this consolidation of our leading film assets is long overdue. Tony and I are committed to the growth and continued success of these historic studios.'

Ivan Dunleavy, chief executive of the enlarged group, said: 'We shall continue to invest in both studios for the future. Both studios have a common customer base, principally the Hollywood majors and UK film and TV producers. By combining the booking of all the stages and support facilities, we will be able to accommodate more productions overall.'

The two studios will continue to retain their individual trading identities, although they will be under common ownership and management. The merger has received clearance from the Office of Fair Trading.

The focus of the management team will be to build on the existing strong relationships with film, television and commercial production companies. Pinewood and Shepperton are flexible facilities, able to service every size of production. With the varying sizes of stages, productions range from two-day advertising shoots to blockbuster feature films. Both studios have built more large sound stages and the combination of the facilities will greatly increase the studio's ability to simultaneously accommodate several large film projects. Pinewood has also launched a state-of-the-art digital television studio.

Additional notes:

1. In 1929, the Irish Free State Treaty was signed at Heatherden Hall, later to become the site of Pinewood Studios.

Two years after starring opposite Sean Connery in *Entrapment* at Pinewood in 1998, Catherine Zeta Jones (early portrait) married screen star and producer Michael Douglas (son of Kirk Douglas).

2. After Charles Boot purchased Heatherden Hall in 1936, he bought the old Cunard liner *Mauritania* that was being broken up to use in the interior fittings in the old mansion at the new studios. They are still there.

3. Construction work for Pinewood Studios commenced in 1935, and the building labourers were paid one shilling and two pence an hour.

4. Pinewood's first Managing Director in 1936 was the Hon. Richard Norton, heir to Lord Grantley. A charismatic figure and descendant of the playwright Sheridan, he was a stooped (due to war injuries), monocled figure, who nevertheless acquired a considerable reputation as a racing motorist and was also able to negotiate finance with skill for Pinewood in its early difficult years.

5. When in 1960 the production of *Cleopatra*, starring Elizabeth Taylor, Richard Burton and Rex Harrison, was moved to Italy due to illness and bad weather, the Pinewood production team of *Carry On Cleo* decided to produce a poster with an Elizabeth Taylor lookalike. 20th-Century Fox was not amused and sued over the latter version's plagiaristic poster.

6. J. Arthur Rank took one look at the title of *Every Night Something Awful* and decided that he was not going to have that outside his cinema. The film, produced by Michael Relph and directed by Basil Dearden in 1959, was retitled *Desert Mice*.

Portsmouth
Hampshire

In 1929, Erle Osborne-Smith converted an old building into a studio, the Kingston Film Studio, and made *Terrors*, a fantasy concerning boys who tunnel their way to Australia and frighten pre-historic monsters *en route*. The film was premiered at Leicester Square, London in 1930.

Also known as the Portsmouth Sound Film Studios Limited, the company specialized in making film models such as volcanoes, monsters and animals.

Port Talbot
West Glamorgan

The Port Talbot Studio operated in the 1940s and produced at least one feature film, *Blue Scar* (1948), directed by Jill Craigie, with Emrys Jones and Rachel Thomas. The author would be most grateful to receive any additional information on Welsh film studios via the publishers.

A note on Walter Haggar – Pioneer Producer

Flair, showmanship, family loyalty and free enterprise – the ideal formula for anyone venturing into the new film industry at the turn of the century. Purpose-built cinemas were yet to come, so venues might be fairgrounds, variety and church halls and, in more than one case, abandoned chapels. Walter Haggar was a larger-than-life travelling showman who, having acquired a camera, made 'locals' of topical and scenic interest, especially in South Wales. He then turned his camera on to fairground celebrities and events, which became comic scenes and stories.

Frequently, his family would be called in to support the current production as, for instance, actors, sceneshifters or wardrobe mistresses. It helped if someone in the family could play the piano, music being an essential ingredient of silent film entertainment. For a man without a studio, Haggar's achievements for that period were quite phenomenal. Although his output was naturally less than that of his studio or house-based contemporaries, his films became extremely successful and he commenced storyline production on a grand scale. His *Mirthful Mary series* (1903); *A Desperate Poaching Affray* (1903); *The Salmon Poachers* (1905); and *Life Of Charles Peace* (1905) were much sought after by other exhibitors and generally acclaimed as important film contributions of their era.

Rotherhithe
Southwark, London

In 1975, director Christine Edzard and producer Richard Goodwin moved into two disused warehouses in Rotherhithe in London, where they set up a picture research library, built and equipped a small film studio and assembled a small team with whom they made three short films, which Christine Edzard scripted and directed: *The Little Match Girl*; *The Kitchen*; and *Little Ida*. In 1980, Oliver Stockman joined Sands Films, the production company based at the studio, to collaborate on television films. In 1983, the company launched its most ambitious project, *Little Dorrit*, based on the novel by Charles Dickens and conceived as a two-part feature film. The six-hour film was released in the UK to critical and commercial success in 1987, winning Derek Jacobi the *Evening Standard* British Film Award for Best Actor. In 1988, it was voted Best Picture by the Los Angeles Film Critics as well as receiving BAFTA nominations, two Oscar nominations for the Best Supporting Actor (Alec Guinness) and Best Screen Adaptation (Christine Edzard), and the Orson Welles Award for Best New Director. Projects for the 1990s at the Rotherhithe Studios included *The Fool*; *The Long Day Closes*; *A Dangerous Man*; and *As You Like It*, filmed in a modern setting and costumes, starring Emma Croft, James Fox, Cyril Cusack, Griff Rhys Jones, and Andrew Tiernan, produced and directed by Christine Edzard. The studios have grown in size since the 1970s, with two stages and all the necessary facilities to service independent film production. It also has associated workshops and is operational all year round with a permanent team of 20 people, many of whom have been involved with Sands for more than a decade. The studios also boast a very large stock of scenery, props and period costumes.

St Albans
Hertfordshire

The Alpha Company, with A. Melbourne Cooper as its Managing Director, made film advertisements at the St Albans Studio in 1908.

St Anne's-on-Sea
Lancashire

Although it is known that an aircraft factory at St Anne's-on-Sea was converted into a studio in the early 1920s and that the Lancashire Screen Productions commenced negotiations to film there, it is not clear whether the premises were ever used for film production.

Sheffield
South Yorkshire

In *The History of British Film 1896–1906*, Rachael Low and Roger Manvell quote a description of the Sheffield Photo Company Studio, supplied by Reuter correspondent P. Longhorn: 'This consisted of a stage 18ft from the ground, about 20 ft long by 9 ft wide, the back of the stage was formed by one wall the full length of the stage and approximately 14 ft high, with a further 5 ft of stage floor behind for the on-and-off stage work. This being an open-air studio the wall had to be re-papered for almost every scene taken, and many times when the papering had been finished the light had failed and there was no more work for that day. Owing to this and other difficulties of a like nature, interiors were kept out of as many subjects as possible'.

The leading producer of the company was Frank Mottershaw, who had previously worked as a cameraman for R. W. Paul. His first film, *A Daring Daylight Burglary* (1903), was the unusual length of 275 ft, causing something of a sensation. Within a few weeks of its release, 500 copies were being shown in England and the film was also sold to America. This was followed in 1905 by *The Life Of Charles Peace*, *The Notorious Burglar*, twelve scenes based on fact, where a burglar shoots his mistress's husband and then dons disguises to elude the police. Many of the scenes were actually shot where Peace committed his crimes and even included his dramatic jump from a train while under arrest. Mottershaw's comedies included *Bertie's Courtship*; and his innovative trick and reversing films, *An Eccentric Burglary*, in which police try to catch an acrobatic thief who is able to vanish at will. The 1905 publicity announced that it was 'the most remarkable film ever produced'. The studio continued for most of the decade with productions such as *Banana Skins* and other trick films, but between 1910 and 1913, most of the film industry was becoming centralized in or around London and provincial producers like the Sheffield Photo Company found it almost impossible to compete.

Derek Jacobi as Arthur Clennam in the award-winning *Little Dorrit*, a John Brabourne-Richard Goodwin production directed by Christine Edzard in 1986. Still courtesy of Sands Films Ltd.

Aurele Sydney
as

ULTUS:
THE MAN FROM THE DEAD

The Great Gaumont Exclusive
for which you must reserve
March 20th · Victory Film
produced by the Gaumont Co Ltd

GREAT BRITISH FILM.

GAUMONT · FILM · HIRE · SERVICE
6 DENMAN St · PICCADILLY CIRCUS · LONDON · W · TELE: FILMIRERS · TELEW · LONDON · PHONE REGENT · 4250
BRANCHES: GLASGOW · DUBLIN · CARDIFF · NEWCASTLE · LIVERPOOL · LEEDS · BIRMINGHAM · MANCHESTER · BELFAST

Shepherd's Bush (Lime Grove): In France, Leon Gaumont had been very successful with a series of films built around a mysterious character called 'Fantomas', who always became involved in terrifying situations, inevitably managing to escape in a spectacular fashion. Gaumont asked George Pearson to create a similar character who would appeal to UK audiences. Pearson came across an old Latin dictionary and found his new character within its pages. *Ultus* (1916) – from 'Ultu', an avenger – proved to be so successful that two more films were added to the series in the following year.

Shepherd's Bush

Goldhawk Studio, Hammersmith & Fulham, London

The tiny Goldhawk Studio was founded in 1964 by producer-writer F. J. Robertson for film and television work. The only feature film listed is *The Little Ones*, a drama produced by Freddie Robertson and featuring Dudley Foster and Derek Francis.

Shepherd's Bush

Lime Grove, Hammersmith & Fulham, London

If one had to pick a prominent British studio in the midst of film industry politics and personalities – particularly during the 1930s – then it would surely be Gaumont-British's Lime Grove Studios, Shepherd's Bush, London. With key figures from British film such as Michael Balcon; the Ostrer brothers; C. M. Woolf; Jeffrey Bernerd; and J. Arthur Rank all playing their part in production, distribution and exhibition, it would not be surprising that those who were not prepared to suffer first-degree burns stayed out of the kitchen. The Gaumont Company started in London in 1898 when two brothers, A. C. and R. C. Bromhead decided to distribute the films made by Leon Gaumont in France. Although distribution/renting was the major part of their business at that time, they also went in for film production at a small studio in Shepherd's Bush, and by 1912 they had acquired additional premises there, later building larger studios, Lime Grove, which were opened in 1915. Eventually, in 1922, after prolonged negotiations, the Bromheads bought out the French interests in the agency, Gaumont-British, and it became solely a British company. Prior to 1915, the Bromheads had concentrated on 'actualities' and cartoon production, but with the opening of their new studios, they decided to enter feature films. They engaged Thomas Welsh as their general manager, who in turn employed George Pearson, an up-and-coming producer of the time, who had previously worked for the Samuelson Film Company.

Born in 1875, Pearson was an Oxford-educated schoolmaster, who entered the British film industry in 1912 as a director of educational films. He turned to entertainment features shortly afterwards and soon became recognized as one of Britain's leading silent film directors. He was both a passionate story-teller and a technical innovator, writing and producing many of his own films. He was certainly instrumental in guiding the British film industry in its formative years and helped to popularize British productions in the US.

In the three years that he was with the company, Pearson had two great successes from an important series called the Ultus films. In France, Leon Gaumont had been very successful with a series of films built around a mysterious character called 'Fantomas', a sort of Robin Hood figure, always ready to take the law into his own hands for what he considered to be good reasons. This character was always involved in terrifying situations, and would inevitably manage to escape in spectacular fashion. Gaumont asked Pearson to create a British equivalent for UK audiences, and as he stood by a bookshelf, he came across an old Latin dictionary and found his new character within it pages. *Ultus* (from 'Ultu' – an avenger) was born. The following year, 1917, two Ultus films were made, accompanied by Pearson's four-reel adaptation of Temple Thurston's novel *Sally Bishop*, with Aurele Sydney (who had played Ultus) starring opposite Peggy Hyland. However, in 1918, Pearson decided to leave the Gaumont Company, and together with his General Manager, Thomas Welsh, formed the Welsh-Pearson Film Company, setting up his own studio at Craven Park, Clapham.

With the horrendous loss of life in the First World War, many British studios found it difficult to keep going due to the lack of actors and technicians. Pearson's departure from Lime Grove caused something of a production crisis for the company, and although some *Brimstone* and *Eve* comedies with Eileen Molyneaux

Shepherd's Bush Studios, 1918. The young man on the left of the camera has a confident look about him. The world came to know him as Oscar-winning cinematographer, Freddie Young.

were produced, the studio had to wait until 1919 to release two rather more important features: *The Key Of The World*; and *Pallard, The Punter*, which was based on a novel by Edgar Wallace.

Hoping to revitalize the company, the Bromhead brothers engaged Will Kellino, a former British circus clown and father of film director Roy Kellino, to direct a thriller, *The Fall Of The Saint*, with Gerald Lawrence and Josephine Earle.

Gaumont's *Bonnie Prince Charlie*, made in 1923, gave two West End stage stars the opportunity to further their careers. Gladys Cooper, a delicate English beauty who had been the soldiers' pin-up in the First World War, played Flora Macdonald, and matinée idol, playwright, screenwriter and composer Ivor Novello, played Bonnie Prince Charlie. Although Miss Cooper appeared in a number of silent films, her major screen career really began in Hollywood in 1940 where for three decades she played distinguished character roles exemplifying British dignity, and was three times nominated for an Academy Award.

In 1926, the Bromheads, with financial backing from the Ostrer brothers, decided to enlarge and amalgamate their company with an authorized capital of £2,500,000. Accompanying the Bromheads and the Ostrers on the board were Simon Rowson of Ideal Productions and the renter C. M. Woolf, who handled the Gainsborough output. Within the newly-registered Gaumont-British Picture Corporation were the Bromheads' Gaumont Company, with its studios and distribution business; Woolf's renting firm; Ideal, another renting and production firm; and a number of cinemas. Thus the foundations were laid for a giant film operation which incorporated production, distribution and exhibition, a pattern that J. Arthur Rank was to follow in the 1930s.

In his autobiography, the actor James Mason wrote of the Ostrer brothers: 'Isidore had the brain, and Mark was comfortable in white tie and tails. There was David, the oldest, who was married to a mid-European wife and was allowed to look after foreign sales. He looked like an unsuccessful Ruritanian Pretender in a UFA film. Then came Maurice, who was Isidore's shadow, and lastly, you got Harry, who having been a school teacher, became the literary department at the studios. The five of them

Shepherd's Bush: English beauty Gladys Cooper, who had been the soldiers' pin-up in the First World War, appeared in *Bonnie Prince Charlie* in 1923.

Shepherd's Bush: The Gaumont-British Lime Grove Studios at Shepherd's Bush after being rebuilt in 1932 at a cost of over £500,000.

had one opinion and one brain'. James Mason later married Pamela Kellino (née Ostrer), the daughter of Isidore Ostrer.

Towards the end of 1926, the Shepherd's Bush Studios were enlarged, and Maurice Elvey was brought in to develop production. His first film for Gaumont-British was *Mademoiselle From Armentieres*, which he directed and starred John Stuart and

Shepherd's Bush: American actress Estelle Brody became a firm favourite with British audiences, and is seen here in the title role of *Mademoiselle From Armentieres* in 1926.

the American Estelle Brody. Elvey helped to develop Estelle Brody's career, and she became a star in British silent films. Elvey's other films under the Gaumont-British banner from the mid- to late 1920s included *Hindle Wakes*, again with Estelle Brody and John Stuart; *Roses Of Picardy*, with the popular star Lillian Hall-Davis, John Stuart and Marie Ault; and *Quinneys*, with stars Alma Taylor, Cyril McLaglen and Ursula Jeans.

Sadly, at this time, British film production had to pander to the 'Quota Quickies' system, and the Shepherd's Bush Studios were to have their share of poor films. *This Marriage Business*, a comedy with a weak story-line about a newly-wed who poses as a burglar to scare his flighty wife, was one of these box-office failures, despite a cast including Owen Nares, Estelle Brody and young Polly Ward.

Michael Balcon had founded Gainsborough Pictures at Islington in 1924, and four years later, Gainsborough was absorbed into the Gaumont-British Picture Corporation to form a conglomerate that owned nearly 300 cinemas. By 1929, talkies were revolutionizing the film industry, and Gaumont decided to rebuild their studios at Lime Grove at a cost of £500,000. A huge white-faced block, with a flat roof (ideal for filming) towering nearly 90 feet above the pavement, the new building incorporated five production stages; star dressing rooms, dressing room accommodation for 600 artistes; laboratories with output capacity of 2,000,000 ft a week; three private theatres; an orchestration room; nine film vaults; a 600-seat restaurant; plasterers' and carpenters' workshops; property rooms; and monitor and recording rooms. Extra floors and buildings were added shortly afterwards.

While these renovations were taking place, Gainsborough, with its small two-stage studio at Islington, served as the production arm of Gaumont-British. By 1931, Michael Balcon was dividing his production responsibilities between

Gorgeous American actress, Esther Ralston and Hugh Williams in *Rome Express*, made at the newly-rebuilt Shepherd's Bush studio in 1932. The film was directed by former silent comedian Walter Force and produced by Michael Balcon.

Gainsborough Studios at Islington and Gaumont-British at Shepherd's Bush. Balcon stayed as head of production until 1936, and during these years he developed his contacts and associations with film-makers and technicians – many of whom followed him at the end of the decade to Ealing Studios.

The first film to be made at the 'new' Lime Grove Studios under Balcon in 1931–32 was *Rome Express*, which starred Conrad Veidt and Esther Ralston. The film was directed by a former silent film comedian, Walter Forde. Having started out as a pianist and comedian in vaudeville, Forde graduated to silent pictures where he began directing as well as starring in slapstick shorts. He was probably one of England's greatest comic talents during the early silent period and was immensely popular, though under-estimated over the decades. During the early 1920s, he went to Hollywood, where he worked for Universal before returning to England. From the late 1920s to the early 1940s, he directed many feature films in England, turning out comedies as well as thrillers, and *Rome Express* received favourable notices.

Another film with Conrad Veidt was released in 1933, *I Was A Spy* with Madeleine Carroll and heart-throb Herbert Marshall, this time directed by Victor Saville. Balcon's imaginative production slate encompassed a range of subjects and blossoming talent. *Forever England*, for example, had an island sequence directed by Anthony Asquith; while *O.H.M.S.* gave an opportunity to newcomers Anna Lee and John Mills. *The Guv'nor*, based on a story by Paul Lafitte called *Rothschild*, starred the distinguished stage and screen actor of the period George Arliss as François Rothschild in a tale about a tramp who is made a director of a failing bank because he bears the financier's surname. However, Arliss's

best film for Gaumont in terms of box-office success was *The Iron Duke* in 1935, again produced by Michael Balcon, in which he co-starred with Gladys Cooper and Emlyn Williams. Some of the films that stand out during Balcon's tenure of office in terms of critical acclaim, performances or commercial success were *The Constant Nymph* (1933), based on the book by Margaret Kennedy, with Victoria Hopper and Brian Aherne; *The Man Who Knew Too Much* (1934), directed by Alfred Hitchcock, with Edna Best, Leslie Banks, Peter Lorre and Nova Pilbeam; the controversial *Jew Suss* (1934), again starring Conrad Veidt, Benita Hume, Cedric Hardwicke and Pamela Ostrer; and the film adaptation of John Buchan's thriller *The Thirty-Nine Steps*, a great box-office success of 1935, with Robert Donat and Madeleine Carroll as the romantic leads.

Publicized as 'The Dancing Divinity', actress, dancer and singer Jessie Matthews rose to stardom in musical revues of the late 1920s, and in the early 1930s reached the height of her popularity in films. Her fame spread to America, a high accolade for a British dancer at that time, and she remained one of the most admired and loved screen stars of pre-Second World War. Although she had made *The Good Companions*, based on the novel and play by J. B. Priestley, with a young John Gielgud and Edmund Gwenn, her most famous film, made at Lime Grove, was *Evergreen*. The film was produced by Michael Balcon and directed by Victor Saville in 1934; Matthew's co-stars were the very popular Betty Balfour and Sonnie Hale.

Shepherd's Bush: George Arliss as *The Iron Duke*, a box-office success for Gaumont-British in 1935.

Shepherd's Bush: Alfred Hitchcock delighted film fans in 1935 with an adaptation of John Buchan's thriller *The Thirty Nine Steps*. Madeleine Carroll and Robert Donat were the romantic leads.

The Jessie Matthews and Sonnie Hale romance was one of the most publicized of the 1930s. Hale was a light comedian who seemed to have a magnetic effect on any lady who came within his presence, while Matthews certainly had her own share of sexual allure. The two had met while working in Cochran's successful revue *Wake Up And Dream* in which they sang Cole Porter's famous song 'Let's Do It'. They did – fall in love that is – and their romance affected not only their own immediate circle but also colleagues and friends in the theatre. The problem was that Hale was already married to West End leading lady, Evelyn Laye, a blue-eyed blonde beauty with a starry personality off-stage as well as on. She came from a theatrical background and was ruthlessly professional; by contrast, at 21, Matthews was Laye's junior by seven years and was as dark as Miss Laye was fair, with huge brown, sparkling eyes, a brunette page-boy fringe and a sexy vivacity that men found irresistible. In July 1930, Evelyn Laye's divorce petition came to court before Sir Maurice Hill, and the press-box was packed with reporters. Evelyn Laye was in Hollywood making a film called *One Heavenly Night* for Sam Goldwyn, but Jessie Matthews insisted on accompanying Sonnie Hale to the hearing. Love letters from Jessie to Sonnie Hale were read aloud in open court, and Sir Maurice's final summing-up was stinging in its severity. 'It is quite clear, that the husband admits himself to be a cad, and nobody will quarrel with that, and that the woman Matthews writes letters which show her to be a person of an odious mind'. Evelyn Laye was granted a decree nisi with costs and the press had a field day. Matthews and Hale married in 1931, and were divorced in 1944.

Although the 'Quota Quickies' had helped to keep British studios alive, by the beginning of 1937 it became clear that British films could not capture a big enough share of the American and world markets to ensure the studios' success. Moreover, the fact that the older production companies had not made substantial profits for a number of years was a warning that the investment which had led to the expansion of the industry and concomitant loans was unjustified. Isidore Ostrer announced that: 'Unless we can get a bigger return from the American market for British Pictures, Gaumont-British will be compelled to abandon production'. An even greater shock came with the announcement that Gaumont-British had a debt of nearly £100,000 on the previous year's trading and that the Shepherd's Bush Studios would close, though a limited number of films would continue to be made by Gainsborough at Islington Studios.

J. Arthur Rank and C. M. Woolf came up with a type of rescue package for Isidore Ostrer's failing Gaumont-British film empire. Woolf's renting company, General Film Distributors, had become part-owners of the immense new studio at Pinewood, and the two men suggested to Ostrer that they would take over the distribution of the Gaumont-British films along with his studios, and in return Gaumont-British production would be transferred to Pinewood while a few films could still be made at the Gainsborough Studios, Islington. The transferred productions from Lime Grove to Pinewood included a Hitchcock thriller, *Young And Innocent*; *Gangway*; and *Sailing Along*, musicals starring Jessie Matthews.

West End leading lady and screen star Evelyn Laye. In July 1930, Laye's divorce petition against her husband, Sonnie Hale, came to court and the press had a field day. Letters from the young Jessie Matthews to Hale, described as a 'cad' by the judge, were read in court. Evelyn Laye married leading man Frank Lawton after her divorce. She was the star of *Waltz Time* for Gaumont-British in 1933.

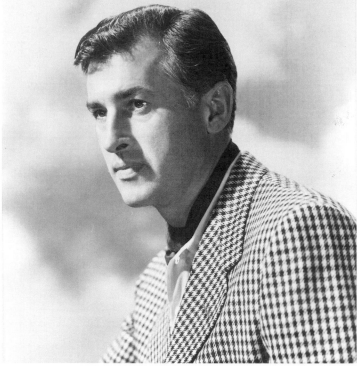

Shepherd's Bush: One of 'the dancing divinity' Jessie Matthews' greatest successes was in *Evergreen* for Gaumont-British (1984), directed by Victor Saville.

Shepherd's Bush: Stewart Granger, co-star of *The Man In Grey* and other Gainsborough films, was very often cast as the swashbuckling hero.

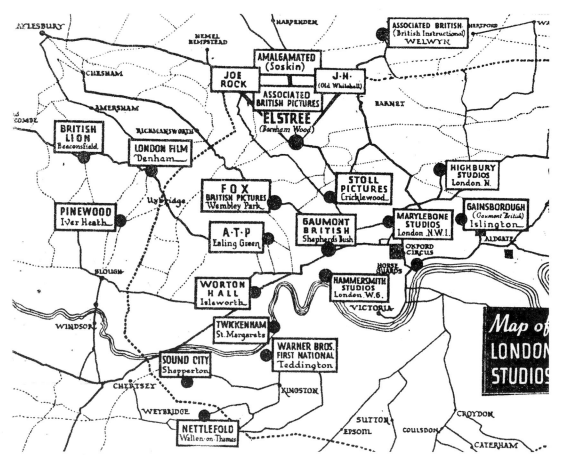

Map of London Studios from the *International Motion Picture Almanack* 1937–38, also including those in the neighbouring counties.

Shepherd's Bush: Jean Kent and Stewart Granger in Gainsborough's *Madonna Of The Seven Moons*, directed in 1944 by top cameraman Arthur Crabtree.

Shepherd's Bush: A munitions factory formed the backcloth to *Millions Like Us*, a 1943 wartime drama starring Patricia Roc and Gordon Jackson.

Shepherd's Bush: Anne Crawford and Eric Portman in *Millions Like Us*, written and directed by Frank Launder and Sidney Gilliat.

Ironically, all these plans were no match for the Second World War, which started in 1939. Many studios were commandeered by the War Ministry, including Pinewood. It was left to the much-respected studio manager-producer Edward 'Ted' Black, who had taken over at Islington on Balcon's departure in 1936, to announce that as there was the likelihood of the huge power chimney at Islington collapsing in an air raid, production would now be transferred to the Lime Grove Studios at Shepherd's Bush. By this time, Black was in an uneasy partnership with Maurice Ostrer. Ostrer was technically head of production, which did not stop Black cheerfully directing enquiries for him to Newmarket racecourse.

By the end of 1941, J. Arthur Rank had become chairman of the Gaumont-British Group, and had also acquired the 251 Gaumont-British cinemas from Isidore Ostrer who retired from the film industry in that year. The other leading protagonist, C. M. Woolf, died in 1942.

Prior to the outbreak of war, 20th Century-Fox, who had long had a financial stake in Gaumont-British, decided to close their own small studio at Wembley and lease the Shepherd's Bush Studios. The services of Edward Black and Maurice Ostrer were retained to work in close liaison with Robert T. Kane, who had formerly been in charge of production for Fox in England. *Kipps*, based on a novel by H. G. Wells, was produced by Edward Black and directed by Carol Reed in 1941. A turn-of-the-century tale of a draper's assistant who inherits money and tries to crash local society, the film starred Michael Redgrave, Phyllis Calvert, Diana Wynyard and Michael Wilding. Another vehicle for 20th-Century Fox, released a year later, was *The Young Mr Pitt*, excellent wartime propaganda with its story of Britain's youngest Prime Minister quelling the threat of invasion from Napoleon. Mr Pitt was played by Robert Donat, his co-stars being Phyllis Calvert, Robert Morley, John Mills and Felix Aylmer. More successes awaited the Shepherd's Bush, Lime Grove Studios. Fox's agreement with the studios ran out in mid-1942, and it was left to Ted Black and Maurice Ostrer to develop and expand film production. Despite the difficult relationship between the two men, and Ostrer's 'man about town' image, they were determined to succeed. Ostrer was convinced that what the public wanted more than anything else in wartime Britain was escapism; subjects that took away the worry of war, ration books and gasmasks. He instigated a number of costume melodramas and romances, made under the Gainsborough label, which proved to be some of the

Shepherd's Bush: *The Man In Grey* was the first of the Gainsborough melodramas to rocket heart-throbs James Mason and Stewart Granger to greater stardom, along with their co-stars Phyllis Calvert and Margaret Lockwood. Here Phyllis Calvert as the neglected wife of James Mason, the bounder, accepts a family heirloom from her husband.

Shepherd's Bush: Margaret Lockwood in the title role of *The Wicked Lady* (1945), which ran into censorship problems in the States. The Hays Office blocked its distribution, objecting to the expanse of bouncing cleavage revealed by its star, specifically in shots of her riding in a coach. The publicity resulting from this situation was expertly exploited by J. Arthur Rank, who owned the studio at the time.

Sheila Sim and husband Richard Attenborough at the premiere of *Broken Journey*. The film was directed by Ken Annakin at Shepherd's Bush in 1948 and starred Phyllis Calvert.

Shepherd's Bush: Dennis Price as *The Bad Lord Byron*, released in 1949, produced by Aubrey Baring and directed by David McDonald.

most successful films in the history of the studio. A Regency melodrama, *The Man In Grey*, was the first Gainsborough film of this genre, and rocketed heart-throbs James Mason and Stewart Granger to even greater stardom, along with co-stars Margaret Lockwood and Phyllis Calvert. The film's success created a further disturbance in the balance of power between Ostrer and Black, the latter leaving the company in 1942 to join Korda at MGM. With the addition of Jean Kent and Patricia Roc, Ostrer developed a type of repertory company, and made *Madonna Of The Seven Moons*; *Caravan*; and *Jassy*; all around the mid-1940s. However, the most successful of the Gainsborough melodramas was *The Wicked Lady*, produced by R. J. Minney and written and directed by Leslie Arliss. Set in the reign of Charles II, it told the story of the wicked Lady Skelton, played by Margaret Lockwood, who befriends a highwayman, James Mason, and takes to crime and high adventure. The cast also included a lovelorn Patricia Roc, Griffith Jones as the cuckolded husband and Michael Rennie as the dashing cavalier. The film ran into censorship problems in the US when the Hays Office blocked its distribution objecting to the expanse of bouncing cleavage revealed by Roc and Lockwood, specifically in shots of them riding in a coach. J. Arthur Rank, the owner of Shepherd's Bush Studios by 1945, desperately hoped for a crucial American box-office breakthrough, and ordered that the offending scenes be re-shot. Expertly exploiting the publicity, Rank ensured even greater queues around the cinemas in the UK.

However, by the mid-1940s, Maurice Ostrer had 'dangerously narrowed down' his production programme to exclude virtually anything but a handful of melodramas. His contract ended in 1946, and he was replaced by Sydney Box. Sydney and Muriel Box were a British husband-wife team, who produced, directed and wrote their films, and were already well-established in the British film industry by the time of his new appointment as Head of Production with Gainsborough Films. Box complained about the low Gainsborough output, and boasted that he would be able to produce twelve films a year compared to Ostrer's three. Three of his productions included *Holiday Camp*, with Jack Warner, Flora Robson, Dennis Price, Hazel Court and Kathleen Harrison – all firm favourites of the period; *The Man Within*, starring Michael Redgrave, Jean Kent, Joan Greenwood and Richard Attenborough, which had Geoffrey Unsworth as its cinematographer; and *Easy Money*, a four-episode film with Jack Watling, Greta Gynt, Bill Owen and Petula Clark. Other films on Box's production slate included *The Calendar*, with an early appearance from Diana Dors; and Dennis Price appearing as *The Bad Lord Byron* to Joan Greenwood's Lady Caroline Lamb, released in 1949.

Sadly, towards the end of the 1940s even the great Rank empire was beginning to crumble with a massive bank overdraft of £16 million. Extreme measures were called for, and John Davis, an accountant who had joined Rank in 1939, was Pinewood's St George. His only course of action was to slash budgets and sell off everything that did not immediately affect the survival of Rank's Pinewood Studios. Amongst the casualties were the Gainsborough Studios at Islington (2 stages) and Lime Grove Studios, Shepherd's Bush (5 stages). Both studios were closed in 1949, and in the same year, Rank sold the Shepherd's Bush, Lime Grove Studios to BBC Television.

Shepperton

Middlesex, TW17 0QD

For more than 70 years, Shepperton has been the home of some of the all-time great movies. *Richard III*; *The Third Man*; *Becket*; *Oliver!*; *Anne Of A Thousand Days*; *A Man For All Seasons*; *Anna Karenina*; and *The Guns Of Navarone* are among the numerous marvellous British films that have been made there.

In more recent times, titles have included Sidney Pollack's *Out Of Africa*; David Jones's *84, Charing Cross Road*; Lord Attenborough's *Cry Freedom*, *Chaplin*, and *Shadowlands*; Michael Apted's *Gorillas In The Mist*; Kenneth Branagh's *Henry V* and *Frankenstein*; Kevin Costner's *Robin Hood: Prince Of Thieves*; Franco Zeffirelli's *Hamlet*; Brian Henson's *The Muppets' Christmas Carol*; Louis Malle's *Damage*; and Neil Jordan's *The Crying Game*.

In 1689, Thomas Wood, the son of an alderman of the City of London, built Littleton Park, the house that stands at the centre of the site today. The family purchased the title to the manor in 1749, and resided there until the end of the nineteenth century. William IV often took time off from affairs of state to relax in the summer house by the river, as did Queen Victoria's son, the Prince of Wales (later Edward

Left to right: Michael Wilding, Gladys Young and Anna Neagle in *The Courtneys Of Curzon Street* (1947), produced and directed at Shepperton by Herbert Wilcox.

VII), who enjoyed hunting in the grounds. The house was partially burnt down in 1876, and was repaired in the early 1900s by Sir Richard Burbridge, (then the Managing Director of Harrods) who used timber from the old Houses of Parliament. Marbles depicting the victories of Nelson and Wellington were brought from Westminster Abbey and placed in the conservatory. After Sir Richard's death in 1917, the estate was sold to Sir Edward Nicholl, a successful shipping magnate who resided there until 1928.

The film history of the estate began in 1931, when Norman Loudon, a dynamic Scottish businessman, bought Littleton Park with its surrounding 60-acre grounds, which included a beautiful stretch of the River Ash at Shepperton.

Loudon was new to the film industry, but he had had a prosperous camera business which manufactured small 'flicker' books of photographs, which gave an impression of movement when the pages were flicked with the thumb. His company, Flicker Productions, proved so successful that he decided the next step was to enter film production. Littleton Park seemed ideal for a film studio, and its grounds would be magnificent for location purposes.

His new company, Sound City Film Producing & Recording Studios, was founded in 1932, and gave an opportunity to keen, gifted, amateur and sometimes monied men to enter film production.

There was nothing amateurish about Loudon, who ran an extremely efficient organization. By the end of 1932, Sound City had registered five productions, three shorts for MGM and two features, *Watch Beverley*, directed by Arthur Maude; and *Reunion*, directed by Ivor Campbell. The authentic country house, complete with conservatory and ballroom, acres of park and woodlands and two new sound stages, quickly attracted production companies including the Wainwright Brothers; Embassy Pictures; Argyle Talking Pictures; and Fitzpatric Pictures, to the rapidy-expanding studios.

Sound City, as the studios were known, also beckoned young, enthusiastic directors such as George King, J. L. Freer-Hunt, Ralph Ince, J. D. Cousins, W. P. Lipscombe, and John Baxter. Baxter, a confirmed Christian socialist, became an influential producer and director, making realistic dramas and comedies of the 1930s and 1940s which pointed to the 'new wave' school of the 1950s and 1960s. Having acted as an assistant on *Reunion*, he then directed *Doss House*, an observation of human suffering among 'down and outs'. His other films at Shepperton during the 1930s included *Song Of The Plough*, with Stewart Rome; the appropriately-titled *Taking Ways*, based on a sketch, 'Light-Fingered Freddy'; *Birds Of A Feather*, made under his own company's banner, Baxter and Barter, starring Sir George Robey; *Hearts Of Humanity*, with Eric Portman; *Song Of The Road*; and *Talking Feet*.

At 21 years of age, John Paddy Carstairs made his first Shepperton film, *Paris Plane*, with John Loder and Molly Lamont, released in 1933; and in 1937, he also directed *Double Exposures*, with Ruby Miller and Julian Mitchell.

By the end of 1934, the £5,000 paid by Norman Loudon for the 60-acre estate and mansion was producing dividends and the demand for Sound City facilities necessitated substantial expansion. Loudon firmly believed in the power of publicity, and

Paulette Goddard as the scheming Mrs Cheveley in Oscar Wilde's *An Ideal Husband,* produced and directed by Alexander Korda at Shepperton in 1947–48.

his excellent Sound City brochure of 1935 reflected a keen business mind at work. Its major thrust was to demonstrate the use made of the wonderful locations in the studios' grounds by external companies as well as Sound City. So, the brochure showed the whole of the Tower of London reconstructed in the tank for *Colonel Blood*; a dockland scene with Will Fyffe for *Rolling Home*; George Arliss marshalling his troops in Gaumont-British's *The Iron Duke*; Clifford Mollison about to fall into the river in BIP's *Mr Cinders*; a scene from *Sanders Of The River* for London Films, with a jungle reconstruction along the Shepperton and Iver banks; an entire Sussex village for Fox-British's *Once In A New Moon*; Irish countryside in Twickenham Studios' production of *Lily Of Killarney*; Ealing Studios under canvas for their production of *Three Men In A Boat*; and Conrad Veidt looking decidedly lost in Sound City's woodlands in the Twickenham Studios' production of *The Wandering Jew*.

The Cinematograph Films Act of 1927 stipulated that for ten years a rising proportion of British films should be rented and exhibited in the United Kingdom. This meant that an increased number of films were made cheaply and quickly to comply with the Act. They became known as 'Quota Quickies', and while they were good for British film production, they did little to enhance the reputation of British films. This is not to say that all 'Quota

Shepperton: Lobby still for *Room At The Top* (1958).

Quickies' were bad; indeed, they certainly provided a marvellous training ground for actors, technicians, producers and directors. But, in the main, films made between 1927 and 1937 were understandably known as either 'quality' or 'quota'. The Act had also encouraged American studios and companies to set up UK operations, and churn out quota films to feed their own home market as well as Britain's. Thus, they would either rent a UK studio space or part of one for a given period, or use available space as their production schedules dictated.

Norman Loudon, a tough, shrewd, resourceful businessman with undoubted charm, took full advantage of the situation. In the period to 1937, Sound City at Shepperton was used for a great many quota films by both UK producers and directors and American companies and studios. Loudon's strategy proved so successful that, in 1936, after a short period of closure for modernization, the studios reopened with seven sound stages (including two of 18,000 sq ft), twelve cutting rooms, three viewing theatres, scene docks and workshops, while the old house was refurbished to provide hotel and restaurant facilities. That year, 22 productions took advantage of the new services on offer at Shepperton, one of which was *Sabotage*, from the distinguished director of the 1920s and 1930s, Adrian Brunel; while a young, handsome James Mason appeared in *Mill On The Floss*, with Victoria Hopper, Frank Lawton and Geraldine Fitzgerald. Other productions up to and including 1939 were *Sweeney Todd, The Demon Barber Of Fleet Street*, starring the appropriately-named Tod Slaughter; *The Last Adventurers*, directed by Roy Kellino; *Wake Up Famous*, with actor-comedians Nelson Keys and Gene Gerrard; *Life Of Chopin*, directed by James A. Fitzpatrick; and *Sexton Blake And The Hooded Terror*, directed by George King and starring Tod Slaughter and Greta Gynt. Probably one of the best-remembered films from Sound City in the 1930s was *French Without Tears*, released in 1939, of which Graham Greene wrote: 'There is always something a little

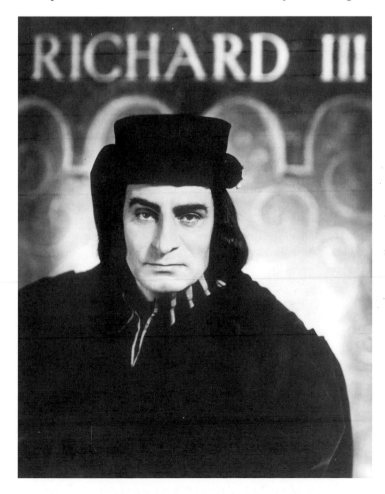

Shepperton: Laurence Olivier as the spine-chilling *Richard III,* which he produced and co-directed with Anthony Bushell in 1955.

Shepperton: An adaptation of Jean Anouilh's play *Becket,* released in 1964, provided brilliant screen entertainment in the hands of Richard Burton, in the title role, and Peter O'Toole as King Henry II.

Two *Pink Panther* films were made at Shepperton in the 1970s, both starring the inimitable Peter Sellers as the blundering Inspector Clouseau.

shocking about English levity. The greedy exhilaration of these blithe young men when they learn that another fellow's girl is to join them at the establishment where they are learning French – the scramble over her luggage, the light-hearted badinage – the watery and libidinous eye – that national mixture of prudery and excitement – would be unbearable if it were not for Mr Asquith's civilised direction'. The film was based on a play by Terence Rattigan with a screenplay by Anatole de Grunwald, and the cast included Ray Milland, Ellen Drew, Guy Middleton and Roland Culver.

Quiet Wedding was one of the last productions to be partly made at Shepperton before filming was interrupted by the Second World War. A splendid cast, including much-loved character actors A. E. Matthews, Athene Seyler, Roland Culver and Bernard Miles, was headed by Margaret Lockwood in a film written by Terence Rattigan and directed by Anthony Asquith. Filming commenced in 1940, as did the Blitz and the Battle of Britain. The War Office considered Shepperton Studios a safe location as it was 14 miles from the centre of London. However, they had failed to consider that the huge Vickers-Armstrong aircraft factory was producing Spitfires and Wellington bombers a few miles across the river and was a prime target for the German air raids. Filming was constantly interrupted and stray bombs fell into the studio grounds. Eventually, the Vickers-

Armstrong factory did receive a direct hit and was put partially out of commission when they moved part of their operation to the requisitioned Walton film studios. At this point, the War Office came up with a clever strategy: if you can't beat them, fox them. They immediately requisitioned the Shepperton Studios, and the skills of its craftsmen were put to work making replicas of aircraft that were to be used in the Middle East as decoys, plus fake guns and landing strips. A number of other British studios were also commandeered by the Ministry of Defence for food and equipment storage and for the production of camouflage materials and weaponry.

In 1945, Norman Loudon announced the re-opening of Sound City's six-stage studio, although he was to retire from the film industry within 12 months. In the same year, Sir Alexander Korda severed what had been a brief connection with MGM, and brought London Film Productions out from under the wing of that company. London Films then purchased the controlling interest in British Lion, reconstructing the board with Hugh Quennell as Chairman and Arthur Jarratt as Managing Director. In April 1946, British Lion acquired a 74 per cent controlling interest in Sound City (Films) Limited for £380,000, together with its studios at Shepperton. British Lion also had a 50 per cent interest in the Worton Hall Studios at Isleworth. Sound City (Films) Limited was renamed the British Lion Studio Company,

American leading actor, Kevin Costner, who played the title role in *Robin Hood: Prince Of Thieves* at Shepperton in 1990.

American film star Robert de Niro had the title role in *Mary Shelley's Frankenstein,* made at Shepperton in 1993.

and in 1946, this company acquired the whole undertaking of Worton Hall Studios (1944) Limited. These new acquisitions superseded British Lion's studio at Beaconsfield in Buckinghamshire, which was taken over by the government on a 21-year lease. British Lion was now in a position to become a powerful post-war factor in British film production. Its studio facilities were greater than those of ABPC and second only to the Rank Group. An additional twist to the Korda takeover was to come. Korda had owed a vast sum of money to the Prudential Assurance Company from his previous studios at Denham, and had had the negatives of his films seized when they foreclosed. The Prudential thought that the negatives were of little value and were quite delighted when he offered to buy them back for a modest sum after the war.

One of the early films made at Shepperton under the new regime was an adaptation of Oscar Wilde's *An Ideal Husband*, produced and directed by Alexander Korda in 1947. The film starred Paulette Goddard, Michael Wilding, Glynis Johns, Diana Wynyard and Hugh Williams, with Cecil Beaton making his debut as an art director. The next film produced by Korda was *Anna Karenina*, directed by Julien Duvivier and starring Vivien Leigh, Ralph Richardson and Kieron Moore.

The highly successful Wilcox romances *The Courtneys Of Curzon Street*, and *Spring In Park Lane*, starring the popular

team of Anna Neagle (Wilcox's wife) and Michael Wilding were made in 1947 and 1948 respectively. From the same period came *The Fallen Idol*, partly made at Worton Hall. This collaboration between Graham Greene and director Carol Reed ranks as a British film classic. The story of an ambassador's son who witnesses the accidental death of the wife of the butler whom he idolizes produced sterling performances from Bobby Henrey as the boy and Ralph Richardson as the butler. Other films directed by Carol Reed at Shepperton between 1948 and 1967 were the outstanding *The Third Man*, a Reed-Greene thriller set in war-torn Vienna, backed by insistent zither music by Anton Karas, and starring Orson Welles, Joseph Cotten, Valli, and Trevor Howard; *An Outcast Of The Islands: The Man Between*, with James Mason, Hildegarde Neff, and Claire Bloom, which the *Daily Express* described as: 'A cold-hearted film about people with cold feet'; *A Kid For Two Farthings*, set in the East End of London and giving Diana Dors a chance to shine; an adaptation of Graham Greene's novel *Our Man In Havana*, starring Alec Guinness, Noël Coward, Burl Ives and Maureen O'Hara; and the Academy Award-winning smash-hit *Oliver!*, Lionel Bart's musical version of Dickens' *Oliver Twist*.

In 1948, the new Cinematograph Films Act announced that the quotas for British films in the coming year would be 45 per cent for first features and 25 per cent for supporting programmes. These

Shepperton: Producer and director Richard Attenborough directs Anthony Hopkins as C. S. 'Jack' Lewis on the set of *Shadowlands.* Photograph by Keith Hamshere, Copyright Shadowlands Productions, 1993.

figures were unduly high, considering that they had been fixed only one month before the President of the Board of Trade reported a 'stoppage' in production through lack of finance, and it was unlikely that British exhibitors would be unable to comply. The President of the Board of Trade, Harold Wilson, was asked if the British Film Industry agreed that they could supply 45 per cent of the first feature films stipulated in the Act, and the far from reassuring reply that appeared in Hansard was: 'This industry never agrees on anything as between producers and exhibitors'. The truth of the matter was that these quotas, the last signs of an arrested boom, were plans fixed on paper and were never implemented on the studio floor. To alleviate the situation, one month later in July, the Board of Trade announced that the National Film Finance Corporation (NFFC) would be created to lend money for film production. Sir Alexander Korda approved of the idea, and, using the same persuasive charm that had mesmerized The Prudential Assurance Company in the 1930s, he managed to obtain a long-term loan which amounted to £3 million. However, British Lion incurred high production losses, which were worsened late in 1950 when the Republic Pictures Corporation of America ended their relationship with the company. The financial crisis reached a peak in 1954 when the NFFC called in their loan, appointing a receiver and manager. It was then disclosed that all of the British Lion's share capital of £1,205,000 had been lost. British Lion Films

Limited was formed in January 1955 to take over the assets of its insolvent predecessor. The new company's main function was not film production but the provision of distribution and financial guarantees for independent producers. Among those appointed to a re-organized board of directors were practical film-makers such as Roy and John Boulting, Frank Launder and Sidney Gilliat, all of whom were to make a number of films at the studios. These included Sidney Gilliat's *The Constant Husband*, *Fortune Is A Woman*, and *Left, Right And Centre*; Frank Launder's *Geordie* and *Blue Murder At St Trinians*; and another comedy in the same vein, *Pure Hell At St Trinians*; the Boulting Brothers' suspense thriller *Seven Days To Noon*; *Josephine And Men*, starring the 1930s matinée idol Jack Buchanan; the irresistible comedy *Private's Progress*; the much-acclaimed satirical farce *I'm Alright, Jack*, which starred Ian Carmichael, Peter Sellers, Irene Handl, Richard Attenborough, Terry-Thomas, and Margaret Rutherford; *Carlton-Browne Of The F.O.*; and *The Family Way*, starring John Mills with his daughter Hayley.

The films made at Shepperton in the 1950s and 1960s reflected the influence of the strong independent companies, producers and directors who used the studios, rather than the former paternal dominance of Alexander Korda who died of a heart attack in 1956. Further landmark films of which the British film industry can be justly proud date from that period to the present day.

Shepperton: Helena Bonham-Carter and Kenneth Branagh in *Mary Shelley's Frankenstein*, which Kenneth Branagh also directed. Photo by David Appleby.

Two films directed by David Lean in the 1950s command particular attention: *The Sound Barrier*, a riveting story with marvellous air sequences, featuring finely-drawn performances from Ralph Richardson, Nigel Patrick, Ann Todd and Dinah Sheridan; and the delightful *Hobson's Choice*, about a tyrannical Victorian bootmaker from Lancashire who is brought to heel by his plain but frank daughter and her poor though determined husband, the characters brilliantly portrayed by Charles Laughton, Brenda de Banzie and John Mills.

Hollywood came to Shepperton in the 1950s with *Pandora And The Flying Dutchman*, Ava Gardner, at the height of her great beauty, co-starring with James Mason. In his autobiography, Mason writes of the behaviour of the film's director, Albert Lewin: 'He did not bark his orders. He was a cool Führer. Unfortunately, for him, he was also a deaf Führer. Although he wore a hearing-aid, he missed much muttering by the malcontents around him, and he often printed shots in which the actors had not even said their lines correctly'. Despite impeccable photography from Jack Cardiff, the film was not well received by the critics. In 1952, the great John Huston directed some scenes of *The African Queen* in the grounds of the studio. The film starred Katharine Hepburn and Humphrey Bogart, who won an Oscar for his portrayal of the hard-drinking captain, Charlie Allnutt. Later that year, Huston directed the *Moulin Rouge* at

Shepperton, based on the life of Toulouse-Lautrec with José Ferrer in the title role. Gregory Peck, David Niven, Stanley Baker, Anthony Quinn and Anthony Quayle were brought to Shepperton in 1960 to film a story about a wartime team sent to destroy two giant guns on a Turkish island. *The Guns Of Navarone* was directed by J. Lee-Thompson, with splendid photography from Oswald Morris.

Anyone seeing Laurence Olivier's 1955 performance as *Richard III* at the Old Vic would have thought that it was an impossible task to transfer the hypnotic evil that he conveyed to his stage audience to the screen. With excellent performances from a supporting cast that included Claire Bloom, Ralph Richardson, John Gielgud and Alec Clunes, plus William Walton's music, Olivier succeeded splendidly. Two of his problems during the 13-week shoot at Shepperton and on location were how to make 500 men look like 60,000 for the wide screen, and how to pacify Alexander Korda. Korda, whose London Films was backing the production, was already deeply in debt, and would telephone him on a daily basis with the words: 'Larry, you must cut, you know? You ruin me, you know.'

John Osborne's *The Entertainer* provided a complete contrast for Olivier, who played the seedy, washed-up, music-hall comedian, Archie Rice. Released in 1960, it was directed by Tony Richardson and the supporting cast included Joan

Cate Blanchett starred as a vulnerable *Elizabeth* to a passionate Robert Dudley, played by Joseph Fiennes in Alison Owen's production at Shepperton in 1996. Photo Alex Bailey. Copyright Polygram Filmed Entertainment.

Plowright (who was to become Lady Olivier), Brenda de Banzie, Albert Finney, Alan Bates, Shirley Anne Field and Thora Hird. Olivier returned to Shepperton in 1964–65 to play *Othello*, of which the *Observer* wrote: 'What the director does is keep the camera moving among the actors with the most intelligent precision'. The director in this case was Stuart Burge and the cinematographer, Geoffrey Unsworth. Laurence Olivier and Maggie Smith received Academy Award nominations for their performances.

Laurence Olivier (later Lord Olivier) was presented with an honorary Academy Award in 1979 'for the full body of his work, for the unique achievements of his entire career, and his lifetime of contribution to the art of film'.

The Austrian-American director Otto Preminger cast David Niven, Deborah Kerr, Jean Seberg and Mylene Demongeot in his Shepperton production of *Bonjour, Tristesse*, which he also directed. Based on the novel by Françoise Sagan, the film was not well received, described by the film critic/author Alexander Walker as: 'Sagan not so much translated as traduced – opened out, smartened up, the sickness overlaid with Riviera sun-tan', while the *Financial Times* chimed in with 'Long, untidy, muddled and mushy'. The great Charles Chaplin's *A King In New York*, also released in 1957, fared little better. This story of a penniless European king who finds himself at odds with the American way of life was directed by Chaplin, who also played the title role. However, Chaplin was king of the silent movies, not of talkies, and unhappily, *The New Yorker* thought it: 'Maybe the worst film ever made by a celebrated film artist'.

The Angry Silence, one that resulted from the victimization and 'sending to Coventry' of a factory hand by his work mates, was the basis of a powerful 1960 drama. Having created Beaver Films, Richard Attenborough and Bryan Forbes co-produced it as their first feature and, important for the British film industry at that time, adopted a new policy of deferred payment for the artists, which enabled the film to be made for the astonishingly low sum of £97,000. *The Angry Silence* was directed by Guy Green, and Bryan Forbes received an Academy Award nomination for the screenplay, which allowed Richard Attenborough's skills as a contemporary actor to come to the fore. Bryan Forbes went on to write and direct another Shepperton production in 1962, *The L-Shaped Room*, with Leslie Caron, Cecily Courtneidge, Emlyn Williams and Tom Bell. The film was produced by Richard Attenborough and James Woolf. Both James and John Woolf (who had founded Romulus Films in 1949) were the sons of leading producer-distributor C. M. Woolf, who had died in 1942. *The Angry Silence* and *The L-Shaped Room* were examples of films that echoed the social and economic changes that had shaken but not stirred the 1950s. In the late 1950s and 1960s, reality became the essence of the 'New Wave' school. Films of this genre made at Shepperton included *Room At The Top*, directed by Jack Clayton and produced by John and James Woolf, starring Simone Signoret, Laurence Harvey and Heather Sears; John Schlesinger's *A Kind Of Loving*; *Billy Liar*; and *Darling*, in which Julie Christie won an Oscar for her role of Diana, an ambitious, amoral model, co-starring with Dirk Bogarde and Laurence Harvey.

The financial standing of British Lion Films Limited improved steadily from 1955 to 1961. Early in 1961, there was a new departure as British Lion and Columbia formed BLC Films to be responsible for marketing the films of both companies in the UK, an arrangement which lasted until 1967. In 1963, the company reported its fourth profitable year in succession and announced that £600,000 of the government loan had been paid off. However, in 1964, the government sold the company back into private enterprise to a group headed by Michael Balcon, in spite of considerable opposition within the film industry. Profits dropped by £86,000 in the first year and in September 1965, Balcon was succeeded as chairman by Lord Goodman.

Four excellent costume dramas came from Shepperton during the 1960s. A version of Jean Anouilh's play *Becket*, released in 1964, provided brilliant screen entertainment with Richard Burton in the title role and Peter O'Toole as Henry II. The star supporting cast included John Gielgud, Donald Wolfit, Sian Phillips, Pamela Brown and Martita Hunt. In *Anne Of The Thousand Days*, Richard Burton jumped some centuries to play Henry VIII, desperately wanting to divorce his queen of nearly 20 years in order to marry the dazzling Anne Boleyn (Genevieve Bujold). The divorce of Henry VIII was again the theme for *A Man For All Seasons*, released in 1966. This time, the emphasis was on Sir Thomas More (Paul Scofield), who opposed the king's divorce, thus sparking off a train of events that eventually led to his execution. With a cast that included Wendy Hiller, Robert Shaw, Orson Welles, Leo McKern, Susannah York and Nigel Davenport, and directed

Julie Walters, as the ballet teacher, loses patience with *Billy Elliot* (Jamie Bell), who against great odds achieves his ambition to become a ballet dancer. Directed at Shepperton by Stephen Daldry in 1999. Photo courtesy and copyright Universal Pictures and U.I.P.

Jumping for joy: *Billy Elliot* (Jamie Bell) in a Shepperton production of 1999. Photo courtesy and copyright Universal Pictures and U.I.P.

Julia Roberts and Hugh Grant starred in *Notting Hill*, the story of a bumbling British bookseller falling in love with a glamorous American film star. Directed by Robert Mitchell at Shepperton in 1998. Photo Clive Coote. Copyright Universal Pictures Ltd, 1999.

Kenneth Branagh as Berowne and Alicia Silverstone as the Princess in his delightful and audacious interpretation of *Love's Labour's Lost*, in which he replaced some of the more difficult Shakespearean dialogue with the songs of Cole Porter and George Gershwin. Photo Laurie Sparham. Copyright Intermedia 2000.

by Fred Zinnemann, the film was awarded six Oscars for Best Picture, Director, Actor, Screenplay, Costumes and Cinematography. Moving on to the reign of Charles I, *Cromwell*, directed by Ken Hughes, was reported to have received the highest sum ever paid by the Russians for a British film, an estimated £100,000. Possibly this historical drama concerning Britain's king, his quest for supreme authority, the ensuing Civil War, and his subsequent execution, had a certain appeal. There was definitely an uncanny likeness between Alec Guinness and portraits of Charles I. Richard Harris played the Roundhead leader, *Cromwell*, who put his faith in God and kept his gunpowder dry.

Costume drama apart, there were a number of other distinguished productions at Shepperton in the 1960s including Stanley Kubrick's *Dr Strangelove, Or: How I Learned To Stop Worrying And Love The Bomb*, a black comedy dealing with the public concerns of 1963. The film will long be remembered for the performances of Peter Sellers and George C. Scott, who played the General with immortal lines such as: 'I don't say we wouldn't get our hair mussed, but I do see no more than ten-to-twenty million people killed'. In the same year, *The Servant*, a study of corruption, was directed by Joseph Losey. With a powerful screenplay by Harold Pinter, it was a remarkable piece of film entertainment and had outstanding performances from Dirk Bogarde, James Fox and Wendy Craig. *The Pumpkin Eater* (1964) directed by Jack Clayton and based on Penelope Mortimer's novel, was another thought-provoking production. Anne Bancroft played a compulsive mother of eight who finds that her third marriage is on the rocks when she discovers proof of her husband's infidelity. The excellent supporting cast included Peter Finch, James Mason, Maggie Smith and Cedric Hardwicke. Richard Burton, Claire Bloom, Oskar Werner, Michael Hordern and Sam Wanamaker came to Shepperton in 1964–65 for the filming of *The Spy Who Came In From The Cold*. Produced and directed by Martin Ritt, it was one of the first 'realistic' examples of the seedy, unglamorous world of modern spies as conveyed in John le Carré's novel.

An increase in the company's profits was announced in 1967. In the following year, the BBC bought British Lion's library of feature films, and by 1969, with John Boulting as Managing Director, the company seemed to be in a healthy financial condition. However, the number of new films distributed was declining, and by 1971, represented scarcely more than a trickle. A new chapter in British Lion's history was opened in April 1972 when Barclay Securities, headed by the financier John Bentley, took over the organization.

In the mid-1960s, two new stages were constructed at Shepperton to increase capacity. Although film production was to decrease dramatically at all British studios in the 1970s due to poor investment incentives and the state of the world economy (Shepperton lists just two films for 1979), there were nevertheless a number of notable films from the studio during that decade. Vanessa Redgrave, the daughter of Rachel Kempson and Michael Redgrave, starred in the title role of *Mary, Queen Of Scots*, which was directed by Charles Jarrott. Another film of the early 1970s was *The Day Of The Jackal*,

Kenneth Branagh and Natascha McElhone lead the dance in *Love's Labour's Lost*, made at Shepperton in 1998. Photo Laurie Sparham. Copyright Intermedia 2000.

based on Frederick Forsyth's bestseller. Directed by Fred Zinnemann, the film starred Edward Fox, who gave a memorable performance as the sinister but charming assassin. There were two *Pink Panther* films at Shepperton in the 1970s, both starring the inimitable Peter Sellers as the blundering Inspector Clouseau, and Herbert Lom, continually on the verge of a nervous breakdown. Henry Mancini's music won almost as much credit for the success of the films as their director Blake Edwards. In 1978–9 there was tight security on the stages at Shepperton for *Alien*, a science-fiction film with a difference. The secrecy on this Ridley Scott film was due to the development of Oscar-winning special effects by Brian Johnson, Nick Allder, Denys Ayling and H. R. Giger.

Between 1970 and 1993, Richard Attenborough (Lord Attenborough) made some of his finest films at Shepperton. These included *Young Winston*, starring Simon Ward, John Mills, Anne Bancroft, Jack Hawkins and Anthony Hopkins; the 8-Oscar winner *Gandhi* (1982), with an impeccable performance from Ben Kingsley in the title role, strongly supported by Edward Fox, Candice Bergen, John Gielgud and John Mills; the part-thriller, part-social conscience film *Cry Freedom*, starring Kevin Kline, Penelope Wilton, Denzel Washington and Alec McCowen; *Chaplin*, a film biography of the London-born silent star, with a fine performance from Robert Downey Jnr in the title role and Geraldine Chaplin, the daughter of Charles, giving a beautifully-drawn characterization as the mother of Charles Chaplin. In 1994, Lord Attenborough's adaptation of William Nicholson's play *Shadowlands*, starring Anthony Hopkins and Debra Winger, was released to critical and public acclaim.

In 1984, the manor of Littleton acquired a new overlord when

Lee International paid £3.6 million for the studios. The Lee Group invested a considerable sum of money in refurbishing the facilities, and plans were drawn up for new workshops, which were built in 1987. Hand Made Films also based their production arm at the studios. In 1987, the studios became part of Lee Panavision Inc. Fine films continued to be made at Shepperton during the 1980s such as *The Elephant Man* and *Little Lord Fauntleroy*, an immaculately-made film for television directed by Jack Gold, with wonderfully underplayed performances from Alec Guinness, Connie Booth, Ricky Schroder, Eric Porter and Colin Blakely preventing this adaptation of Frances Hodgson Burnett's novel from being sickly-sweet. Further big productions at Shepperton during the decade were *The Missionary*, directed by Richard Loncraine; *The Company Of Wolves*, directed by Neil Jordan; David Lean's *Passage To India*; *Out Of Africa*, directed by Sydney Pollack and starring Meryl Streep and Robert Redford; *Gorillas In The Mist*, starring Sigourney Weaver and directed by Michael Apted; and Kenneth Branagh's first film production, *Henry V*, which he directed as well as playing the title role.

Also among the 1980s productions at the studios were Michael Blakemore's *Privates On Parade*; Michael Radford's film of the George Orwell novel *1984*; *84 Charing Cross Road*, a pleasing adaptation of the now famous book in which a New York woman conducts a long correspondence with a bookseller in London, with Anne Bancroft, Anthony Hopkins and Judi Dench, directed by David Jones; and Jack Clayton's *The Lonely Passion Of Judith Hearne*, starring Maggie Smith.

The 1990s saw Franco Zeffirelli's interpretation of *Hamlet*, a fresh, sumptuous production starring Mel Gibson as Hamlet,

Brad Pitt (L) and Robert Redford co-star in *Spy Game*, a thriller directed by Tony Scott at Shepperton in 2000/2001. A Zaltman Films production for Universal Pictures/Beacon Pictures. Photo: Keith Hamshere.

Glenn Close, Alan Bates, Paul Scofield and Helena Bonham-Carter; Kevin Costner starring as *Robin Hood: Prince Of Thieves*; *Three Men And A Little Lady*, a sequel to the successful *Three Men And A Baby*, with Tom Selleck, Steve Guttenburg, Ted Danson, Nancy Travis and Christopher Cazenove, which was directed by Emile Ardonilo; Neil Jordan's Oscar winner, *The Crying Game*; the acclaimed director Louis Malle's *Damage*; Lord Attenborough's *Chaplin* and *Shadowlands*; and *Mary Shelley's Frankenstein*, directed by Kenneth Branagh and starring Robert de Niro. Although the immensely successful *Four Weddings And A Funeral* was filmed mainly on location, it did have a production office at Shepperton and one of the studios' stages was used for filming. This award-winning 1994 romantic comedy was directed by Mike Newell and produced by Duncan Kenworthy, starring Hugh Grant and Andie McDowell; the marvellous supporting cast included Kristin Scott-Thomas and Simon Callow. Another award-winning film (using 2 stages) in 1994 was the brilliant *The Madness of King George*, starring Nigel Hawthorne, Helen Mirren and Ian Holm, directed from Alan Bennett's screenplay by Nicholas Hytner.

Production schedules for 1994–95 included Sylvester Stallone in *Judge Dredd*: *Restoration*, with Robert Downey Jnr and Meg Ryan; Mel Gibson's *Braveheart*; and *Carrington*, with Emma Thompson and Jonathan Pryce; as well as increasingly important television films, programmes and commercials. In February 1995, a consortium led by British film directors Ridley and Tony Scott purchased the studios. The production slate for that year included actor/director Kenneth Branagh's *Hamlet* with Kate Winslet as his Ophelia and the award-winning production of *Sense and Sensibility*. Directed by Ang Lee, with an Oscar-winning screenplay from Emma Thompson, moving score from Patrick Doyle, and superlative photography from Michael Coulter, the impressive star cast included Emma Thompson, Kate Winslet, Hugh Grant, Alan Rickman, Greg Wise, Harriet Walter, Gemma Jones, Elizabeth Spriggs, and Robert Hardy. Owen Gleiberman of *Entertainment Weekly* wrote that the critically acclaimed production 'luminously brings to life Austen's vision of the dance of the sexes. The final romantic epiphany is a stunner, at once rapturous and funny.'

In 1996 Alan Parker filmed part of *Evita* with Madonna at Shepperton, and Richard Attenborough directed *In Love and War*. These were followed in 1997 by *Sliding Doors* (also partly made at Pinewood), directed by Peter Howitt; and Alison Owen's award-winning, powerful production of *Elizabeth*, directed by Shekhar Kapur and starring Cate Blanchett, Joseph Fiennes and Richard Attenborough.

Shepperton's reputation was further enhanced in 1998 by the outstanding success of *Shakespeare in Love*. Directed by John Madden, Gwyneth Paltrow and Joseph Fiennes matched their dramatic skills against Judi Dench, who portrayed a mischievous Queen Elizabeth I. The film won seven Oscars, including Best Picture, Best Actress (Gwyneth Paltrow), Best Supporting Actress (Judi Dench) and Best Original Screenplay (Marc Norman and Tom Stoppard). In the same year *Notting Hill*, starring Julia Roberts and Hugh Grant and with a sharp screenplay by Richard Curtis, was directed by Roger Mitchell. The producers were anxious to stress that it was not a follow-up to *Four Weddings and a Funeral*, and the storyline of a bumbling, British bookseller falling in love with a glamorous American film star certainly appealed to an international audience. Other 1998 productions included Ridley Scott's *Gladiator*, which topped the Screen International Poll for December 2000, and won an Oscar in 2001; Neil Jordan's *The End of the Affair* with Ralph Fiennes and Julianne Moore; and Kenneth Branagh's audacious *Love's Labours Lost*, which he starred in as well as directed, with backing from the Arts Council of England through the Pathé Pictures Lottery franchise. Branagh chose to set the film in the 1930s and also replaced some of the more difficult dialogue with the songs of Cole Porter and George Gershwin.

Heading for the new millennium, in 1999 Glen Close again played the villainess in *102 Dalmations*; this was followed by *Billy Elliot*, which received excellent notices. It starred Jamie Bell as the boy from a mining town in the north of England, who, against great odds, eventually achieves his ambition to become a ballet dancer. As well as capturing a splendid performance from Bell, Stephen Daldry's direction also caught moving performances from Gary Lewis, who played Billy's father, and Julie Walters as the ballet teacher.

In February 1995, a consortium led by British film directors Ridley (left) and Tony Scott purchased the studios. Photo courtesy Shepperton Studios, 2000.

The studio's production listings for 2000 and 2001 included *Mummy II*, directed by Stephen Sommers for Universal Pictures; *The Four Feathers*, directed by Shekhar Kapur; *Spy Game*, directed by Tony Scott; *Possession*, for Warner Bros; and *Chocolat*, directed by Lasse Hallström and starring Juliet Binoche, Judi Dench and Alfred Molina.

2001 marked the 70th anniversary of the purchase of the Shepperton Studio site by the film producer Norman Loudon. It now boasts the greatest array of purpose-built large stages in Europe and there is a continuous building programme. Shepperton is also the home of over 80 specialist film/TV companies, providing services such as drapes, model making, agencies, camera hire etc. to support the studio's productions. Other facilities include backlots of 16 and 20 acres, and five theatres.

Still commanding pride of place, the old Manor of Littleton has undergone careful restoration, while recent landscaping of the gardens and improvements to the grounds enhance its elegant and historic past.

On Sunday 11 February 2001, Europe's two leading film and television studios, Pinewood and Shepperton, announced their merger, valuing the combined business at more than £100 million. The combination of the two studios created a facility that can compete on a global scale for Hollywood productions and offers producers an unrivalled level of service, flexibility and comfort. 3i, Europe's leading venture capital company is the majority shareholder in the combined business.

Michael Grade, executive chairman of the enlarged group, said: 'The two studios have been competing for years against each other. In an increasingly global market, this makes no sense. Together, we can enhance Britain's share of the international movie making business.'

Shepperton was acquired in January 1995 by an investor group headed by Ridley and Tony Scott and Candover Partners. Since the acquisition, more than £17.9 million has been invested in Shepperton studios. Candover is selling its interest in Shepperton to Pinewood's shareholders. Ridley and Tony Scott will remain active shareholders in the enlarged group and continue as co-chairmen.

Ridley Scott said: 'Britain remains a great place to make movies – this consolidation of our leading film assets is long overdue. Tony and I are committed to the growth and continued success of these historic studios.'

Ivan Dunleavy, chief executive of the enlarged group, said: 'We shall continue to invest in both studios for the future. Both studios have a common customer base, principally the Hollywood majors and UK film and TV producers. By combining the booking of all the stages and support facilities, we will be able to accommodate more productions overall.'

The two studios will continue to retain their individual trading identities, although they will be under common ownership and management. The merger has received clearance from the Office of Fair Trading.

The focus of the management team will be to build on the existing strong relationships with film, television and commercial production companies. Pinewood and Shepperton are flexible facilities, able to service every size of production. With the varying sizes of stages, productions range from two-day advertising shoots to blockbuster feature films. Both studios have built more large sound stages and the combination of the facilities will greatly increase the studio's ability to simultaneously accommodate several large film projects. Pinewood has also launched a state-of-the-art digital television studio.

Shoreham
Bungalow Town, Shoreham, West Sussex

Utilizing part of an old fort on the south coast of England, the Sunny South and Sealight Film Company was founded in 1913 by F. L. Lyndhurst, a scenic artist, and Will Evans. Their films, which included *Building A Chicken House* and *The Jockey* (1914), proved to be very popular. Shortly afterwards, the studios were occupied by Sidney Morgan's Progress Film Company. Morgan developed his own modest stock company, which included his daughter and leading lady Joan Morgan, who appeared in *Lady Noggs*; *Lilac Sunbonnet*, with Pauline Peters and Warwick Ward; and *A Lowland Cinderella* (1921), with Ralph Forbes, in the early 1920s.

Shoreham was the only studio in the UK to rely on daylight after the First World War in 1918. It was destroyed by fire in 1922.

Southall
Gladstone Road, Ealing, London

In 1924, G. B. Samuelson converted an aeroplane hangar in Southall into a dark stage, but it appears to have been used very little until the 1930s. It was then hired for some modest 'Quota Quickie' film productions including *Dodging The Dole*, directed by Arthur Murtz; and *Children Of The Fog* (1937), starring Barbara Gott and directed by Professor Leopold Jessner, with cinematography by Eugene Schufftan, an outstanding lighting cameraman of German, French, British, and American films, who invented the Schufftan process, an optical trick shot which was named after him.

After the Second World War, the studios were acquired by the Alliance Film Studios Limited, who also owned the Twickenham and Riverside Studios. Productions in the latter half of the 1940s included *Dancing With Crime*, directed by John Paddy Carstairs and starring Richard Attenborough, Sheila Sim, and Barry K. Barnes; and *Things Happen At Night*, an Alliance Studios production with Gordon Harker, Alfred Drayton, and Robertson Hare.

In 1946, the well-known and respected documentary film-maker John Grierson was appointed joint Executive Producer of Group 3 at Southall Studios where he remained until 1954. One of his productions was *Time Gentlemen Please*, directed by Lewis Gilbert. In 1954, the studio commenced television productions with shorts starring Boris Karloff; and *Lyons Abroad* with Bebe Daniels and Ben Lyon. By 1956, the three stages employing 47 personnel were listed as a television production centre.

Southwark

Jacob Street Studios, Mill Street, Southwark, London

Converted from an old dog biscuit factory in 1984, in the 1980s the four-stage Jacob Street Studios in Southwark were involved in the filming of *Highlander*, with Christopher Lambert; *Personal Services*, starring Julie Walters and Alec McCowen, directed by Terry Jones; and *Prick Up Your Ears*, directed by Stephen Frears, with Vanessa Redgrave, Gary Oldman and Alfred Molina; and in the 1990s, *The Cement Garden*, with Sinead Cusack, Charlotte Gainsbourg and Andrew Robertson. The studio also produces television productions and commercials.

Stamford Hill

Hackney, London

Will Barker (full name, William George Barker) moved swiftly from being a 'free show' amateur producer, director and cameraman in 1896, to becoming a professional visionary. By 1901, he had founded the Autoscope Company and in the same year, built his open-air studio, consisting of a stage, two scaffolding rods and a backcloth at Stamford Hill. These humble beginnings yielded a quick profit, and were superseded in 1904 by his studio at Ealing, a location that was to earn itself a very special place in the history of the British film industry.

In 1906 the Warwick Trading Company, of which Barker had become the Managing Director, took over the Autoscope Company.

Surbiton

Park Road, Kingston-upon-Thames

The ballroom in Regent House, an old mansion, provided the setting for this one-stage studio formed in 1918 by the Stoll Film Company Limited. Their first production was *Comradeship*, produced by Maurice Elvey, starring stage actor Gerald Ames and Lily Elsie. By 1920, Stoll had moved to a larger studio at Cricklewood, and cinematographer Geoffrey Malins had formed the Garrick Film Company and was using the Surbiton Studio. Although Malins made a number of comedy films, in the main his productions were shorts and educational films, which included *Our Girls And Their Physique*. Stoll retained the ownership of the studio until 1923 when it was taken over by British Instructional Films.

Tamworth

Staffordshire

Producer Widgey Newman, who made 'Quota Quickies' for the American RKO company and others, used the Dryden Studio at Tamworth in 1932 to make *Game Of Chance* for Equity British, a silent movie with synchronized music, which starred John Argyle.

Teddington

Broome Road, Richmond-upon-Thames

In 1912, a company called EcKo first used the grounds of an isolated riverside mansion at Teddington called Weir House to make films. Much of the filming, including the *Nobby* series, was done in the greenhouse, and featured such stars as Charles Austin, Jack Edge and Billy Merson. EcKo's output was about one film per week, each film being around 500 ft long, and prints were sold at four old pence per foot by agent film renters and exhibitors.

In 1914, American-born film pioneer Charles Urban installed himself at Bushey Lodge at Teddington and acquired Weir House for the Kinemacolor Company. Urban was mainly responsible for the development of newsreel-style reportage and scientific and educational films, and had also been particularly instrumental in the success and promotion of G. A. Smith's invention of Kinemacolor. Urban's tenancy was a short one, however, due to the termination of his five-year monopoly on the use of Kinemacolor later in the year. The Kinemacolor Company changed its name to 'Homeland' and moved to the Boathouse Inn Studio at Kew Bridge (south side) where it proceeded to make comedies with Lupino Lane and Billy Merson.

At the end of the First World War in 1918, Weir House was leased and later purchased by Master Films Limited, whose ambitious dramatic and historical productions included *Calvary*, with Henry Victor; *Corinthian Jack*, starring Victor McLaglen, Warwick Ward and Dorothy Fane; *Daniel Deronda*, with Clive Brook; *Hobson's Choice*; *A Peep Behind The Scenes*; and *La Poupée*, based on the comic opera by Edmund Audrien, starring Flora le Breton.

Master Films extended the greenhouse, turning it into a real glass-house studio, with dressing rooms, workshops, scene docks

Teddington: The wreckage of the Warner Brothers Studios after being bombed in 1944.

Tallulah Bankhead in *His House In Order,* an adaptation of a play by Sir Arthur Pinero that was made under the Ideal banner in 1927–28 at Teddington.

Teddington: Burt Lancaster as the eighteenth-century swashbucking *Crimson Pirate* (1952), a Warner Brothers production co-starring Eva Bartok.

and a tiny preview theatre. In 1927, the Ideal Film Company, who had formerly leased the Neptune Studios at Elstree, merged with Gaumont-British and leased the Teddington Studios. Their tenancy was short due to a fire that partly destroyed the studios in 1929, but *His House In Order* was one film that was made under the Ideal banner in 1927–28. It was produced by Meyrick Milton from a play by Sir Arthur Pinero and starred Tallulah Bankhead and Ian Hunter.

In the late 1920s, Henry Edwards and E. G. Norman purchased the Weir House Studios at Teddington for £15,000, extending the silent studio and building another in which they installed the RCA 'Sound on Film' system. Edwards made talking pictures under the name Teddington Film Studios Limited and also hired the complex out to independent producers.

In 1931, Warner Brothers first leased and then purchased the two-stage Teddington Studios to make their British quota films. Headed by Irving Asher, Warner Brothers and First National (to give them their full title) immediately spent £100,000 on extending the studios, adding a further two stages and modernizing the camera, sound and lighting systems. The old Weir House also experienced changes. Its 40 rooms turned into offices, long galleries, guest rooms, a lofty dining hall and finely-tapestried drawing rooms; while the neglected grounds became beautifully cultivated gardens with lawns sweeping down to the river and tennis courts.

From 1931 to the outbreak of war in 1939, Warner Brothers ran the studio with streamlined efficiency. The object of the studios over that period was to make between 120 and 140 low-budget films that would fulfil Warner Brothers' 'Quota Quickie' obligations, so enabling them to show their important American films at British cinemas. They were not looking for quality, as such films were, after all, a secondary feature in a programme that would consist of a major film, a 'Quota Quickie', a newsreel, a cartoon, trailers and a sing-along organ recital in the interval. However, as with other studios, the 'Quota Quickies' provided an invaluable training ground for producers, directors, technicians and actors. Mario Zampi worked at Warners as an editor from 1931; Florence Desmond appeared in Irving Asher's production of *High Society*; *High Finance* starred Ida Lupino; an adaptation of A. E. W. Mason's novel, *Her Imaginary Lover*, was the perfect vehicle for Laura La Plante and Lady Tree; heart-throb Errol Flynn put in an early appearance with Eve Gray in *Murder At Monte Carlo*, directed by Ralph Ince; comedian-turned-director Monty Banks starred Edmund Gwenn in *Father And Son*; Lilli Palmer appeared in *Crime Unlimited*; Maurice Elvey directed Sir Seymour Hicks and Chili Bouchier in *Change For A Sovereign*; variety-hall comedian 'Cheeky Chappie' Max Miller joked his way through *Don't Get Me Wrong*; Michael Powell directed *Girl In The Crowd*, and Ben Lyon starred with Jane Baxter in *Confidential Lady*, which was directed by Arthur Woods. The powerful drama *They Drive By Night*, edited by Leslie Norman and starring Emlyn Williams, was also directed by Arthur Woods before the outbreak of the Second World War.

The studios closed at the commencement of hostilities, but opened again some months later under the management of Doc Salomon. Until the studios received a direct hit from a flying bomb in 1944, productions completed there included *The Night Invader*, a propaganda pot boiler with Anne Crawford and David Farrar; a racing yarn entitled *The Hundred Pound Window*, with Richard Attenborough and Niall MacGinnis; *The Dark Tower*, with Herbert Lom and William Hartnell; and *Flight From Folly*, a variation on *Random Harvest*, directed by Herbert Mason with Pat Kirkwood and Sydney Howard.

Production was suspended after the bombing, but the studios were rebuilt and opened again in 1948. Meanwhile, in 1946, Warner Brothers had acquired a vast share bulk in the Associated British Picture Corporation from the John Maxwell estate, placing themselves in an unassailable position. The ABPC Studios at Elstree were part of the Associated British Picture Corporation empire, and shortly afterwards, all major Warner production was moved to Elstree. Teddington was again closed during 1951 and 1952, and it would seem that the last major film production there was *The Crimson Pirate*, an eighteenth-century swashbuckling yarn starring Burt Lancaster and Eva Bartok. During the shooting, Lancaster had the occasional quarrel with the studios' General Manager, and threatened to hang him outside his office window by the scruff of his neck. A big, strong man, Lancaster was true to his word, and the situation was not helped by the fact that the office in question was on the first floor of the administration block.

In 1955, ABC Television Limited purchased the two-stage studios to use the services of star actors in London, making such classic series as *The Avengers*; *Armchair Theatre*; and *Callan*. In 1968, ABC and Rediffusion Television amalgamated to form Thames Television, resulting in further expansion of the Teddington Television Studios and facilities.

Thames Ditton
Portsmouth Road, Thames Ditton, Surrey

These premises at Portsmouth Road, Thames Ditton consisted of one glass-roofed stage studio, and was used for filming during the First World War first by the Comedy Combine Company, then by Harry Lorraine who made a *Detective Daring* series there and finally by the Climax Film Company. Subsequently, the site was used mainly as a processing and printing laboratory.

Torquay
Watcombe Hall, Torquay/Babbacombe, Devon

Hoping to found an English Hollywood, Dallas Cairns, a producer-actor, formed the Cairns Torquay Film Company at Watcombe Hall, Torquay in 1919, building a dark and light studio at a cost of £40,000, which was completed in the early part of 1920. In the same year came the studio's first film, *Unrest*, which starred Dallas Cairns and Mary Dibley, with a small role going to Marjorie Hore, the daughter of a Brixham banker. The film cost £6,000 to make and the company immediately ran into financial difficulties with production at the studio ceasing soon afterwards.

In 1946, plans were submitted to renovate the premises as the new Torquay Studios. Planning permission was given but then rescinded after a deputation of Torquay councillors visited Ealing Studios in London and complained about 'what went on in the way of noise'. It was also noted that 'the unions would be unwilling to move so far afield from London'. After serving as a store for beach floats, the studio in the grounds of Watcombe Hall was pulled down and the house became a convalescent home.

Three Mills Island
Three Mill Lane, London E3 3DU

Based in a major new media complex, Three Mills Island Studios are located on a 17-acre island site consisting of nine acres of landscaped open space and eight acres of 18th-, 19th- and 20th-century industrial architecture. Among these are a Grade One listed tidal mill (recently restored), a Grade Two listed Clock Mill with two kiln oast houses, a large gin distillery (containing four original 300-year-old copper stills) and a collection of listed Georgian and Victorian buildings, all within a cobbled conservation area.

The studios are owned by the Workspace Group, a property company that specialises in the provision of accommodation for small businesses. Founded in 1987 and floated on the London Stock Exchange in 1993, the Group then went on to acquire Three Mills Island and invested over £8 million in the site. In the same year (1993) Edwin Shirley, a former actor and businessman, saw – like many famous studio proprietors before him – the potential for a film and television studio. He then founded Edwin Shirley Productions Ltd, the management company for the Three Mills Island Studios and successfully managed to attract film and television companies to his new production centre.

Features shot at the studios from 1994 to 1996 included *Proteus* with Craig Fairbrass, directed by Bob Keen; *Innocent Sleep* with Michael Gambon heading the cast, directed by Scott Mitchell; and *Brazen Hussies* starring Julie Walters, Robert Lindsay and Julian Clary. In 1997, Derek Jacobi starred in the Cannes Film Festival entry, *Love is the Devil*; director Christine Ezzard made *The Nutcracker* (the first film in the UK to be shot on Imax 3D); SKA Productions, responsible for the surprise hit (in 1998) of *Lock, Stock and Two Smoking Barrels*, directed by Guy Ritchie, based themselves at the studios; and the British Film Institute made *Speak Like a Child*. The following year British director and screenwriter, Mike Leigh (noted for improvising scripts with his

Publicity brochure, courtesy Three Mills Island Studios.

Three Mills Island Studios.

actors, and for his comment, 'Given the choice of Hollywood or poking steel pins into my eyes, I'd prefer the latter') made *Topsy-Turvy*, which won two Oscars for Best Costume and Best Make-up. For his tale of the making of *The Mikado* and a behind-the-scenes peek at theatre life in the late 1800s, Leigh cast Jim Broadbent as the notoriously bad-tempered Gilbert and Allan Corduner as the respected classic composer Sullivan.

Additional films in 1998 included *24 Hours in London* with Gary Olsen and Anjela Lauren, in which director Alexander Finbow set out to show a very different side to the city than the usual tourist shots; and *Mad Cows*, adapted from Kathy Lette's best-selling novel, directed by Sara Sugarman and starring Anna Friel, Greg Wise, and Joanna Lumley. Heading for the turn of the century, Three Mills Island played host to such films as Julian Simpson's first feature, *The Criminal*, a conspiracy-type thriller; *Sexy Beast* for British producer Jeremy Thomas, a drama directed by Jonathan Glazier starring Ben Kingsley; and *Honest*, a tale involving London's underworld gangs, directed by David A. Stewart; all were made in 1999/2000.

From the time of its inception onwards, the Three Mills Island Studios has developed a strong and diverse television, commercials, and pop promo presence in the industry. Television productions range from the *Kavanagh QC* and *Bad Girls* series for Carlton TV, *Letting Go* for BBC drama, and *Twinkletoes* for Channel 4 Children's TV. Their commercials section provides an impressive list of clients such as Kellogs, Eurostar, RAF, Halifax, Birds Custard, American Express, and British Telecom.

The studios are a ten-minute drive from London City Airport and are situated just off the A102M Blackwall Tunnel approach road, or a five-minute walk from Bromley-by-Bow tube station. There are currently 15 studios, varying in size from 3,960 square ft to 13,920 square ft, with ceiling heights up to 38 ft and all with car and truck access. Each studio offers production offices, wardrobe and hair and make-up facilities. All have a three-phase electricity supply of 400 amps per phase. Buildings have been renovated at Three Mills to provide high-standard offices and post-production services.

Twickenham

Eel Pie Island, Richmond-upon-Thames

This tiny part-glass, one-stage studio at Eel Pie Island, converted from an old boat builders' shed, commenced production in 1912. *Folly Comedies* from the Phoenix Film Company starred Fred Evans as Lieutenant Pimple in such titles as *Lieutenant Pimple And The Stolen Submarine*; and *Lieutenant Pimple's Sealed Orders*. In 1917, Hagen and Double made a series of *Kinekature* comedies. Comedian Lupino Lane appeared in a number of these, but by 1919 the company had gone bankrupt.

Twickenham

St Margaret's, Richmond-upon-Thames

'A Club For Professionals'

In 1913, the London Film Company, founded by Dr Ralph Jupp, heralded their first release, *The House Of Temperley*, from their new studios at Twickenham. Well regarded in the industry, Jupp

Twickenham (Eel Pie Island): *Folly Comedies* starred Fred Evans as Lieutenant Pimple in a 'send-up' of Lieutenant Daring, the screen hero of 1912.

Twickenham: Ivor Novello pledges himself to Gladys Cooper while C. Aubrey Smith (right) looks on in *The Bohemian Girl,* made for the Alliance Company in 1922.

owned a chain of purpose-built cinemas which later became part of the Gaumont-British Group. His 1912 acquisition of an old skating rink at St Margaret's, Twickenham for conversion into a film studio for his own productions seemed a logical step.

With a guaranteed capital of £40,000 and an eye to the US market, the new company's advertising manager was despatched to America to engage experienced producers and directors. The result included producers Harold M. Shaw and George Loane Tucker, who had recently directed the controversial *Traffic In Souls* in Hollywood. Jupp also acquired the services of actor John

East as a casting manager, and through him, hired Percy Nash, an experienced producer. As adaptations were very much in favour at the time, Harold Shaw was given the job of mounting a full-scale production of *The House Of Temperley* based on Arthur Conan Doyle's novel *Rodney Stone.* The film starred Ben Webster and was very successful. Aware of the established competition from companies such as Hepworth, British and Colonial, Barker and Cricks, and Martin, the London Film Company decided to put the emphasis on stylish productions. They produced a steady flow of films in their first year which included Lillian Logan, one of their

In 1913, the newly-formed London Film Company heralded their first release from their studios at Twickenham: *The House Of Temperley.* Formerly a skating rink, the studio was the largest in the UK at that time.

Twickenham: Anette Benson starred with Jack Buchanan in *Confetti* (1927), a romance for First National British Pictures.

Popular actor and director Henry Edwards became a director of Twickenham Film Studios in 1928 and appeared in a number of their films.

Celebrated stage and screen actor Ben Webster, who was married to the equally famous Dame May Whitty, is seen here in *The Lyons Mail*, produced and directed by Arthur Maude in 1931 at Twickenham.

stock players, with Henry Ainley in *Bachelor's Love Story*; *Branscombe's Pal*; *The Cage*, again with Lillian Logan, Charles Rock, and Gerald Ames; the well-received *Child O' My Heart*; and *Clan Carty*, with Walter Gay and Edward O'Neill. Distinguished stage actors of the day were the stars of two further notable films: *Trilby*, with Sir Herbert Tree as Svengali; and *Turtle Doves*, with Langhorne Burton.

Certainly, Dr Ralph Tennyson Jupp must have been delighted with his first year's output. A medical specialist from the north of England who had seen service in the Boer War, Jupp had entered film exhibition because he was appalled at the inadequate ventilation and poor hygiene of the local picture houses. He was determined to erect purpose-built cinemas instead of converting buildings such as old churches and halls and was equally concerned that his productions should have a higher degree of polish and expertise than those of his competitors.

However, by 1914, Jupp was to lose the services of John East and Percy Nash who had decided to open their own Neptune Studios at Elstree – the first of the studios that would become part of 'the British Hollywood'.

With the war in progress and American films flooding the home market, Twickenham experienced heavy losses in 1915–16, despite a number of excellent productions from the Americans Harold M. Shaw and George Loane Tucker, as well as from British producers such as Maurice Elvey. These included *Two*

Columbines and *VC*, both produced by Shaw and starring his wife, Edna Flugrath; *The Prisoner Of Zenda*, based on Anthony Hope's novel and produced by Tucker, with a star cast that included Henry Ainley, Jane Gail, and Gerald Ames; Maurice Elvey's *When Knights Were Bold*, with Janet Ross and Gerald Ames; and *The King's Outcast*, produced by Ralph Dewsbury.

Despite a small up-turn in profits, the problems continued. Jupp's health was failing, and he was forced to hand over the management of the company to his cousin F. E. Adams. Moreover, in the war years, good studio and administrative staff were difficult to come by, and although Tucker was made Managing Director, it was not long before he was to make his way back to the States in the wake of his leading lady, Jane Gail. Harold Shaw departed for African film productions, accompanied by his wife, Edna Flugrath, who had become one of Twickenham's leading stock players. For a period of time, the Ideal Company leased the studio's one stage (165 ft x 75 ft) with producers Fred Paul and Maurice Elvey making films such as *Dombey And Son*; an adaptation of Sir Arthur Pinero's play *The Gay Lord Quex*, with Lillian Braithwaite, Ben Webster, and Irene Vanbrugh; *Her Greatest Performance*, starring Ellen Terry, Edith Craig, and Dennis Neilson-Terry; and *Masks And Faces*, made to raise funds for the building of The Royal Academy of Dramatic Art, featuring stars of the day such as Sir Johnston Forbes-Robertson, Irene Vanbrugh, Gerald de Maurier, Gladys Cooper, Matheson Lang, and Ellaline Terriss.

Julius Hagen produced *Condemned To Death*, directed by Walter Forde at Twickenham in 1932. Described as a story of a mystery killer, the film had a cast including (left to right) Jane Welsh, Edmund Gwenn, and Gordon Harker.

Twickenham: A modest cover-up for the popular Gracie Fields in *This Week Of Grace* (1933), which also starred Henry Kendall and John Stuart.

In 1918, Jupp sold his interests in Provincial Cinematograph Theatres to Sir William Jury (who had been knighted in the same year for his services for supplying films to all of the war fronts), and two years later, with just one more year to live, Jupp sold Twickenham Studios to the Alliance Company.

The newly-formed Alliance Company appears to have been big on ideas but short on experience. Its Board of Directors included the actors A. E. Matthews and Gerald du Maurier and publisher Sir Walter de Frece. The big ideas consisted of the acquisition of the British Actors Film Company, of which A. E. Matthews was a director, plans to build a British Hollywood-style studio city at Harrow Weald Park, distribution in the US from the First National Exhibitors and, in the meantime, a busy production schedule at both its small studio at Bushey (acquired with the British Actors Film Company) and its new Twickenham Studios. Seeking to emulate the big American studios, after buying Twickenham for £35,000 they then spent another £23,000 on installing new lighting equipment. Only the best was good enough for Alliance, and they hired excellent actors such as Ivor Novello, Gladys Cooper, Ellen Terry and C. Aubrey Smith to appear in *The Bohemian Girl*. Both this film and the subsequent *Carnival*, partly made at Bushey, had lavish sets. Although *Carnival* did extremely well at the box-office, its success came too late to save Alliance, whose resources were stretched in too many directions. In 1922, the company went out of business.

Between 1923 and 1928, the studios were leased or rented to various film companies. The Astra Film Company made a number of productions there, including *Miriam Rozella*, starring Owen Nares; the Hepworth star, Alma Taylor, appeared in *The Shadow Of Egypt*; popular Henry Edwards, who was married to another Hepworth star, Chrissie White, appeared in *The Flag Lieutenant*, directed by Maurice Elvey; and matinée idol Jack Buchanan appeared with Betty Faire in *Bulldog Drummond's Third Round*, which was directed by Sidney Morgan. In 1925, Herbert Wilcox produced and directed *The Only Way* based on Charles Dickens' novel *A Tale of Two Cities*, in which Sir John Martin Harvey played Sydney Carton. Two years later, Wilcox made the popular *Mumsie* at Twickenham, starring heart-throb Herbert Marshall, Pauline Frederick and Nelson Keys.

There was a further change at Twickenham in 1927. Henry Edwards, who had starred in the Astra-National film *The Flag Lieutenant*, paired up with another employee of the company, producer Julius Hagen, and they decided to found their own company. The new enterprise was registered as Neo-Art, and Hagen and Edwards proceeded to hire Twickenham Studios. In 1928, Hagen founded Twickenham Film Studios Limited, of which he became Chairman and Managing Director. Henry Edwards and film director Leslie Hiscott also became directors of Twickenham Film Studios Ltd, and over the coming years, Edwards would appear in and Hiscott would direct a great number of the Twickenham films. Julius Hagen, however, remained firmly at the helm. Hagen had started his professional career as an actor and had then worked for the English branch of the Essenay Company, where he was given the job of breaking down the British boycott on the Charles Chaplin films. After Essenay had angered Reuters by deciding to deal directly with Exhibitors, Hagan moved to Universal Pictures, and from there to Astra-National where he had become a production executive.

Twickenham Film Studios Limited's first production under the banner of Strand Pictures was a silent comedy, *Ringing The Changes* (to be re-titled *The Crooked Staircase*), directed by Leslie Hiscott and starring Henry Edwards. Early in 1929, they went into production on *To What Red Hell*.

Twickenham: Albert Finney speculates on the *Saturday Night And Sunday Morning* as a good-time factory worker, pursuing somebody else's wife (Rachel Roberts). An important contribution to modern film-making, it was directed by Karel Reisz in 1960.

The Beatles brought international recognition to the two-stage Twickenham Studios in 1964. 800 screaming teenagers converged at its gates in the hope of seeing their idols during the filming of A *Hard Day's Night*.

However, talkies had arrived and were about to change the entire face of film production. Spurred on by Edwards, Hagen agreed to install RCA sound equipment, and the film starring Sybil Thorndike, Bramwell Fletcher and John Hamilton was completely remade as a 'full talking picture'. However, quite apart from the many technical problems experienced by all studios with the coming of sound, Twickenham backed on to a railway line. A roof look-out had to be employed to signal the approach of a train via a red light to the studio below and filming would cease until the green 'all clear' was given.

Akin to many of its contemporaries, Twickenham in the 1930s was dominated by the need to produce the notorious 'Quota Quickies'. Nevertheless, these low-budget productions provided a valuable training ground for producers, directors, artists and technicians.

Considering that Twickenham was just a one-stage studio with an outside lot (another was added in 1934), Julius Hagen produced an amazing number of films there. Given the customary low quality of the 'Quota Quickies', he was still able to attract good actors and directors as well as other companies to his studios. *At The Villa Rose*, based on the novel by A. E. W. Mason, was made for Warner Brothers; *The Call Of The Sea*, starred the husband-and-wife team of Henry Edwards and Chrissie White; silent film comedian Walter Forde made his directorial debut with *Lord Richard In The Pantry* in 1930; Guy Newall directed *Rodney Steps In* and *Chinese Puzzle*, starring Elizabeth Allan and Austin Trevor in the early 1930s; and Leslie Hiscott's films included *Double Dealing*; *Alibi*; and *The Missing Rembrandt*, based on Sir Arthur Conan Doyle's story, starring Miles Mander and Ian Fleming.

In his delightful autobiography *Up In The Clouds, Gentleman Please*, Sir John Mills gives a wonderful description of filming *The Ghost Camera* at Twickenham in 1933. 'The studio had two films going on at once, and owing to lack of space one was shot at night and one during the day. *The Ghost Camera* was on the day-shift. The atmosphere when I walked onto the set at 8 o'clock the first morning was almost indescribable: the night-shift staggered out at 7.30 am, leaving in their wake an aroma – a delicate blend of cigarette butts, orange-peel, stale beer, make-up and several unmentionable gasses. The schedule for the picture was eight days; they never went over. If at any time it looked as if they might, the producer solved the problem by tearing some pages out of the script'. Starring with John Mills in this film directed by Barnard Vorhaus were Henry Kendall and Ida Lupino, daughter of Stanley Lupino, who became a big star in America (usually in 'long-suffering' roles) and later a film director.

Other films in the first half of the 1930s were *I Lived With You*; *The Lost Chord*; and *The Wandering Jew*, all directed by Maurice Elvey; *The Man Who Changed His Name*; *Lord Edgware Dies*; *Squibs*, with popular star Betty Balfour; and *The Private Secretary*, all from actor-turned-director, Henry Edwards; *Lazybones*, directed by Michael Powell; and *The Morals Of Marcus*, which seems to have been a family affair, the scenario by Miles Mander and directed by Miss Mander. The host of stars in these productions included Ivor Novello, Ida Lupino, Elizabeth Allan, Conrad Veidt, Anne Grey, Peggy Ashcroft, and Matheson Lang. Comedians Leslie Fuller and Flanagan and Allen also filmed at Twickenham, as did Gracie Fields who starred in *This Week Of Grace*.

British production went through a particularly difficult period in the late 1930s, and Twickenham, along with a number of other studios, found itself on the verge of collapse. Further borrowing for JH (Julius Hagen) Productions to invest in such films as *Spy Of Napoleon*, starring Richard Barthelmess; Boris Karloff in *Juggernaut*; and *The Man In The Mirror*, with the splendid

Michael Caine starred in *The Eagle Has Landed*, adapted from the novel by Jack Higgins and directed by John Sturges at Twickenham in 1976.

Warren Beatty, who wrote and appeared in *Reds* (1981) at Twickenham. He also directed the film, for which he received an American Academy Award.

Edward Everett Horton, did not alleviate the situation. Although Hagen tried hard to save his studios, the Westminster Bank called in the receivers in January 1937. The studio was sold quickly and perhaps too cheaply to the Studio Holdings Trust who immediately loaned it back to Hagen. There is no doubt that Hagen ran his small studio with great efficiency, but the receivers' report criticized the salaries given to the studio's directors, production costs and, indeed, Hagen's own salary. Hagen struggled to produce a few more films, but he was already in the hands of the money-lenders and by 1938 the studio was closed. Hagen, a ruined man, died one year later.

There was very little activity at Twickenham during the short period between Julius Hagen's death and the outbreak of the Second World War in 1939, and during hostilities, the studio received a direct hit. In 1946, The Alliance Film Studios Limited was formed, which controlled several studios – Southall, Riverside and Twickenham. On the Board of Directors was James Carter, the ex-Managing Director of Studio Holdings Trust, which had bought Twickenham after Julius Hagen's company had gone into receivership. Peter Noble's *British Film Year Book, 1949–50* mentions only one film at Twickenham Studios, *Just William's Luck* (1948) with William Graham, Garry Marsh and Jane Welsh, and it seems likely that Riverside and

Southall were favoured against the tiny, and probably still damaged, Twickenham Studios.

During the 1950s, the studios were used mainly for half-hour shorts and television productions. In 1959, Guido Coen, having spent ten years with Two Cities Film as Company Secretary and Production Executive, took up an appointment at the studios and subsequently became their Executive Director. Without doubt, the decade that followed was a major landmark in the studios' history. *Saturday Night And Sunday Morning*, which starred Albert Finney as the good-time factory worker pursuing somebody else's wife (Rachel Roberts), was an important contribution to modern film-making. It was directed by Karel Reisz, and co-produced by Tony Richardson and Harry Salzman. The production ran into financial difficulties, and it was only due to the fact that Twickenham Studios advanced a credit of £25,000 in deferred rentals that it was able to continue. However, it was probably the Beatles who brought international recognition to the two-stage studios. In 1964, 800 screaming teenagers converged at the gates, creating an unprecedented and unplanned public relations exercise. The film attracting the attention was *A Hard Day's Night*, directed by Richard Lester. Michael Caine, Stanley Baker and Jack Hawkins followed in the Beatles' footsteps with *Zulu* in the

Left to right: Richard Harris, Roger Moore, Richard Burton and Hardy Kruger in the Euan Lloyd production of *The Wild Geese* (1978), directed at Twickenham by Andrew V. McLagen, the son of actor Victor McLagen.

Twickenham: British leading lady Joan Collins began her screen career in the 1950s and became particularly well known for her role in the American television series *Dynasty*. She is seen here in the title role of *The Bitch* (1979), of whose character she wrote: 'She appears to have the world by the balls, but underneath she's trying to solve the problem of loneliness'.

Twickenham: An adaptation of John Fowles's novel *The French Lieutenant's Woman* proved to be the cinematic talking point of 1981, and gave Jeremy Irons the opportunity to star with Meryl Streep, seen here. The film had a haunting score by Carl Davis and was directed by Karel Reisz.

same year, and Caine came back to the studios in 1966 to make the smash hit *Alfie*, in which he played a cockney Lothario. According to its director, Lewis Gilbert, 'Paramount thought it was a good bet because it was going to be made for $500,000. Normally the sort of money spent on executive cigar bills'. In 1967, Joseph Losey directed Dirk Bogarde in *Accident*, with a screen play by Harold Pinter.

As well as directing the Beatles' first Twickenham film, *A Hard Day's Night*, at Twickenham Studios, Richard Lester went on to direct a second, *Help!*; and in 1974 and 1975, directed *Juggernaut*, 'an elaborate suspense spectacular', with Omar Sharif, Anthony Hopkins, David Hemmings and Richard Harris; and *Royal Flash* starring Malcolm McDowell, Oliver Reed and Alan Bates. One year later, Michael Caine in the company of Donald Sutherland, Robert Duvall and Jenny Agutter filmed Jack Higgins's novel, *The Eagle Has Landed*, which was directed by John Sturges. Four films in 1978–79 were notable either for their international casts, directors and/or production. *The Wild Geese*, directed by Andrew V. McLaglen in 1978, was the story of four British mercenaries in a central African state and starred Richard Burton, Roger Moore, Richard Harris, Hardy Kruger and 1940s heart-throb Stewart Granger. 1979 produced *Yanks*, with Vanessa Redgrave, Richard Gere and Rachel Roberts, directed by John Schlesinger; part of the film *Reds*, for which Warren Beatty received an Academy Award for Best Director as well as starring in the film with Diane Keaton and Jack Nicholson; and *The Bitch*, with Joan Collins, who went on to become a mega-star on American television.

Twickenham: Shirley MacLaine, the impish American leading lady and sister of Warren Beatty, took the title role in *Madame Sousatzka* (1988).

Twickenham: Bored housewife Shirley Valentine (Pauline Collins) takes a journey of self-discovery and romance in the 1989 film of the same title, directed by Lewis Gilbert.

Twickenham continued its international film profile into the 1980s. The decade started with Agatha Christie's *The Mirror Crack'd*, featuring an all-star cast including Elizabeth Taylor, Rock Hudson, Tony Curtis, Edward Fox, Kim Novak, Angela Lansbury and Geraldine Chaplin. An adaptation of John Fowles's novel *The French Lieutenant's Woman* proved to be the cinematic talking point of 1981, giving Jeremy Irons the opportunity to star with Meryl Streep in Karel Reisz's sensitively directed film. Jeremy Irons was to appear in another Twickenham film in 1982 based on Harold Pinter's play *Betrayal*; and in the same year *Eureka*, *The Lords Of Discipline* and a remake of *Witness For The Prosecution* were all made at the studios. Other Twickenham films of the 1980s include *1984*, written and directed by Michael Radford, with John Hurt, Richard Burton and Cyril Cusack; *The Holcroft Covenant*, with Michael Caine and Anthony Andrews; Shirley MacLaine in

Madame Sousatzka; the highly-successful award-winning *A Fish Called Wanda*, directed by the distinguished Charles Crichton and starring John Cleese, Jamie Lee-Curtis, Kevin Kline and Michael Palin; and the equally-successful award-winning *Shirley Valentine*, the story of a bored housewife who abandons her husband to enjoy a holiday romance in Greece, starring Pauline Collins, Tom Conti and Julia McKenzie, and directed by Lewis Gilbert.

In common with other studios, Twickenham also produces television productions and commercials. Its facilities include three stages, dubbing theatres, projection rooms, cutting rooms, production offices, star apartments, restaurant and bar, plus many more production facilities.

A private company, Twickenham Studios is affectionately known as 'a club for professionals'. Former Executive Director Guido Coen was once quoted as saying 'We stand on our record', and no one can argue with that.

Walthamstow
Hoe Street, Walthamstow, Waltham Forest, London

Converted from an old skating rink, the Hoe Street Studio at Walthamstow was acquired by British and Colonial Films in 1913. British and Colonial were particularly famous for their *Lieutenant Daring* series, a rival to Clarendon's Lieutenant Rose. Harry Lorraine took the title role in such stories as *Lieutenant Daring And The Mystery Of Room 41*; *Lieutenant Daring Avenges An Insult To The Union Jack*; and *Lieutenant Daring And The Ship's Mascot*, although, as with James Bond 007 many decades later, a different actor would play the leading character from time to time.

With the outbreak of war in 1914, the Managing Director of this one-stage studio, J. B. McDowell, was called away on active service as an official war cinematographer. During McDowell's absence, Maurice Elvey used the premises to make such films as *It's A Long Way To Tipperary*, a morale-booster starring Elizabeth Risdon and A. V. Bramble; and *Her Luck In London*, a crime story of blackmail and intrigue. Other features included *The World's Desire*, starring West End actress Lillian Braithwaite, but by 1916 there was very little production at Hoe Street.

Walthamstow (Hoe Street): British and Colonial films were particularly famous for their *Lieutenant Daring* series starring Harry Lorraine, a rival to Clarendon's Lieutenant Rose. *Lieut. Daring R.N. And The Photographing Pigeon* was directed by Charles Raymond in 1912.

The post-war boom produced *Twelve-Ten* (1919), directed by Herbert Brenon, with James Carew, Ben Webster and Marie Doro; *The Magic Skin* (1920), directed by George Edwardes Hall, a 'fantasy' with Dennis Neilson-Terry and Yvonne Arnaud; and *The Temptress*, a romance with Langhorne Burton. However, the studio did not prosper. By the end of that year, the complex was rented out to Granger-Binger, and in 1921, to H. W. Thompson. The studio came under the management of Julius Hagen in 1923, who made short films starring Victor McLaglen, Jack Buchanan and José Collins there. Victor McLaglen also starred in *Heart Strings*, a romance directed by Edwin Greenwood. These productions did not prove successful, and the studios and company were placed in the hands of the receivers in 1924.

Walthamstow
Whipps Cross, Walthamstow, Waltham Forest, London

This tiny studio, a glass-covered stage over workshops, was built by the Precision Film Company in 1910 for their film version of *East Lynne*, with a screenplay by Mrs Henry Wood. The company was run by the Gobbett Brothers, and in 1912, they leased out the studio to Lewin Fitzhamon, who had previously worked with Hepworth, under his banner, Fitz Films. The studio only survived until 1914.

Walthamstow
Wood Street, Walthamstow, Waltham Forest, London

This studio was founded in 1914 by Cunard Films, who built a first-floor glass studio over a workshop and laboratory. According to the film journals of the time, the company made a number of 'refined' drama films starring Gladys Cooper and popular actor of the day, Owen Nares, as well as short films, all of which were released during the early war years. In 1916, Broadwest, who ranked alongside film companies of the day such as Hepworth, Barker and British and Colonial, bought the studio and its equipment. Broadwest was already in the process of building up its own stock company with box-office draws Ivy Close, Violet Hopson and Gerald Ames and Walter West was also hired to produce a number of films. The Scottish-Canadian stage actor and London matinee idol of the 1920s, Matheson Lang appeared in *The Merchant Of Venice*; while Muriel Martin-Harvey featured in *The Answer*, based on *Is God Dead*, a novel by Newman Flower. *The Ware Case*, released in 1917, starred Matheson Lang, Violet Hopson and Ivy Close. By the end of the war in 1918, Broadwest was recognized as one of the UK's most important film-makers, but nevertheless, along with a number of production companies, they ran into financial difficulties after the post-war boom. Although they continued to make such films as *Christie Johnstone*, a Scottish romance with Clive Brook, the distinguished British leading man of stage and screen who always played the perfect gentleman (though with the occasional caddish lapse), by 1921 Broadwest had gone into liquidation. The studio was leased out for some years to the makers of short films, and in 1926 it was sold to British Filmcraft for this purpose. In 1928, Sir John Martin-Harvey starred in *The Burgomaster Of Stilemonde*, based on the play by Maurice Maeterlinck, but British Filmcraft was dissolved in 1930.

Interior of the Broadwest Film Company's studios at Wood Street, Walthamstow, between 1916 and 1921.

Walthamstow (Wood Street): Violet Hopson, the early British screen star, appeared in *The Ware Case* (1917) with Matheson Lang, produced and directed by Walter West.

Walton-on-Thames
Surrey

In 1899, at the age of 25, Cecil Hepworth leased a house in Walton-on-Thames for £36 a year, and turned it into a film studio.

As a child, he had travelled with his father, a Victorian magic lantern lecturer, and was soon entranced by limelight, photography and image. Some years later, he developed negatives and story-lines for his own shows, which were accompanied by his sister Effie at the piano. A pioneer and inventor dealing with exhibition machinery and photographic equipment, he also wrote one of the first books devoted to the cinema, *Animated Photography, or The ABC of the Cinematograph*, published in 1897. He was then employed by the Charles Urban Company before deciding to set up his own studio and company, Hepwix, at Walton.

His first offerings were principally 'actualities', that is, local news items such as 'The Ladies' Tortoise Race'; 'Drive Past of Four-in-Hands'; and 'Procession of Prize Cattle', all 50 ft films obtained locally entailing little cost except that of the film stock. The first films to be made at his new studio with its one 15 ft x 8 ft stage were *The Egg-Laying Man*, a trick film in which Hepworth's head filled the whole screen; and *The Eccentric*

Dancer, in which slow-motion photography was probably used for the first time. Another innovation was *The Bathers*, the second half of which Hepworth reversed, showing the bathers diving feet first out of the water and on to the diving board. His filming of Queen Victoria's funeral procession and the coronation procession of Edward VII shortly afterwards was a remarkable achievement for its time.

Hepworth then went on to make an ambitious 800 ft film, *Alice In Wonderland* (1903), breaking away from the 50 ft tradition. Cutting-room assistant Mabel Clark played Alice, and Hepworth's new wife took the role of White Rabbit. The successful *Rescued By Rover* was an even bigger family affair: Hepworth's wife wrote the story and played the distraught mother; the Hepworth's baby, all of eight months, was the heroine; Rover was the family dog who rescues her; and Hepworth, in frock coat and tall hat, played the harassed father. It was also the first film in which Hepworth employed professional actors, and Mr and Mrs Sebastian Smith, playing the flirtatious soldier and the villainess who steals the baby, each received half-a-guinea for their labours, a sum that included their fares from London. A blockbuster of its time, the film had to be shot three times because the negatives were worn out in the making of the 400 prints that were necessary to satisfy public demand.

'I really got into film-making through pure cheek! My elder sister was an actress, and during the summer of 1907 she was on tour with Seymour Hicks when a letter came from the Hepworth studios asking if she would act in a film. I wrote back to say that she was away, but would I do in her place, I was only twelve-years-old, but they accepted me, that's how I began my film career.'

Chrissie White's description of how she started to work for Hepworth – subsequently becoming one of Britain's first film stars along with Alma Taylor, another of Hepworth's discoveries – is a typical example of the relaxed atmosphere at the studios. Her letter of engagement read 'Come if fine', and if by the time she arrived at the studios it was raining and filming had to be abandoned, she would help in the processing rooms, joining up

Cecil Hepworth set up his own film laboratory at Walton-on-Thames and started to produce films in 1899. By the turn of the century, the Hepworth Manufacturing Company was making approximately 100 films a year, a figure that had doubled by 1906.

the lengths of film. It seems that no one was given preferential treatment; if a job needed to be done, then everyone helped in whatever way they could.

Nevertheless, the Hepworth studios did develop Britain's first star system, and with the immensely popular *Tilly* series, usually featuring Chrissie White and Alma Taylor, it was not long before the studio had its own stock company, which included these two schoolgirls, rapidly developing into beautiful young women, as well as Stewart Rome, Violet Hopson and Gladys Sylvani – billed as the Hepworth Picture Players.

By 1905, Hepworth had built a large glass studio adjoining the original house. It was made of Muranese glass, which diffused the sunshine and killed shadows without greatly diminishing the amount of light. The studio was built on the first floor above the level of the surrounding houses, and the space underneath was devoted to printing and developing rooms, drying rooms, and a mechanics' workshop. In his memoirs, Hepworth described the studios as: 'One small room in front between the main dark-room and the road was the perforating room, with half-a-dozen motor-driven Debrie perforators, for it was not until considerably later that the film-stockmakers took over the perforating as a part of

their responsibility . . . I also put down a sort of railway for the wheeled camera-stand to run on, to make what are now called "tracking shots" which had not by then been heard of'. Hepworth also invented the Vivaphone, a gramophone mounted with the camera. The actors danced and mouthed the words of songs while the camera turned, and when the film was shown the record was played at the same time.

Hepworth was gradually giving up camera work in order to concentrate on the supervision of the studio, and his two technicians and cameramen Geoffrey and Stanley Faithfull (by name as well as by nature) came into their own, while Bert Haldane directed a number of comedies for the company including *Wealthy Brother John*, starring Chrissie White and Gladys Sylvani in 1911. Between 1911 and 1914, Hepworth made a number of adaptations of Charles Dickens' novels including *Oliver Twist*; *The Old Curiosity Shop*; and *David Copperfield*. Other films included *The Vicar Of Wakefield*, with Violet Hopson, Harry Royston, Warwick Buckland and Chrissie White; *Dora*, based on the poem by Alfred Tennyson; *The Love Romance Of Admiral Sir Francis Drake*, starring the Hepworth Picture Players; and the melodrama *Rachel's Sin*, with Gladys Sylvani and Hay Plumb.

Unlike his contemporaries at other British studios, Hepworth was one of the few producers who managed to keep production going for the duration of the war (1914–18). He started off by making a number of propaganda shorts with the aim of encouraging people to buy War Bonds or save bones for salvage. Hepworth also continued to rent out his studio to visiting companies. One of these was Ivy Close Films, founded by Elwin Neame during the war years. Their first film was *Dream Paintings*, in which Neame's wife, Ivy Close, the mother of director Ronald Neame and the winner of a *Daily Mirror* beauty competition, posed gracefully in and as a number of classical subjects. Another company at Walton-on-Thames, one that was to have particular significance for Chrissie White, was Turner Films, which had been founded by American star Florence Turner and her manager and producer, Larry Trimble. Trimble directed films for Hepworth, including *The Awakening Of Nora*, which starred Alma Taylor and heart-throb of the period, Stewart Rome, who was paid the grand sum of £10 per week for his leading role. The Turner Company aimed to produce one film per month, and their first production in 1913 was *Rose Of Surrey*, starring Florence Turner and Frank Powell, again directed by Larry Trimble. Soon afterwards, Henry Edwards, a stage actor and writer who had worked for Hepworth in *The Man Who Stayed At Home*, also starring Chrissie White and Alma Taylor, caught Miss Turner's eye and he was invited to join her company at Walton. He went on to produce and appear in a number of films with her, including *A Welsh Singer*, in which Edith Evans had a small part. However, by 1917, the very versatile Miss Turner, known as the Vitagraph Girl, was ready to return to the safety of her home shores and Henry Edwards was left without a leading lady. At the same time, Chrissie White had been offered a contract from a London play producer, and was thinking of leaving films. On hearing this, Edwards proposed that they should team up, and the pair made the Edwards series

The Final Stage. Left to right: Garage with Inspection Theatre over; Drying Rooms (with escape balcony around) and No. 2 Studio behind; Negative Assembly, tail end of No. 1 Studio; Offices beyond, with original Villa at end

Hepworth's completed Walton-on-Thames studio in 1905.

of Hepworth films until the company collapsed late in 1923. In that year, he made another proposal of a different nature, and they were married in 1924. This husband-and-wife team had an enthusiastic public following. Some time later, Edwards started his own film company and moved to Twickenham Film Studios.

The popularity of Hepworth films such as *My Old Dutch*; *Far From The Madding Crowd*; *The Great Adventure*; *Sweet Lavender*; and *Barnaby Rudge* remained undiminished until the end of the war. But, inevitably, changes were in the air. Stewart Rome, one of the stalwart Hepworth players, announced after his demobilization that he would not be going back to the Hepworth studios, but would instead be joining the Broadwest stock company. Violet Hopson, an early Hepworth player, headed off to form her own film company, and rival production companies such as the London Film Company, who had suspended operations for part or all of the war, announced elaborate programmes. In order to stay abreast of this new surge of output, Hepworth formed the Hepworth Picture Plays Limited in 1919, and in the following year, raised further monies for what was to be an ultimately ill-fated expansion programme.

In 1919, a young man who had been wounded in the war and was unsure of his future was given a part in a Hepworth film called *Sheba*, starring Alma Taylor, James Carew and Gerald Ames. A year later, and still towards the bottom of the cast list, he appeared in *Anna The Adventuress*. His name was Ronald Colman, and after the completion of the film, he went to America where he was spotted by Lillian Gish, who gave him a supporting role in *La Tendresse* on Broadway. He then went on to appear in American films as a sophisticated romantic lead, and, with the coming of sound, his hallmark, a low, distinctive English voice, drew rhapsodic reviews. He will probably be best remembered for his performances in *A Tale Of Two Cities*; *The Prisoner Of Zenda*; and *Random Harvest*.

Although filming continued at the Hepworth Studios, life was becoming increasingly difficult for Hepworth and all UK producers after the collapse of the post-war boom. Despite these difficulties, *The Amazing Quest Of Ernest Bliss*, a five-episode series starring Henry Edwards and Chrissie White, was released in 1920, and in 1922, with the company in dire financial straits, Hepworth made his second version of *Comin' Thro' The Rye* at an astonishing cost of £10,000. The film, starring Alma Taylor, James Carew and Shayle Gardner, was released in 1923, and six months later, Cecil Hepworth and the Hepworth Picture Players were declared bankrupt.

Anyone with an interest in film cannot help but feel outraged on reading Hepworth's gentlemanly account of the behaviour of

Walton-on-Thames: Britain's first film stars, schoolgirls Alma Taylor (left) and Chrissie White, who both grew up to be beautiful screen actresses. They are seen here in the famous *Tilly* series.

the receivers. The senior receiver was a man without knowledge of the film business and lacking in experience of how much stock and equipment could realize through the appropriate channels. The contents of Hepworth's engine-house – diesels and generators, the compressing plant, the travelling gantry and a switchboard which alone had cost £3,250 – were all sold together for £950. The two studios with freehold land, together with all accessories, the four printing and developing machines, the drying machines, the electric-lighting apparatus and cameras went for £4,000 as a going concern, and the debenture holders got only seven shillings in the pound. The most bitter blow was the sale of the negatives, all the negatives that Hepworth had issued in 24 years. In Hepworth's own words: 'They were sold to a man who did not know how to use them, who eventually re-sold them to be melted-down for "dope" for aeroplane wings. And with them, the said gentleman was given the rights of such copyright subjects as *Alf's Button*.'

Cecil Hepworth struggled on, continuing to work in educational films and in various Commonwealth countries. He died in 1953.

The departure of Hepworth dramatically changed the style and personality of the studios at Walton. In 1926, the press

Walton-on-Thames: Hepworth rented out his studio to visiting companies such as Ivy Close Films, founded by Elwin Neame and his beautiful actress wife Ivy Close (mother of director Ronald Neame).

announced that it had been purchased by Archibald Nettlefold of the Birmingham industrial family (later part of Guest Keene and Nettlefold). A recreational farmer in his spare time, Nettlefold had long had a close association with the stage as a lessee and manager of the Comedy Theatre, where he had produced a number of successful plays. One of the few theatrical producers to take up the screen at that time, he had founded Anglia Films in 1923 and bought the Hepworth Studios after making a couple of disastrous films. Nettlefold hoped to carry on the Hepworth Studios with its former employees, but with yet another failure on his hands, *The House Of Marney*, made at Walton, he changed his course of direction. Walter Forde, the former silent comedian, was put to work in the renamed Nettlefold Studios.

Forde's first two comedy features, which he directed and starred in with Pauline Johnson and Frank Stanmore, were *Wait And See* and *What Next?* His last silent feature film, well received by the press, was *Would You Believe It!* Nettlefold failed to respond quickly to the challenge of the talkies and sound equipment was not installed until late 1930.

Almost inevitably, Nettlefold, along with many other studios, became a battery station for Quota films. In his autobiography, *A Life in Movies*, Michael Powell explains that: 'In 1931, the only people interested in backing Quota films were the big American companies who had hundreds of films to unload and couldn't, unless they shared the bill with a British film. To achieve this they were prepared to finance second features made in England. They drove a hard bargain and the going rate for the intrepid producers and financiers of these Quota-Quickies was one pound per foot of film, cash on the table.' Powell's directional debut was on a film called *Two Crowded Hours*, which entered the history of motion pictures as a Quota-Quickie for Fox made at the Nettlefold Studios at Walton. Powell directed 19 films, from 1931 to 1936, of differing lengths and various sponsors, many of which were made at the Walton-on-Thames studios.

By 1932, Nettlefold claimed to be the first British studio to have installed the new high-fidelity recording system, and it was widely used by independent producers such as Paramount, Ideal, United Artists and indirectly, the Butcher's Film Service, backers of low-budget pictures, for Quota production. Among the offerings from these companies in the 1930s were *The Officers Mess* (1931), with Elsa Lanchester; *Self-Made Lady* (1932), directed by George King and starring Louis Hayward; *Prince Of Arcadia* (1933), with Carl Brisson and Ida Lupino; *Virginia's Husband* (1934), with Reginald Gardiner and Enid Stamp-Taylor;

Walton-on-Thames: After several years on the London stage and working in British film studios in such productions as Hepworth's *Anna The Adventuress* (1920), Ronald Colman departed for the United States and became America's English heartthrob of the 1930s.

MY FAVOURITE ROLE

Alma Taylor as "Drusilla Whyddon" *in* The Forest on the Hill.
Chrissie White as "Val" *in* Possession.
Henry Edwards as "Dippy" *in* Broken Threads.
Gerald Ames as "Dr. Purnell" *in* Sunken Rocks.
James Carew as "Timothy Snow" *in* the Forest on the Hill.
Gwynne Herbert as "Mrs. Grey" *in* The City of Beautiful Nonsense.
John MacAndrews as "Bill" *in* Alf's Button.
Eileen Dennes as "Isobel" *in* Alf's Button.

Walton-on-Thames: A page from *Hepworth Picture Play Magazine*, June 1920.

Walton-on-Thames: Film crew at the Nettlefold Studios c.1929, with actor-director Walter Forde on the left.

Twice Branded (1936), with James Mason and Eve Grey; *Father Steps Out* (1937), a George Smith production, from a story by Henry Holt with a young Dinah Sheridan; and *Spies Of The Air*, a John Corfield production starring Roger Livesey. Two other John Corfield productions in 1939 were *Laugh It Off*, with Tommy Trinder; and *Night Journey*. In the late 1930s, the music-hall artists Arthur Lucan and his wife, Kitty McShane, alias Old Mother Riley and her wayward daughter Kitty, appeared in a Butcher's production at Walton, *Old Mother Riley In Paris*.

Walton-on-Thames: Hepworth star Alma Taylor.

By 1940, Walton, along with many other British studios, had been commandeered by the Ministry of Works for the war years. The Vickers-Armstrong aircraft factory on the borders of Kingston-upon-Thames received a direct hit and moved part of their operations to the Walton studios. They built two new hangars, which were used for filming after the war. The *Kinematograph Year Book of 1946* lists the studios' proprietors as the executors of Archibald Nettlefold, but when the studios were back in 1947, boasting three sound stages, they were now owned by Ernest G. Roy who was also in charge of production. The studios continued to produce modest films; among the 1940s releases were *The Hills Of Donegal*, with Dinah Sheridan and Moore Marriott; *The First Gentleman*, with Cecil Parker and Jean-Pierre Aumont, which was directed by Alberto Cavalcanti; and *Calling Paul Temple*, an adaptation of a popular radio series of the time. With an open door hiring policy, the studios fared little better in the 1950s, producing films with the occasional star performance such as *The Sleeping Tiger*, with Dirk Bogarde and Alexis Smith; *Dance Little Lady*, with Mai Zetterling; *Trilby*, starring Hildegarde Neff; and *Tiger By The Tail*, with Larry Parks and Constance Smith.

By the end of the 1950s, Nettlefold's fortunes had completely declined due to the popularity of television and a lack of production funding. This once unique studio was never able to claim a strong personality once the life presence of Cecil Hepworth had disappeared. It closed in 1961 and was pulled down soon afterwards. All that is left of the studio is the power block that housed the generators, which is now the Playhouse Theatre, used for amateur productions and dances. Hepworth might be pleased about that, particularly as it stands in the renamed Hepworth Way.

Welwyn

Hertfordshire

In 1928, the newly-registered British Instructional Films (Proprietors) commenced building a studio at Welwyn. The company's background derived from feature films; and they had an educational films department, headed by the outstanding Mary Field, which had produced a well-crafted, successful, factual series, *Secrets Of Nature*.

The Managing Director of the company and studio was Bruce Woolfe, a producer and director who had entered the film industry in 1910 and was associated with many of the pioneer British documentaries. In 1919, he had founded British Instructional Films, and produced early educational films such as the *Secrets Of Nature* series, going on to make such pictures as *Ypres*; *Mons*; and *Battles Of Coronel And Falkland Islands*. In 1925, the control of British Instructional passed into other hands, leading Woolfe to form British Instructional Films (Proprietors) in 1927. The writer John Buchan was made a member of the board shortly afterwards.

Although the *Secrets Of Nature* series continued to be made at the new studio, the company decided to concentrate almost entirely on fiction. Woolfe was brilliant at attracting well-educated and well-connected young men to Welwyn, including Anthony Asquith, whose father had been Prime Minister from 1908 to 1916.

Educated at Winchester and Oxford University, Asquith had stayed in Hollywood with Mary Pickford and Douglas Fairbanks for three months, before returning to England and entering films in 1926 with British Instructional Films. His first opportunity to direct, in association with A. V Bramble, came with *Shooting Stars*, starring Annette Benson, Brian Aherne, Chili Bouchier, and Donald Calthrop.

The Celestial City, based on a novel by Baroness Orczy, was the first film to be made entirely at the studio, and Asquith directed their first 'sound film', *A Cottage On Dartmoor*. It was, in fact, a silent film to which some dialogue and music had been added by the Klangfilm Company in Germany, as sound production facilities were not installed at Welwyn until 1929. In technical

A sinister Francis L. Sullivan (left) confronts Ralph Richardson in *The Return Of Bulldog Drummond,* directed by Walter Summers for BIP at Welwyn in 1934.

terms, Asquith fared much better with *Tell England,* trade-shown in 1931, though commercially it was not a great box-office success. Even the most patriotic audiences roared with laughter at this stiff upper lip story of school chums who join up and mostly die at Gallipoli. Nevertheless, after such a remarkable debut, there was never any question as to Asquith's abilities, it was simply a case of biding his time until the industry and the public were ready for him. In the late 1930s and the 1940s he came into his own.

In 1930, a larger sound stage was added to Welwyn Studios, and in the same year, British International Pictures, headed by John Maxwell, the owner of the Elstree Studios, absorbed British Instructional Films into their rapidly-expanding group. Woolfe had been led to believe that the studio would continue with imaginative and educational projects. However, the next film directed by Asquith, *Dance, Pretty Lady,* although well-crafted and with Frederick Ashton as its choreographer, again had poor box-office returns. Maxwell was an astute businessman who did not appreciate such 'films for the intelligentsia'. His decision to purchase both the Elstree and the Welwyn Studios would have been nudged on by the knowledge that the Federation of British Industries had inaugurated a campaign to secure statutory protection for the British film-producing industry. The protection was in the form of the Cinematograph Films Bill of 1927, which called upon cinemas to include 20 per cent British films in their programmes; while film renters were required to obtain a similar percentage of British films for distribution. This led to the establishment of the 'Quota Quickies', the mainly low-budget 'B' classified films, usually the second feature of a cinema's programme. Disillusioned, Woolfe left the studio and went to work for Gaumont-British. For the rest of the decade, Welwyn was used principally for the overflow from the Elstree Studios and was also hired out to other producing companies.

A great number of 'Quota Quickies' were made at Welwyn during the 1930s, but whatever their merits, they gave a number of young stars, directors and technicians the opportunity to learn their trade. Director Walter Summers made *The Return Of Bulldog Drummond,* with a pretty, young Ann Todd and Ralph Richardson; Margaret Lockwood had her opportunity to shine with Greta Nissen and Patric Knowles in *Honours Easy,* directed by Herbert Brenon with Ronald Neame as its cameraman. In the second half of the 1930s, Dinah Sheridan and Jimmy Hanley appeared in *Landslide;* and Pat Kirkwood starred in *Save A Little Sunshine,* directed by Norman Lee. In 1938, Maureen O'Hara appeared with Binkie Stuart and Tom Burke in *My Irish Molly;* while in 1939, Bela Lugosi filmed *Dark Eyes Of London* at Welwyn, with Hugh Williams and Greta Gynt.

Welwyn was one of the few studios that was not requisitioned at the outbreak of war in 1939; and as John Maxwell's other studio at Elstree had been commandeered by the War Office, he switched production to Welwyn.

So, with gas masks, ration books, blackout curtains and the Home Guard at the ready, Welwyn struggled through the war years. Personnel came and went, as producers, directors, technicians and actors were called up. In 1940, Jack Hawkins appeared with Basil Radford in *The Flying Squad,* based on a novel by Edgar Wallace; and in the same year, Lilli Palmer starred with

Edward Everett Horton always seemed to play immaculate, if bemused, characters in the 1930s. He is seen here in *The Gang's All Here,* made at John Maxwell's Welwyn and Elstree studios in 1939.

Leslie Banks in the thriller *The Door With Seven Locks.* In 1941, ABPC made a comedy, *Spring Meeting,* with an interesting cast list that included Nova Pilbeam, Basil Sydney, Henry Edwards, Sarah Churchill, Enid Stamp-Taylor, Michael Wilding, Margaret Rutherford, and Hugh McDermott. This was followed by a wartime story, *The Tower Of Terror,* with Michael Rennie and Wilfrid Lawson. *Banana Ridge,* again made at Welwyn, was to be particularly significant for actor Michael Denison. In 1947, Robert Lennard, the casting director of ABPC, which owned the Elstree and Welwyn studios, asked actress Dulcie Gray if she could remember a young man who had stood-in at her test for the film which had been released in 1941. 'That shouldn't be too difficult', she told him, 'his name is Michael Denison, he's my husband, and you can find him at home!' Lennard then cast Denison in *My Brother Jonathan,* made at Elstree, which shot him to immediate stardom and a long and distinguished career in films and theatre. In 1942, Leslie Arliss directed James Mason in the thriller *The Night Has Eyes,* and in the following year, a 1940s favourite, Jean Kent, appeared in *Warn That Man.* Towards the end of the war, Herbert Wilcox produced and directed his wife, Anna Neagle in *I Live In Grosvenor Square,* which also starred Rex Harrison; and in 1946, she returned to the studio to make *Piccadilly Incident* with Michael Wilding and A. E. Matthews.

The close of the 1940s produced a spate of interesting and varied features at the studios. *Brighton Rock,* based on the novel by Graham Greene, was produced by Roy Boulting and directed by John Boulting. A youthful Richard Attenborough starred as

Welwyn: Firm favourites of the 1940s, Anna Neagle and Michael Wilding, seen here in *Piccadilly Incident* (1946), the first of their films together. It proved to be so popular that Miss Neagle's husband, producer Herbert Wilcox, promptly cast the pair in a number of films. Lady Luck had evidently smiled upon Michael Wilding as both Rex Harrison and John Mills had been unavailable for the part.

Welwyn: Edith Evans on the set of *The Queen Of Spades,* directed by Thorold Dickinson in 1948.

Pinkie Brown, the teenage leader of a racecourse gang in Brighton, with Carol Marsh, Hermione Baddeley, and William Hartnell. In 1948, Edith Evans and Anton Walbrook starred in *The Queen Of Spades*, which was directed by Thorold Dickinson and produced by Anatole de Grunwald, and in the same year, Peter Ustinov took the role of *Private Angelo*, co-starring with James Robertson Justice in a film directed by Michael Anderson and Ustinov himself. The two last films made at the studios in the 1940s were *No Place For Jennifer*, a drama concerning a twelve-year-old girl who runs away from home on the divorce of her parents, with Leo Genn, Beatrice Campbell, Rosamund John and Janette Scott as Jennifer; and *Last Holiday*, with a screenplay by J. B. Priestley and starring Alec Guinness.

Industry speculation that the Associated British Picture Corporation might sell Welwyn in order to concentrate all production at their Elstree Studios proved well-founded. The final productions made at Welwyn in 1950 were *Murder Without Crime*; *Talk Of A Million*; and classic crime writer Josephine Tey's *The Franchise Affair*, which starred husband-and-wife team Dulcie Gray and Michael Denison. ABPC sold the three-stage studios shortly afterwards, and a tobacco company took over the premises in late 1951.

Wembley

Wembley Park, Brent, London

British Incorporated Pictures was founded in 1927 by the businessmen, Ralph J. Pugh and Rupert Mason, who intended to develop the Palace of Engineering from the Wembley Exhibition as an American-style studio complex. Although the company acquired 35 acres for their film studios, the financial backing fell through, and a year later, the property was bought by an exhibitor who rechristened the site Wembley National Studios.

Around the same time, a small studio was built on the site for De Forest Phono Films, but this burnt down in 1929. The coming of sound had prompted financier I. W. Schlesinger to acquire Phono Films in the late 1920s. He built a new studio at Wembley, again on the same site, and formed a new company, British Talking Pictures. British Sound Film Productions, a subsidiary of British Talking Pictures, was also formed around the same period.

British Sound Film Productions' first feature was *The Crimson Circle*, an Anglo-German production. Friedrich Zelnick directed the silent part of the film and Sinclair Hill the sound portion, and it starred Stewart Rome and Lya Mara. Their second feature, *Dark Red Roses*, again with Stewart Rome, was trade-shown at the end of 1929, billed as a full-talking feature with songs.

By the early 1930s, British Talking Pictures had merged with Associated Sound Film Industries, a £1 million company. Although only able to cope with one production at a time, their well-designed studio at Wembley had 10,000 sq ft of floor space and was blessed with a modern Overhead Gantry Wiring system, as well as easy accessibility to the centre of London.

Unfortunately, the grandiose schemes of the £1 million company did not materialize. Apart from a number of single-reelers made by John Grierson and *The Bells*, with music by

Laurence Olivier as Orlando in *As You Like It* (1936), also starring Elisabeth Bergner. The film was a 20th Century-Fox production, partly made at Wembley.

Gustav Holst, starring Donald Calthrop and Jane Welsh; and *City Of Song*, two ambitious multi-national films trade-shown in 1931, the operation was unsuccessful. As other studios had found to their cost, multi-national and multi-lingual productions proved in the main to be extremely costly and had disappointing box-office returns.

Wembley saw very little activity in 1931, and leased out its facilities to independent producers wanting to make 'Quota Quickies' in order to comply with the 1928 Cinematograph Films Act. The American Fox Film Company needed to make a large number of British films so that they could show their own prestigious American productions, and so they formed Fox-British Pictures in order to make Quota films. Initially, they used Wembley as well as other studios, until in 1934, they took over the lease of the Wembley Studio, buying the complex in 1936.

Wembley became a busy production centre for Fox-British Quota films in the 1930s. In the first half of the decade, these included Alexander Korda's *Wedding Rehearsal*, with George Grossmith, Lady Tree and John Loder; *Two White Arms*, starring Adolphe Menjou; *Money For Speed*, with Ida Lupino; *All At Sea*, featuring Googie Withers and Rex Harrison, directed by Anthony Kimmins; and *Riverside Murder*, with Basil Sydney and Alastair Sim.

Fox-British Pictures employed a number of American film directors at the studios such as Albert Parker, who would later join the Fox board. Productions completed before the Films Act of 1938 included *Sexton Blake And The Bearded Doctor*, starring Donald Wolfit; *Troubled Waters*, directed by Albert Parker, with James Mason; *Wedding Group*, with cinematography by Arthur Crabtree; and *Murder In The Family*, starring Jessica Tandy, this time with Ronald Neame as cinematographer.

However, 20th-Century Fox, Fox-British's American parent company, had seen a number of changes in their home market in the 1930s and were not happy with the new quotas imposed by the 1938 act. As they also used other studios in Britain, it was decided to close Wembley. The political situation in Europe

Wembley: British-born actress Jessica Tandy in the 1938 production of *Murder In The Family*, which also featured Roddy McDowall and Barry Jones.

would not have gone unnoticed by the American majors, and might well have been a factor in their decision. One of their last productions was *Who Goes Next?*, which was directed by Maurice Elvey, with a young Jack Hawkins in its cast.

Before the outbreak of the Second World War, the studio was leased out to independent companies with Admiral Films making *The Spider*, with Diana Churchill; and Beaumont Film Productions making *Toilers Of The Sea*, based on a novel by Victor Hugo, starring Clifford McLaglen.

Once the war started, Wembley gradually faded out of film production. Certainly, it was closed for very long periods, although it appears to have had the same Managing Director, Francis Harley, between 1941 and 1944. The Army Kinematograph Service used Wembley during this time as one of its bases for military training films, with Thorold Dickinson in charge of production. In 1947, the *Kinematograph Year Book* lists Wembley as either having re-opened or planning to re-open with two stages and a total floor area of 12,252 sq ft. William Kupper and L. Munson are also listed as Managing Directors in the *Kinematograph Weekly* magazines of the late 1940s. The Royal Air Force Film Unit used Wembley during this period to make a number of films including *School For Danger*, directed by Wing Commander Edward Baird.

Although the studios were still owned by 20th Century-Fox Films Limited, by 1950 they were being leased to independent companies such as Mercia Film Productions for commercial films, and Rayant Pictures for magazine shorts and commercials. By 1954, the one-stage studio was listed as having only two clerical staff. During 1955–56 they were used by Associated-Rediffusion for television productions.

Westminster
Carlton Hill, Westminster, London

Primarily a post-Second World War studio, Carlton Hill was owned by Nettlefold Films Limited who also ran the Walton-on-Thames Studios. The studio enjoyed a good production schedule in the second half of the 1940s, with independent producers making films that included *Eyes That Kill*; *Jim The Penman*; *The Phantom Shot*, with John Stuart; and *The Monkey's Paw*, with Milton Rosmer and Megs Jenkins, directed by Norman Lee.

In the early 1950s, this one-stage studio played host to producer-director Mario Zampi's Anglofilm Limited, which produced *The Fatal Night* and *They Cracked Her Glass Slipper*. Cullimore-Arbeid Productions Limited also used the studio as their production base.

The studio produced short films and documentaries until 1953 when it moved into television work.

Westminster
Ebury Street, Westminster, London

In 1912, the British Oak Film Company Limited converted an old warehouse into a film studio with one stage of 90 ft x 25 ft. They used the studio until 1914, and it was taken over a year later by the New Agency Film Company Limited. The outbreak of the First World War meant that the studio, along with others, was making newsreels, war films and propaganda items.

In 1917, Lt. Col. John Buchan, who had already written *The Thirty-Nine Steps* and *Greenmantle*, formed the Department of Information on behalf of the government and naturally saw films as an ideal media vehicle. It is interesting to note that a number of his novels were made into films, and that he became the British Film Institute's first Governor. One-reel dramas with a patriotic flavour were also made at the studio under the New Agency and British Oak banners, one of which was *Boys Of The Old Brigade* (1916), based on the well-known army song. In the same year, producer Thomas Bentley made *Beau Brocade* from the novel by Baroness Orczy, starring Charles Rock and Cecil Mannering. After the war in 1918, Artistic Films had leased the studios and were making such films as *Three Men In A Boat* with Johnny Butt, Lionelle Howard and Manning Haynes.

By the end of 1919, George Clark Productions had taken over the studio and were making films starring Guy Newell and his leading lady (and wife), Ivy Duke. These included *The Bigamist*; *Duke's Son*; and *The Lure Of Crooning Water*. The studio had become far too small for George Clark's output by the early 1920s, and he moved the company to his new studio in Beaconsfield.

Westminster
Great Portland Street, Westminster, London

Ex-schoolmaster George Pearson was paid three guineas by Pathé for his first scenarios, some scenes of *The Merry Wives Of Windsor*, in 1911. In the following year, the converted basement studio at Great Portland Street was owned by Pathé to make their Big Ben Productions, produced and directed by George Pearson. One of these was *The Fool* (1913), based on Rudyard Kipling's

Husband-and-wife team, Ivy Duke and Guy Newall in *The Lure Of Crooning Water*, a George Clark production at the Ebury Street Studio, Westminster, in 1920.

poem 'A Fool There Was' and starring Godfrey Tearle and Mary Malone. The company, also known as The Union Film Publishing Company, moved to premises at Alexandra Palace after the start of the First World War.

Westminster
Strand, Westminster, London
This studio is recorded as the first in Britain. It was built at the back of the Tivoli Theatre in the Strand by the Mutoscope and Biograph Company in 1897. Remarkable for its time, the studio had removable glass panels and was mounted on a cup-and-ball fixture that enabled it to be turned in the direction of the sun. The stage could also be rocked for carriage and sea scenes. It is unlikely that the company used the studio for an extended period, as it is known that they moved their operation to Regent Street some time later.

Westminster
Urbanora House, Wardour Street, Westminster, London
This tiny studio at the top of the Charles Urban Company's film printing works was opened in 1908 with a demonstration of Kinemacolor from its Brighton inventor G. A. Smith, a colour

process that had been patented by the Charles Urban Company. The studio appears to have been utilized for experimental purposes.

Whetstone
Hertfordshire
In 1913, British Empire Films and Zenith Films Limited built an all-glass stage in the grounds of Woodlands, an old country house at Whetstone. A great many productions of that period were filmed versions of popular West End plays, and planning a liaison with His Majesty's Theatre and others, they hired the West End stage actors Seymour Hicks and Ellaline Terriss to appear in their films. These included *David Garrick* and *Scrooge*, both of which were made in 1913 and credited as Coliseum Theatre productions. Later that year, Zenith made *Ivanhoe*, produced by Frederick and Walter Melville, which appeared as a Lyceum Theatre production.

The outbreak of war in 1914 meant that Zenith's last production was *Kismet*, and the studio was left in the hands of British Empire Films, who intended to film West End productions. Although a number of short comedies were made by and with Will Evans, Seymour Hicks, and Ellaline Terriss, the company was in the hands of the receivers by the end of 1916.

Bibliography

Ackland, Rodney and Grant, Elspeth, *The Celluloid Mistress*, Wingate, 1954

Armes, Roy, *A Critical History Of British Cinema*, Secker and Warburg, 1978

Balcon, Michael, *A Lifetime of Films*, Hutchinson, 1969

Balcon, Michael, *The Pursuit of British Cinema*, Museum of Modern Art, New York, 1984

Barr, Charles, *Ealing Studios*, Overlook Press, New York, 1980

Betts, E., *The Film Business*, Allen & Unwin, 1973

British Film Industry, Political and Economic Planning (PEP) report, 1952

British Film Institute, *Film and Television Handbook*, 1994

British Film Institute, *National Film Archive Catalogue Part III* (1895–1930)

British Film Institute, 1966 BFI Dossier 18, *Gainsborough Melodrama*

Brown, Geoff, *Launder & Gilliatt*, British Film Institute

Brunel, Adrian, *Nice Work*, Forbes Robertson, 1949

Butler, Ivan, *Cinema in Britain*, A. S. Barnes/Tantivy Press, 1973

Cowie, Peter, *The Concise History of the Cinema*, Zwemmer, 1971

Douglas Eames, John, *The MGM Story*, Octopus Books, 1977

Dundy, Elaine, *Finch, Bloody Finch*, Michael Joseph

Dunham, Harold, BERTIE: *The Life & Times of G. B.* (Bertie) *Samuelson*, not published

East, J. M.,*'Neath the Mask*, Allen & Unwin, 1967

Falk, Quentin, *The Golden Gong*, Columbus Books

Freedland, Michael, *Errol Flynn*, A Barker

Gifford, Denis, *The British Film Catalogue 1895–1970*, David & Charles, 1973

Guinness, Alec, *Blessings in Disguise*, Fontana/Collins, 1986

Halliwell, L., *Halliwell's Television Companion*, Grafton Books, 1986

Halliwell, L., *Halliwell's Filmgoer's Companion*, Grafton Books, 1988

Hawkins, Jack, *Anything for a Quiet Life*, Elm Tree Books

Hepworth, C., *Came the Dawn*, Phoenix, 1951

Higham, Charles, *Marlene*, Granada

International Motion Picture Almanacs, Quigley Publications, 1966

Jackson-Wrigley, Martin and Leyland, Edmund, *The Cinema*, Grafton Books, 1939

Junge, Helmut, *Plan for Film Studios*, Focal Press, 1945

Katz, E., *International Film Encyclopaedia*, Macmillan, 1979

Kendall, Henry, *I Remember Romano's*, Macdonald, 1960

Kine Yearbooks 1946–1959

Korda, Michael, *Charmed Lives*, Penguin Books, 1980

Lang, Matheson, *Mr Wu Looks Back*, Stanley Paul, 1940

Longmans and Green, *The Year's Work in the Film* 1949, published for the British Council by Longmans, Green & Co., 1950

Low, Rachael, *The History Of British Film*, 5 vols, Allen & Unwin, 1948–1985

Marshall, Michael, *Top Hat & Tails*, Elm Tree Books, 1978

Mason, James, *Before I Forget*, Sphere Books, 1982

Matthews, Jessie, *Over My Shoulder*, Mayflower, 1975

Mills, John, *Up in the Clouds, Gentlemen Please*, Penguin Books, 1981

Morley, Sheridan, *Marlene Dietrich*, Elm Tree Books

National Council of Public Morals, *The Cinema Its Present Position & Future Possibilities*, William & Norgate, 1917

Neagle, Anna, *There's Always Tomorrow*, W. H. Allen, 1974

Oakley, C. A., *When We Came In*, Allen & Unwin, 1964

Olivier, Laurence, *Confessions of an Actor*, Coronet, 1984

Oxford Companion to Film, Oxford University Press, 1976

Pearson, George, *Flashback: An Autobiography of a British Film-maker*, Allen & Unwin, 1957

Perry, George, *Forever Ealing*, Michael Joseph, 1984

Perry, George, *Movies from the Mansions*, Elm Tree Books, 1976

Picturegoer's Who's Who 1933, Odhams Press

Pictureshow Annual 1926

Powell, Michael, *A Life in Movies*, Methuen, 1987

Pritchard, Michael, *Sir Hubert Von Herkomer*, Bushey Museum Trust, 1987

Robertson, Patrick, *The Guinness Book of Film Facts and Figures*, Guinness Superlatives Ltd, 1980

Seaton, Roy and Martin, Ray, *Good Morning Boys: Will Hay*, Barrie & Jenkins, 1978

Silverman, Stephen M., *David Lean*, Andre Deutsch, 1989

Sullivan, J. ed., *The British Film Industry Yearbook*, Film Press Limited, 1947

Tabori, Paul, *Alexander Korda*, Oldbourne, 1959

Thornton, Michael, *Jessie Matthews*, Mayflower, 1975

Tims, Hamilton, *Once a Wicked Lady*, Virgin Books

Travers, Ben, *A-Sitting on a Gate*, W. H. Allen

Trewin, J. C., *Robert Donat*, Heinemann, 1968

Truffaut, François, *Hitchcock*, Secker & Warburg, 1968

Walker, Alexander, *Hollywood England*, Michael Joseph, 1974

Walker, John ed., *Halliwell's Film Guide*, HarperCollins, 1994

Warren, Patricia, *British Cinema in Pictures: The British Film Collection*, B. T. Batsford Ltd, 1993

Warren, Patricia, Elstree: *The British Hollywood*, Columbus Books, 1988

Wilcox, Herbert, *25,000 Sunsets*, Bodley Head, 1976

Winchester's Screen Encyclopaedia, Winchester Publications, 1948

Winchester, C., *World Film Encyclopaedia*, Amalgamated Press, 1933

Wood, Leslie, *Miracle of the Movies*, Burke Publishing Co., 1947

Wood, Leslie, *Romance of the Movies*, Heinemann, 1937

Bioscope 1916–1929

Close-Up 1927–1933

Film Weekly 1928, 1929

Kinematograph Weekly

Picturegoer

Progress British Photoplay

Screen International

General Index

Index of Film Names

Index of Film Names

Index of Film Names